Conference on Empirical Methods in Natural Language Processing (EMNLP 2017)

System Demonstrations

Copenhagen, Denmark
9 – 11 September 2017

ISBN: 978-1-5108-4780-4

EMNLP 2017

The Conference on Empirical Methods in Natural Language Processing

Proceedings of System Demonstrations

September 9-11, 2017
Copenhagen, Denmark

Introduction

Welcome to the proceedings of the System Demonstrations session. This volume contains the papers of the system demonstrations presented at the annual meeting of the Conference on Empirical Methods in Natural Language Processing, held in Copenhagen, Denmark from September 7–11, 2017.

The system demonstrations program offers the presentation of early research prototypes as well as interesting mature systems. We received 53 submissions, of which 21 (39%) were selected for inclusion in the program after review by three or four members of the program committee.

We sincerely thank the members of the program committee for their timely help in reviewing the submissions.

Josef Steinberger
Pontus Stenetorp
Sebastian Sulger
Kaveh Taghipour
Nadi Tomeh
Marco Turchi
Maarten van Gompel

Natalia Vanetik
Andrea Varga
Marc Vilain
Yafang Wang
Leo Wanner
Marion Weller-Di Marco
Guillaume Wisniewski

Travis Wolfe
Seid Muhie Yimam
Mo Yu
Liang-Chih Yu
Pierre Zweigenbaum

Table of Contents

Conference Program

Saturday, September 9, 2017

10:30–12:10   *Demo Session*

The NLTK FrameNet API: Designing for Discoverability with a Rich Linguistic Resource
Nathan Schneider and Chuck Wooters

Argotario: Computational Argumentation Meets Serious Games
Ivan Habernal, Raffael Hannemann, Christian Pollak, Christopher Klamm, Patrick Pauli and Iryna Gurevych

An Analysis and Visualization Tool for Case Study Learning of Linguistic Concepts
Cecilia Ovesdotter Alm, Benjamin Meyers and Emily Prud'hommeaux

GraphDocExplore: A Framework for the Experimental Comparison of Graph-based Document Exploration Techniques
Tobias Falke and Iryna Gurevych

SGNMT – A Flexible NMT Decoding Platform for Quick Prototyping of New Models and Search Strategies
Felix Stahlberg, Eva Hasler, Danielle Saunders and Bill Byrne

StruAP: A Tool for Bundling Linguistic Trees through Structure-based Abstract Pattern
Kohsuke Yanai, Misa Sato, Toshihiko Yanase, Kenzo Kurotsuchi, Yuta Koreeda and Yoshiki Niwa

KnowYourNyms? A Game of Semantic Relationships
Ross Mechanic, Dean Fulgoni, Hannah Cutler, Sneha Rajana, Zheyuan Liu, Bradley Jackson, Anne Cocos, Chris Callison-Burch and Marianna Apidianaki

The Projector: An Interactive Annotation Projection Visualization Tool
Alan Akbik and Roland Vollgraf

Interactive Visualization for Linguistic Structure
Aaron Sarnat, Vidur Joshi, Cristian Petrescu-Prahova, Alvaro Herrasti, Brandon Stilson and Mark Hopkins

DLATK: Differential Language Analysis ToolKit
H. Andrew Schwartz, Salvatore Giorgi, Maarten Sap, Patrick Crutchley, Lyle Ungar and Johannes Eichstaedt

The NLTK FrameNet API:
Designing for Discoverability with a Rich Linguistic Resource

Nathan Schneider
Georgetown University
Washington, DC
nathan.schneider@georgetown.edu

Chuck Wooters
Semantic Machines
Berkeley, CA
wooters@semanticmachines.com

Abstract

A new Python API, integrated within the NLTK suite, offers access to the FrameNet 1.7 lexical database. The lexicon (structured in terms of frames) as well as annotated sentences can be processed programatically, or browsed with human-readable displays via the interactive Python prompt.

1 Introduction

For over a decade, the Berkeley FrameNet (henceforth, simply "FrameNet") project (Baker et al., 1998) has been documenting the vocabulary of contemporary English with respect to the theory of frame semantics (Fillmore, 1982). A freely available, linguistically-rich resource, FrameNet now covers over 1,000 semantic frames, 10,000 lexical senses, and 100,000 lexical annotations in sentences drawn from corpora. The resource has formed a basis for much research in natural language processing—most notably, a tradition of semantic role labeling that continues to this day (Gildea and Jurafsky, 2002; Baker et al., 2007; Das et al., 2014; FitzGerald et al., 2015; Roth and Lapata, 2015, *inter alia*).

Despite the importance of FrameNet, computational users are often frustrated by the complexity of its custom XML format. Whereas much of the resource is browsable on the web (http://framenet.icsi.berkeley.edu/), certain details of the linguistic descriptions and annotations languish in obscurity as they are not exposed by the HTML views of the data.[1] The few open source APIs for reading FrameNet data are now antiquated, and none has been widely adopted.[2]

We describe a new, user-friendly Python API for accessing FrameNet data. The API is included within recent releases of the popular NLTK suite (Bird et al., 2009), and provides access to nearly all the information in the FrameNet release.

2 Installation

Instructions for installing NLTK are found at nltk.org. NLTK is cross-platform and supports Python 2.7 as well as Python 3.x environments. It is bundled in the Anaconda and Enthought Canopy Python distributions for data scientists.[3]

In a working NLTK installation (version 3.2.2 or later), one merely has to invoke a method to download the FrameNet data:[4,5]

```
>>> import nltk
>>> nltk.download('framenet_v17')
```

---

[1] For example, one of the authors was recently asked by a FrameNet user whether frame-to-frame relations include mappings between individual frame elements. They do, but the user's confusion is understandable because these mappings are not exposed in the HTML frame definitions on the website. (They can be explored visually via the FrameGrapher tool on the website, https://framenet.icsi.

berkeley.edu/fndrupal/FrameGrapher, if the user knows to look there.) In the interest of space, our API does not show them in the frame display, but they can be accessed via an individual frame relation object or with the fe_relations() method, §4.4.

[2] We are aware of:

- github.com/dasmith/FrameNet-python (Python)
- nlp.stanford.edu/software/framenet.shtml (Java)
- github.com/FabianFriedrich/Text2Process/tree/master/src/de/saar/coli/salsa/reiter/framenet (Java)
- github.com/GrammaticalFramework/gf-contrib/tree/master/framenet (Grammatical Framework)

None of these has been updated in the past few years, so they are likely not fully compatible with the latest data release.

[3] https://www.continuum.io/downloads, https://store.enthought.com/downloads

[4] >>> is the standard Python interactive prompt, generally invoked by typing python on the command line. Python code can then be entered at the prompt, where it is evaluated/executed. Henceforth, examples will assume familiarity with the basics of Python.

[5] By default, the 855MB data release is installed under the user's home directory, but an alternate location can be specified: see http://www.nltk.org/data.html.

Proceedings of the 2017 EMNLP System Demonstrations, pages 1–6
Copenhagen, Denmark, September 7–11, 2017. ©2017 Association for Computational Linguistics

Subsequently, the `framenet` module is loaded as follows (with alias `fn` for convenience):

```
>>> from nltk.corpus import framenet as fn
```

3 Overview of FrameNet

FrameNet is organized around conceptual structures known as **frames**. A semantic frame represents a **scene**—a kind of event, state, or other scenario which may be universal or culturally-specific, and domain-general or domain-specific. The frame defines participant roles or **frame elements** (FEs), whose relationships forms the conceptual background required to understand (certain senses of) vocabulary items. Oft-cited examples by Fillmore include:

- Verbs such as *buy*, *sell*, and *pay*, and nouns such as *buyer*, *seller*, *price*, and *purchase*, are all defined with respect to a commercial transaction scene (frame). FEs that are central to this frame—they may or may not be mentioned explicitly in a text with one of the aforementioned lexical items—are the **Buyer**, the **Seller**, the **Goods** being sold by the **Seller**, and the **Money** given as payment in exchange by the **Buyer**.
- The concept of REVENGE—lexicalized in vocabulary items such as *revenge*, *avenge*, *avenger*, *retaliate*, *payback*, and *get even*—fundamentally presupposes an **Injury** that an **Offender** has inflicted upon an **Injured_party**, for which an **Avenger** (who may or may not be the same as the **Injured_party**) seeks to exact some **Punishment** on the **Offender**.
- A *hypotenuse* presupposes a geometrical notion of right triangle, while a *pedestrian* presupposes a street with both vehicular and nonvehicular traffic. (Neither frame is currently present in FrameNet.)

The FEs in a frame are formally listed alongside an English description of their function within the frame. Frames are organized in a network, including an inheritance hierarchy (e.g., REVENGE is a special case of an EVENT) and other kinds of frame-to-frame relations.

Vocabulary items listed within a frame are called **lexical units** (LUs). FrameNet's inventory of LUs includes both content and function words. Formally, an LU links a lemma with a frame.[6]

---

[6]The lemma name incorporates a part-of-speech tag. The lemma may consist of a single word, such as *surrender.v*, or multiple words, such as *give up.v*.

In a text, a token of an LU is said to **evoke** the frame. Sentences are annotated with respect to frame-evoking tokens and their FE spans. Thus:

[Snape]Injured_party 's **revenge** [on Harry]Offender

labels overt mentions of participants in the REVENGE frame.

The reader is referred to (Fillmore and Baker, 2009) for a contemporary introduction to the resource and the theory of frame semantics upon which it is based. Extensive linguistic details are provided in (Ruppenhofer et al., 2016).

4 API Overview

4.1 Design Principles

The API is designed with the following goals in mind:

Simplicity. It should be easy to access important objects in the database (primarily frames, lexical units, and annotations), whether by iterating over all entries or searching for particular ones. To avoid cluttering the API with too many methods, other information in the database should be reachable via object attributes. Calling the API's `help()` method prints a summary of the main methods for accessing information in the database.

Discoverability. Many of the details of the database are complex. The API makes it easy to browse what is in database objects via the Python interactive prompt. The main way it achieves this is with pretty-printed displays of the objects, such as the frame display in figure 1 (see §4.3). The display makes it clear how to access attributes of the object that a novice user of FrameNet might not have known about.

In our view, this approach sets this API apart from others. Some of the other NLTK APIs for complex structured data make it difficult to browse the structure without consulting documentation.

On-demand loading. The database is stored in thousands of XML files, including files indexing the lists of frames, frame relations, LUs, and full-text documents, plus individual files for all frames, LUs, and full-text documents. Unzipped, the FrameNet 1.7 release is 855 MB. Loading all of these files—particularly the corpus annotations—is slow and memory-intensive, costs which are unnecessary for many purposes. Therefore, the API is carefully designed with lazy data structures to load XML files only as needed. Once loaded, all data is cached in memory for fast subsequent access.

```
frame (347): Revenge

[URL] https://framenet2.icsi.berkeley.edu/fnReports/data/frame/Revenge.xml

[definition]
  This frame concerns the infliction of punishment in return for a
  wrong suffered. An Avenger performs a Punishment on a Offender as
  a consequence of an earlier action by the Offender, the Injury.
  The Avenger inflicting thePunishment need not be the same as the
  Injured_Party who suffered the Injury,  but the Avenger does have
  to share the judgment that the Offender's action was wrong. The
  judgment that the Offender had inflicted an Injury  is made
  without regard to the law.  '(1) They took revenge for the deaths
  of two loyalist prisoners.' '(2) Lachlan went out to avenge
  them.' '(3) The next day, the Roman forces took revenge on their
  enemies..'

[semTypes] 0 semantic types

[frameRelations] 1 frame relations
  <Parent=Rewards_and_punishments -- Inheritance -> Child=Revenge>

[lexUnit] 18 lexical units
  avenge.v (6056), avenger.n (6057), get back (at).v (10003), get
  even.v (6075), payback.n (10124), retaliate.v (6065),
  retaliation.n (6071), retribution.n (6070), retributive.a (6074),
  retributory.a (6076), revenge.n (6067), revenge.v (6066),
  revengeful.a (6073), revenger.n (6072), sanction.n (10676),
  vengeance.n (6058), vengeful.a (6068), vindictive.a (6069)


[FE] 14 frame elements
          Core: Avenger (3009), Injured_party (3022), Injury (3018),
Offender (3012), Punishment (3015)
      Peripheral: Degree (3010), Duration (12060), Instrument (3013),
Manner (3014), Place (3016), Purpose (3017), Time (3021)
  Extra-Thematic: Depictive (3011), Result (3020)

[FEcoreSets] 2 frame element core sets
  Injury, Injured_party
  Avenger, Punishment
```

Figure 1: Textual display of the REVENGE frame. Shown in square brackets are attribute names for accessing the frame's contents. In parentheses are IDs for the frame, its LUs, and its FEs.

4.2 Lexicon Access Methods

The main methods for looking up information in the lexicon are:

```
frames(name)      frame(nameOrId)
lus(name, frame)  lu(id)
fes(name, frame)
```

The methods with plural names (left) are for searching the lexicon by regular expression pattern to be matched against the entry name. In addition (or instead), `lus()` and `fes()` allow for the results to be restricted to a particular frame. The result is a list with 0 or more elements. If no arguments are provided, all entries in the lexicon are returned.

An example of a search by frame name pattern:[7]

```
>>> fn.frames('(?i)creat')
```

---

[7] (?i) makes the pattern case-insensitive.

```
[<frame ID=268 name=Cooking_creation>,
 <frame ID=1658 name=Create_physical_artwork>, ...]
```

Similarly, a search by LU name pattern—note that the `.v` suffix is used for all verbal LUs:

```
>>> fn.lus(r'.+en\.v')
[<lu ID=5331 name=awaken.v>,
 <lu ID=7544 name=betoken.v>, ...]
```

The `frame()` and `lu()` methods are for retrieving a single known entry by its name or ID. Attempting to retrieve a nonexistent entry triggers an exception of type `FramenetError`.

Two additional methods are available for frame lookup: `frame_ids_and_names(name)` to get a mapping from frame IDs to names, and `frames_by_lemma(name)` to get all frames with some LU matching the given name pattern.

```
exemplar sentence (929548):
[sentNo] 0
[aPos] 1113164

[LU] (6067) revenge.n in Revenge

[frame] (347) Revenge

[annotationSet] 2 annotation sets

[POS] 12 tags

[POS_tagset] BNC

[GF] 4 relations

[PT] 4 phrases

[text] + [Target] + [FE] + [Noun]

A short while later Joseph had his revenge on Watney 's .
------------------- ------ ^^^ --- ******* -------------
Time                Avenge sup Ave        Offender


[Injury:DNI]
 (Avenge=Avenger, sup=supp, Ave=Avenger)
```

Figure 2: A lexicographic sentence display. The visualization of the frame annotation set at the bottom is produced by pretty-printing the combined information in the text, Target, FE, and Noun layers. Abbreviations in the visualization are expanded at the bottom in parentheses ("supp" is short for "support"). "DNI" is FrameNet jargon for "definite null instantiation"; GF stands for "grammatical function"; and PT stands for "phrase type".

4.3 Database Objects

All structured objects in the database—frames, LUs, FEs, etc.—are loaded as AttrDict data structures. Each AttrDict instance is a mapping from string keys to values, which can be strings, numbers, or structured objects. AttrDict is so called because it allows keys to be accessed as attributes:

```
>>> f = fn.frame('Revenge')
>>> f.keys()
dict_keys(['cBy', 'cDate', 'name', 'ID', '_type',
'definition', 'definitionMarkup', 'frameRelations',
'FE', 'FEcoreSets', 'lexUnit', 'semTypes', 'URL'])
>>> f.name
'Revenge'
>>> f.ID
347
```

For the most important kinds of structured objects, the API specifies textual **displays** that organize the object's contents in a human-readable fashion. Figure 1 shows the display for the RE-VENGE frame, which would be printed by entering fn.frame('Revenge') at the interactive prompt. The display gives attribute names in square brackets; e.g., lexUnit, which is a mapping from LU names to objects. Thus, after the code listing in the previous paragraph, f.lexUnit['revenge.n'] would access to one of the LU objects in the frame, which in turn has its own attributes and textual display.

4.4 Advanced Lexicon Access

Frame relations. The inventory of frames is organized in a semantic network via several kinds of frame-to-frame relations. For instance, the REVENGE frame is involved in one frame-to-frame relation: it is related to the more general REWARDS_AND_PUNISHMENTS frame by *Inheritance*, as shown in the middle of figure 1. RE-WARDS_AND_PUNISHMENTS, in turn, is involved in *Inheritance* relations with other frames. Each frame-to-frame relation bundles mappings between corresponding FEs in the two frames.

Apart from the frameRelations attribute of frame objects, frame-to-frame relations can be browsed by the main method frame_relations(frame, frame2, type), where the optional arguments allow for filtering by one or both frames and the kind of relation. Within a frame relation object, pairwise FE relations are stored in the feRelations attribute. Main method fe_relations() provides direct access to links between FEs. The inventory of relation types, including *Inheritance, Causative, Inchoative, Subframe, Perspective_on*, and others, is available

```
full-text sentence (4148528) in Tiger_Of_San_Pedro:

[POS] 25 tags

[POS_tagset] PENN

[text] + [annotationSet]

They 've been looking for him all the time for their revenge ,
              *******                                    *******
              Seeking                                    Revenge
              [3] ?                                      [2]

but it is only now that they have begun to find him out . "
                                          *****   ****
                                          Proce   Beco
                                          [1]     [4]
        (Proce=Process_start, Beco=Becoming_aware)
```

Figure 3: A sentence of full-text annotation. If this sentence object is stored under the variable sent, its frame annotation with respect to the target *revenge* is accessed as sent.annotationSet[2]. (The ? under *looking* indicates that there is no corresponding LU defined in the SEEKING frame; in some cases the full-text annotators marked but did not define out-of-vocabulary LUs which fit an existing frame. Also, some full-text annotation sets annotate an LU without its FEs—these are shown with ! to reflect the annotation set's status code of UNANN.)

via main method frame_relation_types().

Semantic types. These provide additional semantic categorizations of FEs, frames, and LUs. For FEs, they mark selectional restrictions (e.g., f.FE['Avenger'].semType gives the *Sentient* type). Main method propagate_semtypes() propogates the FE semantic type labels marked explicitly to other FEs according to inference rules that follow the FE relations. This should be called prior to inspecting FE semtypes (it is not called by default because it takes several seconds to run).

The semantic types are database objects in their own right, and they are organized in their own inheritance hierarchy. Main method semtypes() returns all semantic types as a list; main method semtype() looks up a particular one by name, ID, or abbreviation; and main method semtype_inherits() checks whether two semantic types have a subtype–supertype relationship.

4.5 Corpus Access

Frame-semantic annotations of sentences can be accessed via the exemplars and subCorpus attributes of an LU object, or via the following main methods:

annotations(luname, exemplars, full_text)
sents() **exemplars**(luname) **ft_sents**(docname)
doc(id) **docs**(name)

annotations() returns a list of frame **annotation sets**. Each annotation set consists of a frame-evoking **target** (token) within a sentence, the LU in the frame it evokes, its overt FE spans in the sentence, and the status of null-instantiated FEs.[8] Optionally, the user may filter by LU name, or limit by the type of annotation (see next paragraph): exemplars and full_text both default to True. In the XML, the components of an annotation set are stored in several annotation layers: one (and sometimes more than one) layer of FEs, as well as additional layers for other syntactic information (including grammatical function and phrase type labels for each FE, and copular or support words relative to the frame-evoking target).

Annotation sets are organized by sentence. Corpus sentences appear in two kinds of annotation: exemplars() retrieves sentences with lexicographic annotation (where a single target has been selected for annotation to serve as an example of an LU); the optional argument allows for filtering the set of LUs. ft_sents() retrieves sentences from documents selected for full-text annotation (as many targets in the document as possible have been annotated); the optional argument allows for filtering by document name. sents() can be used to iterate over all sentences. Technically, each sentence object contains multiple annotation sets: the first is for sentence-level annotations, including part-of-speech tagging and in some cases named entity labels; subsequent annotation sets are for

---

[8]In frame semantics, core FEs that are not overt but are conceptually required by a frame are said to be implicit via null instantiation (Fillmore and Baker, 2009).

frame annotations. As lexicographic annotations
have only one frame annotation set, it is visualized
in the sentence display: figure 2 shows the display
for `f.lexUnit['revenge.n'].exemplars[20]`. Full-text
annotations display target information only, allowing the user to drill down to see each annotation
set, as in figure 3.

Sentences of full-text annotation can also be
browsed by document using the `doc()` and `docs()`
methods. The document display lists the sentences
with numeric offsets.

5   Limitations and future work

The main part of the Berkeley FrameNet data that
the API currently does *not* support are **valence
patterns**. For a given LU, the valence patterns
summarize the FEs' syntactic realizations across
annotated tokens. They are displayed in each LU's
"Lexical Entry" report on the FrameNet website.

We intend to add support for valence patterns
in future releases, along with more sophisticated
querying/browsing capabilities for annotations, and
better displays for syntactic information associated
with FE annotations. Some of this functionality can
be modeled after tools like FrameSQL (Sato, 2003)
and Valencer (Kabbach and Ribeyre, 2016). In addition, it is worth investigating whether the API
can be adapted for FrameNets in other languages,
and to support cross-lingual mappings being added
to 14 of these other FrameNets in the ongoing Multilingual FrameNet project.[9]

Acknowledgments

We thank Collin Baker, Michael Ellsworth, and
Miriam R. L. Petruck for helping us to understand
the FrameNet annotation process and the technical aspects of the data, and for co-organizing the
FrameNet tutorial in which an early version of the
API was introduced (Baker et al., 2015). We also
thank NLTK project leader Steven Bird, Mikhail
Korborov, Pierpaolo Pantone, Rob Malouf, and anyone else who may have contributed to the release of
the API by reviewing the code and reporting bugs;
and anonymous reviewers for their suggestions.

References

Collin Baker, Michael Ellsworth, and Katrin Erk. 2007.
SemEval-2007 Task 19: frame semantic structure
extraction. In *Proc. of SemEval*, pages 99–104,
Prague, Czech Republic.

Collin Baker, Nathan Schneider, Miriam R. L. Petruck,
and Michael Ellsworth. 2015. Getting the roles right:
using FrameNet in NLP. In *Proc. of the 2015 Conference of the North American Chapter of the Association for Computational Linguistics: Tutorial Abstracts*, pages 10–12, Denver, Colorado, USA.

Collin F. Baker, Charles J. Fillmore, and John B. Lowe.
1998. The Berkeley FrameNet project. In *Proc.
of COLING-ACL*, pages 86–90, Montreal, Quebec,
Canada.

Steven Bird, Ewan Klein, and Edward Loper. 2009.
*Natural Language Processing with Python: An-
alyzing Text with the Natural Language Toolkit*.
O'Reilly Media, Inc., Sebastopol, CA.

Dipanjan Das, Desai Chen, André F. T. Martins,
Nathan Schneider, and Noah A. Smith. 2014.
Frame-semantic parsing. *Computational Linguis-
tics*, 40(1):9–56.

Charles J. Fillmore. 1982. Frame Semantics. In *Linguistics in the Morning Calm*, pages 111–137. Han-
shin Publishing Co., Seoul, South Korea.

Charles J. Fillmore and Collin Baker. 2009. A frames
approach to semantic analysis. In Bernd Heine and
Heiko Narrog, editors, *The Oxford Handbook of Linguistic Analysis*, pages 791–816. Oxford University
Press, Oxford, UK.

Nicholas FitzGerald, Oscar Täckström, Kuzman
Ganchev, and Dipanjan Das. 2015. Semantic role
labeling with neural network factors. In *Proc. of the
2015 Conference on Empirical Methods in Natural
Language Processing*, pages 960–970, Lisbon, Portugal.

Daniel Gildea and Daniel Jurafsky. 2002. Automatic
labeling of semantic roles. *Computational Linguistics*, 28(3):245–288.

Alexandre Kabbach and Corentin Ribeyre. 2016. Valencer: an API to query valence patterns in
FrameNet. In *Proc. of COLING 2016, the 26th International Conference on Computational Linguistics: System Demonstrations*, pages 156–160, Osaka, Japan.

Michael Roth and Mirella Lapata. 2015. Context-
aware frame-semantic role labeling. *Transactions
of the Association for Computational Linguistics*,
3:449–460.

Josef Ruppenhofer, Michael Ellsworth, Miriam R. L.
Petruck, Christopher R. Johnson, Collin F. Baker,
and Jan Scheffczyk. 2016. FrameNet II: extended
theory and practice.

Hiroaki Sato. 2003. FrameSQL: A software tool for
FrameNet. In *Proc. of ASIALEX 2003*, pages 251–
258, Tokyo, Japan.

---

[9] `github.com/icsi-berkeley/multilingual_FN`

Argotario: Computational Argumentation Meets Serious Games

**Ivan Habernal, Raffael Hannemann, Christian Pollak,
Christopher Klamm, Patrick Pauli, Iryna Gurevych**
Ubiquitous Knowledge Processing Lab (UKP)
Department of Computer Science, Technische Universität Darmstadt
www.ukp.tu-darmstadt.de

Abstract

An important skill in critical thinking and argumentation is the ability to spot and recognize *fallacies*. Fallacious arguments, omnipresent in argumentative discourse, can be deceptive, manipulative, or simply leading to 'wrong moves' in a discussion. Despite their importance, argumentation scholars and NLP researchers with focus on argumentation quality have not yet investigated fallacies empirically. The nonexistence of resources dealing with fallacious argumentation calls for scalable approaches to data acquisition and annotation, for which the *serious games* methodology offers an appealing, yet unexplored, alternative. We present *Argotario*, a serious game that deals with fallacies in everyday argumentation. *Argotario* is a multilingual, open-source, platform-independent application with strong educational aspects, accessible at www.argotario.net.

1 Introduction

Argumentation in natural language has been gaining much interest in the NLP community in recent years. While understanding the structure of an argument is the predominant task of argument mining/computational argumentation (Mochales and Moens, 2011; Stab and Gurevych, 2014; Habernal and Gurevych, 2017), a parallel strand of research tries to assess qualitative properties of arguments (Habernal and Gurevych, 2016b; Stab and Gurevych, 2017). Yet the gap between theories and everyday argumentation, in understanding what 'argument quality' actually is, remains an open research question (Wachsmuth et al., 2017; Habernal and Gurevych, 2016a).

Argumentation theories and critical thinking textbooks, however, offer an alternative view on quality of arguments, namely the notion of *fallacies*: prototypical argument schemes or types that pretend to be correct and valid arguments but suffer logically, emotionally, or rhetorically (Hamblin, 1970). Although this topic was first brought up by Aristotle already some 2,300 years ago, contemporary research on fallacies still does not provide a unifying view and clashes even in the fundamental questions (Boudry et al., 2015; Paglieri, 2016). Nevertheless, there seem to be several types of fallacies, such as *argument ad hominem*,[1] various emotional *appeals*, rhetorical moves of the *red herring*,[2] or *hasty generalization* that are, unfortunately, widely spread in our everyday argumentative discourse. Their powerful and sometimes detrimental impact was revealed in a few manual analyses (Sahlane, 2012; Nieminen and Mustonen, 2014). To the best of our knowledge, there is neither any NLP research dealing with fallacies, nor any resources that would allow for empirical investigation of that matter.

The lack of fallacy-annotated linguistic resources and thus the need for creating and labeling a new dataset from scratch motivated us to investigate *serious games* (also *games with a purpose*)—a scenario in which a task is *gamified* and users (players) enjoy playing a game without thinking much of the burden of annotations (von Ahn and Dabbish, 2008; Mayer et al., 2014). Serious games have been successful in NLP tasks that can be easily represented by images (Jurgens and Navigli, 2014; Kazemzadeh et al., 2014) or that can be simplified to assessing a single word or a pair of propositions (Nevěřilová, 2014; Poesio et al., 2013). More complex tasks such as argument understanding, reasoning, or composing pose several

---

[1] Attacking the opponent instead of her argument
[2] Distracting to irrelevant issues

7

Proceedings of the 2017 EMNLP System Demonstrations, pages 7–12
Copenhagen, Denmark, September 7–11, 2017. ©2017 Association for Computational Linguistics

design challenges centered around the key question: how to make data creation and annotation efforts fun and entertaining in the first place.

To tackle this open research challenge, we created *Argotario*—an online serious game for acquiring a dataset with fallacious argumentation. The main research **contributions** and features of *Argotario* include:

- Gamification of the fallacy recognition task including player vs. player interaction
- Learning by playing and educational aspects
- Full in-game data creation and annotation, all data are under open license
- Automatic gold label and quality estimation based solely on the crowd
- Multilingual, platform independent, open-source, modular, with native look-and-feel on smartphones

2 Background and Related Work

Fallacies have been an active topic in argumentation theory research in the past several decades. While Aristotle's legacy was still noticeable in the twentieth century, a 'fresh' look by Hamblin (1970) showed that the concept of fallacies as arguments 'that *seem to be* valid but are *not* so' deserves to be put under scrutiny.[3] Theories about fallacies evolved into various categorizations and treatments, ranging from rather practical education-oriented approaches (Tindale, 2007; Schiappa and Nordin, 2013) to rhetorical ones in informal logic (Walton, 1995) or pragma-dialectic (Van Eemeren and Grootendorst, 1987). For a historical overview of fallacies see, e.g., (Hansen, 2015).

Surprisingly, the vast majority of current works on fallacies, and especially textbooks, present only toy examples that one is unlikely to encounter in real life (Boudry et al., 2015, p. 432). The distinction between fallacies and acceptable inference is fuzzy and theories do not offer any practical guidance: fully-fledged fallacies are harder to find in real life than is commonly assumed (Boudry et al., 2015). To this account, analysis of fallacies in actual argumentative discourse has been rather limited in scope and size. Nieminen and Mustonen (2014) examined fallacies found in articles supporting creationism. Sahlane (2012) manualy analysed

fallacies in newswire editorials in major U.S. newspapers before invading Iraq in 2003. These two works rely on a list of several fallacy types, such as *ad hominem*, *ad populum*, *appeal to guilt*, *slippery slope*, *hasty generalization*, and few others.

When scaling up annotations and resource acquisitions, serious games provide an alternative to paid crowdsourcing. Recent successful applications include knowledge base extension (Vannella et al., 2014), answering quizes related to medical topics (Ipeirotis and Gabrilovich, 2014), word definition acquisition (Parasca et al., 2016), or word sense labeling (Venhuizen et al., 2013); where the latter one resembles a standard annotation task with bonus rewards rather than a traditional entertaining game. Niculae and Danescu-Niculescu-Mizil (2016) built a game for guessing places given Google Street View images in order to collect data for investigating constructive discussions. An important aspect of serious games for NLP is their benefit to the users other than getting the annotations done quickly: learning a language in *Duolingo*[4] has more added value than killing zombies (despite its obvious fun factor) in *Infection* (Vannella et al., 2014).

3 Argotario: Overview

Architecture and Implementation *Argotario* is a client-server Web-based application that runs in all modern browsers and seamlessly works on smartphones, providing an authentic look-and-feel. Its three-tier architecture consists of a backend MongoDB database, a Python server behind an Apache2 SSL proxy, and a Javascript client built on top of Ionic framework. *Argotario* is **modular** as it allows developers to add new content (worlds, levels, rounds) as independent modules. The game workflow is **configurable** using JSON files, so it can be customized for evaluating new game scenarios. **Security** is ensured by a SSL certificate and securely hashing all passwords with salt. **Localization** utilizes the built-in capabilities of ng-translate so that all texts are stored externally in a JSON file and adding another language to the UI requires only manual translation of these texts.[5] Currently, *Argotario* is available in English

---

[3]Hamblin (1970) criticized the 'standard treatment' of fallacies widely present in contemporary textbooks as being 'debased,' 'worn-out', 'dogmatic' and 'without a connection to modern logic'.

[4]Although Duolingo presents itself as a learning tool, its incentives and competition features make it feel like accomplishing quests in a game.

[5]Needless to say that providing an initial *content* for a new language, such as a list of language-dependent topics, arguments, and fallacies, requires substantial manual work.

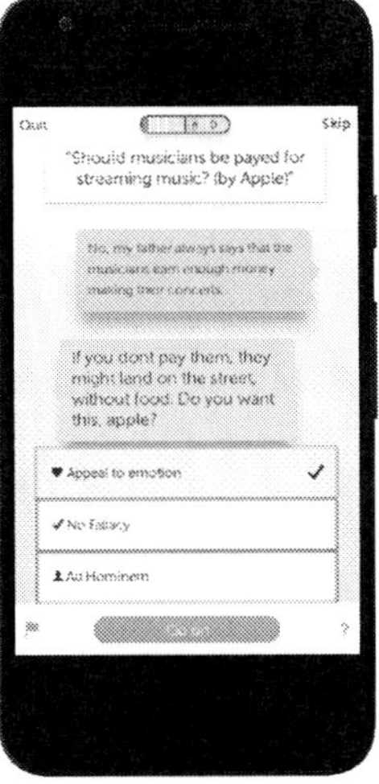
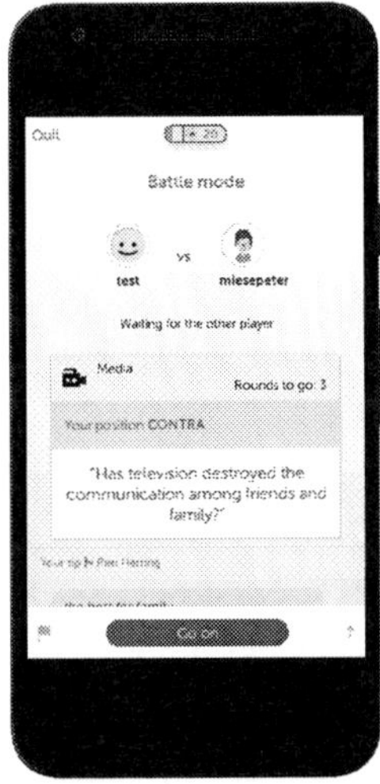

(a) A single *world* with the two first *levels* finished, the third one about to be played, and other to be 'explored'.

(b) The recognize fallacy type *round*.

(c) The *player vs. player* level, now waiting for the opponent's turn.

(d) An example of *hard feedback* in a fallacy recognition round.

Figure 1: Screenshots of *Argotario* taken in a smartphone emulator.

and German.

Game Design We first present the abstract architecture; concrete examples follow in §4. According to Salen and Zimmerman (2004, p. 50), a game is a system consisting of different types of interacting entities that have certain attributes. *Argotario* follows this structure by a hierarchy of **worlds**, **levels**, and game **rounds** (Hannemann, 2015).

A game **round** represents an atomic mini-game in which users take an action and are rewarded with points. Conceptually, each game round follows the same procedure: the users are first faced with *game data*, which they need to interact with. Their response (a choice or free-text input) is then validated with respect to the current game round configuration, similar to form validation on web pages. If the game determines correctness of the response data, it rewards the user with a certain number of points.

A sequence of game rounds form a **level**. To complete a level, all game rounds must be finished, independently of whether the user successfully fulfilled the respective task or not. Whereas game rounds can be re-used in different levels, each level is unique and can be individually designed to fit a certain purpose (i.e., only some types of fallacies are dealt with).

Finally, all levels reside in a **world** which is a wrapper for all included levels, visually resembling a treasure map (see Figure 1a). Their look can be freely customized to be visually appealing and capture a certain atmosphere or theme. There are multiple worlds within the game next to each other.

Users are represented as small circular comic faces (avatars). The first user's **goal** is to finish all levels in all worlds. Initially, the game worlds are covered by a fog, which can be cleared by the user by completing levels. **Ranking** (score) is the second important game goal. Repeating levels allows users to collect more points and hence improve their global rank.

4 Gamifying Fallacy Recognition

The backbone principle of *Argotario* can be summarized as follows. First, since a fallacious argument is one 'that seems to be valid but is not so' (Hamblin, 1970), users must try to 'fool' other users by **writing** a fallacious argument of a given type without being revealed that this is in fact a fallacy. By writing a fallacious argument on purpose with the aim to 'disguise' it as a valid argument, users get sensitive to the very gist of fallacious argumentation (such as rhetorical strategies, linguistic devices, logic, etc.). Second, users learn to **recognize** fallacies in existing arguments—either by revealing the correct fallacy type or stating that the given argument is not fallacious—and get feedback about their 'debunking' skills (see Figure 1b).[6]

In the serious-game terminology of von Ahn and Dabbish (2008, p. 61), recognizing the correct fallacy type combines the *inversion-problem game* (the guesser produces the input that was originally given to the describer') and a modification of the *output-agreement game* (the guesser has to produce the same output as the crowd; details will be discussed later in §4).

Fallacy Types We gathered an inventory of fallacy types suitable for our game scenarios. Given the breadth and variety of fallacy types (Tindale, 2007; Govier, 2010), we conducted several pilot studies to identify types that are (1) common in everyday argumentative discourse, (2) are distinguishable from each other, and (3) have increasing difficulty. The fallacy type inventory in *Argotario* currently contains *ad hominem, appeal to emotion, red herring, hasty generalization, irrelevant authority*, and a non-fallacious argument (Pollak, 2016).

Players learn to recognize different fallacy types gradually, as they accomplish each level. After finishing the first world in which all fallacy types are mastered, users can engage in the *player versus player* world. Here, a dialogue exchange about a given controversy requires users to write fallacious arguments (as in the previous world) and guess which fallacy was used by its opponent (thus getting points for correct answers; details about gold data estimation are explained in the next section). This level is asynchronous; when a user writes a new argument, his opponents gets notification about the turn change, so they do not have to play at the same time (see Figure 1c).

Gold Label Estimation Because all content is created within the game by players with different abilities to write or comprehend argumentation, we treat the data as *noisy* in the first place. First, spam can be reported in all rounds and is submitted to the admins to take action. Second, we rely on MACE (Hovy et al., 2013) for gold label estimation which we seamlessly integrated to the backend. For example, if the user has to write an argument of a given fallacy type, we treat the type only as a single 'vote' and require another four players to guess the correct type of this fallacy in other levels. Only arguments that receive at least five 'votes' are fed into MACE to establish their gold label.

By utilizing crowd voting and spam reporting,

we indirectly aim for high-quality labels. Predicting gold labels can be further parametrized by a *threshold* in MACE, which then provides only gold label estimates for instances whose entropy is below the threshold (Hovy et al., 2013, p. 1125). However, a deep analysis of the data quality is on our current research agenda.

Feedback and Incentives *Argotario* provides two types of feedback: *soft* and *hard* one. For labeling arguments with yet unknown gold label, users get only one point without knowing whether their answer was right (*soft feedback*). For arguments with already estimated gold labels, *hard feedback* (see Figure 1d) is given: if the user makes an error, she receives no reward. Apparently, hard feedback is better from the educational point of view as one knows immediately whether her answer was right or wrong; however, users do not know in advance whether a current assessment gives them a soft or hard feedback, so they are inherently encouraged to try their best.

We also built in several sorts of incentives to keep the player engaged. First, *Argotario* shows the overall leaderboard as well as *weekly* ranks to ensure newcomers have chances to succeed, see (Ipeirotis and Gabrilovich, 2014) for details. Players of the week are publicly shown and receive a small monetary prize. Second, debunking fallacious arguments to familiar topics is reportedly entertaining for players interested in rhetoric, argumentation, or public deliberation, according to user feedback obtained after few classroom runs.

5 Benchmarking

So far we tested *Argotario* in serveral user studies and beta-testing sessions. The first study on early versions of *Argotario* examined the effect of hard feedback and the lack thereof on overall users' engagement in the game. We found that the soft feedback has no significant negative impact on the users' experience[7] (Hannemann, 2015).

In a subsequent study, we benchmarked the player vs. player level using Amazon Mechanical Turk (AMT). We asked workers to play a specially configured version of *Argotario* in order to 'win' 20 points required for submitting the HIT. As the player vs. player round needs two dialogue turns of

---

[7]Two user groups (20 and 17 participants, respectively) with the same game configuration but with either only soft or hard feedback; final questionnaire with Likert-scale questions; Mann-Whitney-U non-parametric test.

two users and thus two or more people actively participating over a longer period of time, we also implemented a naive *bot* for this study.[8] At the same time, we promoted the game on social media and attracted some non-paid users. Using this process, we could quickly test the entire game mechanism with a larger crowd, identify potential drawbacks, and gather about 1,160 hand-written fallacious arguments. We also experimented with various price per HIT ($1–$2) with respect to average playing time. While the number of rejected low-quality HITs remained negligible for all configurations, we did not observe any correlation between HIT prices and playing times ($\approx$ 18–26 min). Our interpretation is that the HIT price for benchmarking studies should be fair and reflect the study time but does not influence the quality (Pollak, 2016).

6 Conclusions and Outlook

Argotario is a serious game that serves several purposes. First, it is a software tool for computational linguistics research, as it focuses on fallacies in argumentative discourse, an important part of qualitative criteria in computational argumentation. Second, it is software supporting learning and education. Its main educational purpose is to raise awareness—not only that fallacies do exist but they might be easily overlooked and misused in everyday argumentation. Finally, *Argotario* is also a data-acquisition and annotation tool that applies successful techniques for quality estimation from crowd-sourcing approaches. All content is created by users within the game, as opposed to usual annotation tools.

In the long run, we expect that *Argotario* provides a feasible method for data acquisition as compared to standard crowdsourcing. First, a purely monetary-driven perspective is not always the deciding factor of playing additional levels, as shown by Eickhoff et al. (2012). Second, 'experts' from the crowd motivated by the potential for achievement can help engage in participation (Ipeirotis and Gabrilovich, 2014).

In the current version, *Argotario* is still a proof of concept. Its capabilities need to be verified at a large scale in order to reveal patterns in the game dynamics with impact on the overall user experience and quality; these cannot be easily anticipated on small-scale benchmarks (§5). In this regard, any manual intervention (such as spam removal) needs to be automated.

Argotario is accessible at www.argotario.net along with tutorial videos and runs in any modern web-browser, preferably on smartphones. It is also open-source, source codes under ASL license are available at GitHub.[9]

Acknowledgments

This work has been supported by the Volkswagen Foundation as part of the Lichtenberg-Professorship Program under grant № I/82806, by the German Institute for Educational Research (DIPF), by the GRK 1994/1 AIPHES (DFG), and by the ArguAna Project GU 798/20-1 (DFG).

References

Luis von Ahn and Laura Dabbish. 2008. Designing games with a purpose. *Communications of the ACM*, 51(8):57.

Maarten Boudry, Fabio Paglieri, and Massimo Pigliucci. 2015. The Fake, the Flimsy, and the Fallacious: Demarcating Arguments in Real Life. *Argumentation*, 29(4):431–456.

Carsten Eickhoff, Christopher G. Harris, Arjen P. de Vries, and Padmini Srinivasan. 2012. Quality through flow and immersion: gamifying crowdsourced relevance assessments. In *ACM SIGIR*, pages 871–880, New York, USA. ACM Press.

Trudy Govier. 2010. *A Practical Study of Argument*, 7th edition. Wadsworth, Cengage Learning.

Ivan Habernal and Iryna Gurevych. 2016a. What makes a convincing argument? Empirical analysis and detecting attributes of convincingness in Web argumentation. In *EMNLP*, pages 1214–1223, Austin, Texas.

Ivan Habernal and Iryna Gurevych. 2016b. Which argument is more convincing? Analyzing and predicting convincingness of Web arguments using bidirectional LSTM. In *ACL (Volume 1: Long Papers)*, pages 1589–1599, Berlin, Germany.

Ivan Habernal and Iryna Gurevych. 2017. Argumentation Mining in User-Generated Web Discourse. *Computational Linguistics*, 43(1):125–179.

---

[8]We trained a fallacy classifier system on existing arguments in the database using a Convolutional Neural Network based on GloVe embeddings (Pennington et al., 2014) and Keras framework, so the *bot* tried to recognize a fallacy in its opponent arguments during the player vs. player discussion. For generating an answer, it simply looked up an existing fallacy to the given topic. On the one hand, it disobeyed the discourse flow, as it obviously did not coherently respond to its opponent. On the other hand, it allowed us to deploy the game as a HIT on AMT and get a sufficient number of player vs. bot games in a short time.

---

[9]https://github.com/UKPLab/argotario

Charles L. Hamblin. 1970. *Fallacies*. Methuen, London, UK.

Raffael Hannemann. 2015. Serious games for large-scale argumentation mining. Master Thesis, Techische Universität Darmstadt.

Hans Hansen. 2015. Fallacies. In Edward N. Zalta, editor, *The Stanford Encyclopedia of Philosophy*, summer 2015 edition. Metaphysics Research Lab, Stanford University.

Dirk Hovy, Taylor Berg-Kirkpatrick, Ashish Vaswani, and Eduard Hovy. 2013. Learning whom to trust with MACE. In *NAACL-HLT*, pages 1120–1130, Atlanta, Georgia.

Panagiotis G. Ipeirotis and Evgeniy Gabrilovich. 2014. Quizz: Targeted Crowdsourcing with a Billion (Potential) Users Panagiotis. In *WWW'14*, pages 143–154, Seoul, South Korea. ACM.

David Jurgens and Roberto Navigli. 2014. It's all fun and games until someone annotates: Video games with a purpose for linguistic annotation. *TACL*, 2(1):449–463.

Sahar Kazemzadeh, Vicente Ordonez, Mark Matten, and Tamara L Berg. 2014. ReferItGame: Referring to Objects in Photographs of Natural Scenes. In *EMNLP*, pages 787–798, Doha, Qatar.

Igor Mayer, Geertje Bekebrede, Casper Harteveld, Harald Warmelink, Qiqi Zhou, Theo van Ruijven, Julia Lo, Rens Kortmann, and Ivo Wenzler. 2014. The research and evaluation of serious games: Toward a comprehensive methodology. *British Journal of Educational Technology*, 45(3):502–527.

Raquel Mochales and Marie-Francine Moens. 2011. Argumentation mining. *Artificial Intelligence and Law*, 19(1):1–22.

Zuzana Nevěřilová. 2014. Annotation game for textual entailment evaluation. In *CICLing*, pages 340–350, Kathmandu, Nepal.

Vlad Niculae and Cristian Danescu-Niculescu-Mizil. 2016. Conversational Markers of Constructive Discussions. In *NAACL-HLT*, pages 568–578, San Diego, CA, USA.

Petteri Nieminen and Anne-Mari Mustonen. 2014. Argumentation and fallacies in creationist writings against evolutionary theory. *Evolution: Education and Outreach*, 7(1):11.

Fabio Paglieri. 2016. Don't worry, be gappy! On the unproblematic gappiness of alleged fallacies. In *The psychology of argument*, chapter 9, pages 1–20. College Publications, London.

Iuliana-Eena Parasca, Andreas Lukas Rauter, Jack Roper, Aleksandar Rusinov, Guillaume Bouchard, Sebastian Riedel, and Pontus Stenetorp. 2016. Defining Words with Words: Beyond the Distributional Hypothesis. In *RepEval*, pages 122–126, Berlin, Germany.

Jeffrey Pennington, Richard Socher, and Christopher Manning. 2014. Glove: Global vectors for word representation. In *EMNLP*, pages 1532–1543, Doha, Qatar.

Massimo Poesio, Jon Chamberlain, Udo Kruschwitz, Livio Robaldo, and Luca Ducceschi. 2013. Phrase detectives: Utilizing collective intelligence for internet-scale language resource creation. *ACM Trans. on Interactive Intelligent Systems*, 3(1):1–44.

Christian Pollak. 2016. Serious games for learning fallacy recognition. Master Thesis, Techische Universität Darmstadt.

Ahmed Sahlane. 2012. Argumentation and fallacy in the justification of the 2003 War on Iraq. *Argumentation*, 26(4):459–488.

Katie Salen and Eric Zimmerman. 2004. *Rules of Play: Game Design Fundamentals*. MIT Press.

Edward Schiappa and John P. Nordin. 2013. *Argumentation: Keeping Faith with Reason*, 1st edition. Pearson UK.

Christian Stab and Iryna Gurevych. 2014. Identifying argumentative discourse structures in persuasive essays. In *EMNLP*, pages 46–56, Doha, Qatar.

Christian Stab and Iryna Gurevych. 2017. Recognizing Insufficiently Supported Arguments in Argumentative Essays. In *EACL (Volume 1, Long Papers)*, pages 980–990.

Christopher W. Tindale. 2007. *Fallacies and Argument Appraisal*, critical reasoning and argumentation edition. Cambridge University Press, New York, NY, USA.

Frans H. Van Eemeren and Rob Grootendorst. 1987. Fallacies in pragma-dialectical perspective. *Argumentation*, 1(3):283–301.

Daniele Vannella, David Jurgens, Daniele Scarfini, Domenico Toscani, and Roberto Navigli. 2014. Validating and Extending Semantic Knowledge Bases using Video Games with a Purpose. In *ACL (Volume 1: Long Papers)*, pages 1294–1304, Baltimore, Maryland USA.

Noortje J. Venhuizen, Valerio Basile, Kilian Evang, and Johan Bos. 2013. Gamification for Word Sense Labeling. In *IWCS (Short Papers)*, pages 397–403, Potsdam, Germany.

Henning Wachsmuth, Nona Naderi, Ivan Habernal, Yufang Hou, Graeme Hirst, Iryna Gurevych, and Benno Stein. 2017. Argumentation Quality Assessment: Theory vs. Practice. In *Proceedings of the 55th Annual Meeting of the Association for Computational Linguistics (ACL 2017)*, page (to appear). Association for Computational Linguistics.

Douglas Walton. 1995. *A Pragmatic Theory of Fallacy*. The University of Alabama Press, Tuscaloosa, AL.

An Analysis and Visualization Tool for
Case Study Learning of Linguistic Concepts

Cecilia Ovesdotter Alm, Benjamin S. Meyers, Emily Prud'hommeaux

Rochester Institute of Technology

{coagla,bsm9339,emilypx}@rit.edu

Abstract

We present an educational tool that integrates computational linguistics resources for use in non-technical undergraduate language science courses. By using the tool in conjunction with evidence-driven pedagogical case studies, we strive to provide opportunities for students to gain an understanding of linguistic concepts and analysis through the lens of realistic problems in feasible ways. Case studies tend to be used in legal, business, and health education contexts, but less in the teaching and learning of linguistics. The approach introduced also has potential to encourage students across training backgrounds to continue on to computational language analysis coursework.

1   Introduction

The computational linguistics community makes available software resources for performing structural and meaning-related linguistic analysis on language input. While these tools and models are commonly used in research contexts and have long been used in computational linguistics instruction (Meurers et al., 2002; Baldridge and Erk, 2008), they also have a role to play for enhancing non-computational pedagogy in linguistics.

We present an educational innovation that aims to provide students in undergraduate language science classes with case-based active learning opportunities by enabling them to actively confront linguistic concepts and methods encountered in textbooks and class discussions (or as supplementary materials to stimulate learning) in hands-on tasks that emphasize the applied nature of the study and practice of language science. Computational linguistics software resources tend to be

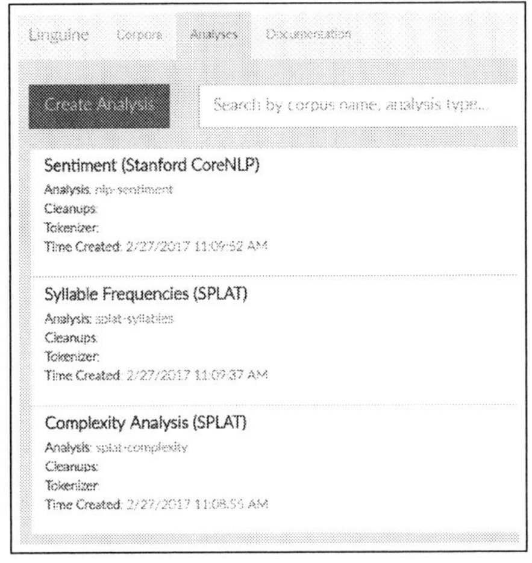

Figure 1: Linguine's tab-based interface showing the Analyses tab with three completed analyses.

designed for tech-savvy users and expect knowledge acquired in computational, or computational linguistics, curriculum or similar contexts. They often require some understanding of technical details about computer programming and computational linguistics principles and methods. While there are web-based linguistic corpus resources, the interaction potential for users tends to be limited to functionalities such as key-words-in-context searches or look-up of relatively simple structural patterns, as opposed to providing students across majors with the ability to conduct, assess, and critique analyses built on models developed in the computational linguistics community.

Linguine [1] is a web-based tool with a user-friendly interface (Figure 1) tailored to educational use in language science coursework. [2] It draws on natural language processing resources in the open domain in order to provide users with the capabilities to study a range of linguistic structural and semantic patterns in written language input.

---

[1] Demo: tinyurl.com/ritlinguine   [2] github.com/ritlinguine

13

Proceedings of the 2017 EMNLP System Demonstrations, pages 13–18

Copenhagen, Denmark, September 7–11, 2017. ©2017 Association for Computational Linguistics

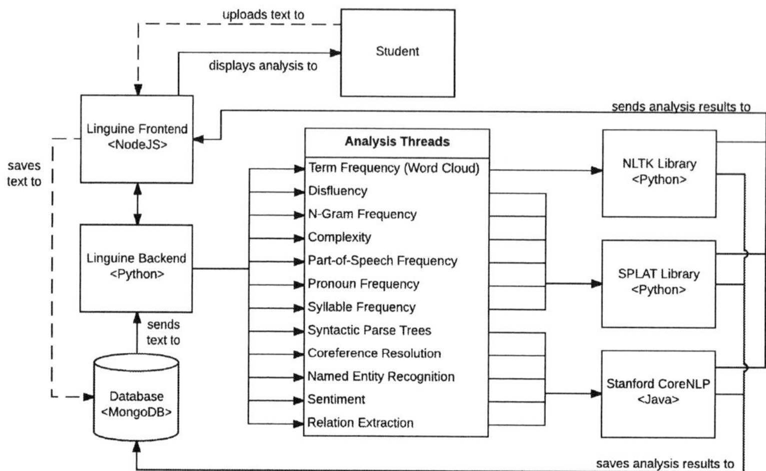

Figure 2: Linguine framework overview. Dotted lines represent text upload. Solid lines represent analysis generation. NodeJS forwards the users's analysis request to Python, which locates the text in the database, performs preprocessing by analysis, and sends the processed text to the appropriate framework for analysis. Generated analyses are stored for later use. NodeJS generates the appropriate visualization.

The motivation for Linguine includes (1) making computationally driven language analysis accessible to non-computing majors in undergraduate linguistics courses; (2) enabling practical, formative opportunities for linguistically informed analysis; and (3) guiding students to perform user-friendly analyses and presenting intuitive visualizations of automatically processed results to make them more readily interpretable. Thus, Linguine contrasts with resources such as the CLARINO Language Analysis Portal (Lapponi et al., 2013) in its pedagogical purpose and its pairing of analyses with visualizations. Linguine also enables a broader set of language analysis functionalities.

This work's main innovation is the applied pairing of this tool with case studies as active learning vehicles in language science. The case studies task students with seeking evidence-based solutions to and recommendations for linguistically grounded real-world problems. They also aim to train students in oral and written communication about their analysis, recommendations, and critical observations. While the case study method is a recognized learning tool in domains such as business and law, it is rather unusual to see it used extensively in the linguistics curriculum. This approach thus differentiates itself from standard ways of teaching linguistics concepts and analysis. Linguine's functionalities and visualizations support and facilitate the situational problem solving and

hands-on critical thinking that case studies enable. Adopting the case study method further seeks to nurture student experiences in utilizing linguistics to address and reason over relatable problems in society. Students can also increase their understanding of the limitations and potential utility of language technologies.

In this paper, we describe Linguine and how it contributes to using case study pedagogy in language science. We also report on instructor observations in conjunction with student surveys to provide insights into the utility of the case study model with the Linguine system.

2　Learning Linguistics with Linguine

Linguine is a web application designed for an educational purpose. It provides an easy-to-use interface, allowing interaction with preloaded default or custom-uploaded plain texts for performing language-based analysis. Figure 1 shows the interface for selecting the resulting analysis. For analysis functionalities, Linguine leverages widely available resources for performing natural language processing, including NLTK (Bird et al., 2009), Stanford CoreNLP (Manning et al., 2014), and SPLAT [3], along with the web technologies, NodeJS [4] and d3 [5]. Aspects that set Linguine apart are its focus on enabling class activities and ac-

---

[3] http://splat-library.org　　[4] https://nodejs.org/en/about/
[5] https://d3js.org/

tive learning and its ability to transform machine-processed results into intuitive visualizations. Visualizations depend on the analysis performed and include sentence-by-sentence display of syntactic trees, data summary tables, tool-tips displaying sequential annotations, and colorful markup in text. Users can inspect results in a structured representation within the tool. Results can also be downloaded in JSON format for off-line analysis by users with the necessary background.

Figure 2 shows the data flow between Linguine's components. The architecture is composed of a Python server that interacts with a NodeJS server and a MongoDB [6] database. These components run as system services on a RHEL7 virtual machine. The Python server receives analysis requests from the NodeJS server. It obtains the relevant text from the database and performs preprocessing operations. Preprocessed text is passed to a queue for analysis. Analyses are carried out in parallel using the expected resources. Analysis time depends on the size of the text and the type of analysis. At present, Linguine is an English-focused environment, aimed at language science coursework offered by computational linguists faculty in an English department. However, its framework enables incorporating additional resources for text-based analyses. For example, models trained on other languages, or potentially other forms of unstructured data, could be integrated with adapted visualizations.

The SPLAT library computes statistics on n-grams, part-of-speech tags, syllables, and disfluencies. SPLAT also calculates linguistic complexity measures, including content and idea densities, Flesch readability, Flesch-Kincaid grade level, and type-token ratio. Examples of visualizations produced by Linguine using SPLAT functionality are shown in Figures 3, 4 (left), and 6 (right). Using output from Stanford CoreNLP, Linguine incorporates analysis options requiring sophisticated modeling, including syntactic trees with sentiment labels (Figure 5) and named entity recognition (Figure 6, left). Analyses are saved to the database, allowing users to return to visualizations without having to reprocess their analysis.

The integration of technologies required managing asynchronous communications between Python and Linguine's other subsystems. Data transfer within Linguine is handled by Tornado [7],

---

[6] https://www.mongodb.com/
[7] http://www.tornadoweb.org/en/stable/

Q	This case study activity...
1	was engaging.
2	had clear instructions.
3	was related to the course material.
4	involved a reasonable time commitment.
5	was a valuable learning experience.
6	enhanced my understanding of linguistic concepts.
7	reinforced theoretical concepts from class with an application.
8	let me use linguistic approaches to problem solving.
9	had me engaged in critical thinking.
10	involved a useful reporting experience.
Q	**Using the provided web tools and input...**
11	was straightforward.
12	went hand-in-hand with the case instructions.
13	enhanced my thinking about the case resolution plan.
14	was interesting.
15	was a good learning experience.

Table 1: Satisfaction agreement statements.

a Python framework that transfers information as HTTP requests. At present, the tool is envisioned for use by a 25-person class. Detailed analysis of resource utilization for different user group sizes is left for future work.

3 Case Studies

We have so far developed three case studies for two course contexts: an overview course of language science fundamentals and an English language history course. Combining case studies with the functionality of Linguine provides students with fictional yet realistic scenarios to solve using active inquiry with linguistic data. Each case study comprises a set of design elements, following a template that enables task clarity and effective design and prototyping:

- The case description includes a narrative that sets up a problem and provides background about the data needed to perform language-based analysis in Linguine for gathering evidence. This includes step-by-step analysis instructions with questions to answer, as well as guidelines for presenting work, preparing written reporting, and completing a quiz, in addition to an evaluation rubric.

Tag	Frequency	Word types (capitalization maintained)
PRP$	1	her
.	1	.
NNP	1	Monday
VBD	1	saw
PRP	2	I her
IN	1	on
VBG	1	walking
NN	1	dog

1st-Person 2nd-Person 3rd-Person

Pronoun	Frequency	Type
I	1	Personal, Singular
HER	2	Personal/Possessive, Singular/Plural

I saw her walking her dog on Monday.

Figure 3: Visualizations: *I saw her walking her dog on Monday.* POS (left); pronoun frequencies (right).

Complexity Metric	Value
Content Density:	1.206
Idea Density:	0.499
Flesch Readability:	72.000
Flesch-Kincaid Grade Level:	10.700
Type-Token Ratio:	0.469 (283 / 603)

Score	Grade Level
> 100.0	< 5th Grade
100.00-90.00	5th Grade
90.0-80.0	6th Grade
80.0-70.0	7th Grade
70.0-60.0	8th-9th Grade
60.0-50.0	10th-12th Grade
50.0-30.0	College Undergraduate
30.0-0.0	College Graduate

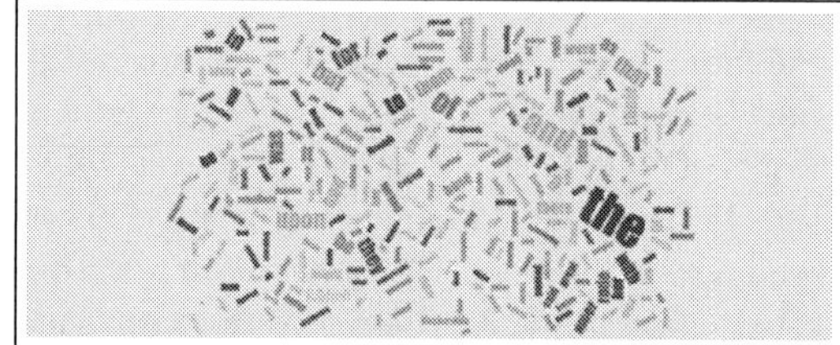

Figure 4: Complexity metrics (left) and term frequencies (right) for a Sir Arthur Conan Doyle excerpt.

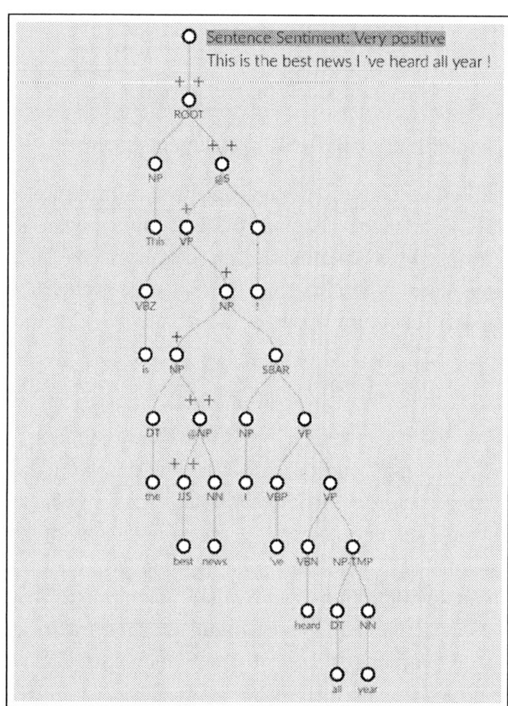

Figure 5: Syntactic tree with sentiment labels for *This is the best news I've heard all year!*

- Data that has been selected and prepared for out-of-class and in-class analysis.

- Two readings that students can consult for reasoning about a case: an applied, broad-audience reading vs. an academic reading.

The case studies are expanded with a develop-ment and teaching guide that outlines the motivation for text selection, details preprocessing on the texts, and includes expected answers to their questions. The initially developed case studies are:

- *The Language of Dementia*: Students analyze a selection of picture descriptions from the DementiaBank corpus (Becker et al., 1994) with the goal of assisting a medical researcher in identifying linguistic markers of Alzheimer's disease. Readings include Szatloczki et al. (2015); Goldstein et al. (2010).

- *Historical Varieties of English*: Students examine excerpts of literature across time periods to assist school teachers in choosing grade-appropriate readings for their classes. Readings include, e.g., Perera (1980).

- *Formality in Business Communications*: In roles as analysts for a training agency, students use email data (Klimt and Yang, 2004; Pavlick and Tetreault, 2016, added later) to critically envision guidelines for workplace communications. Readings include Pavlick and Tetreault (2016); Lebowitz (2015).

4 Results of Case Study Exploration

Students in an introductory linguistics course worked with Linguine in assigned teams first on *The Language of Dementia* and a few weeks later on *Formality in Business Communications*. For both cases, students used Linguine and engaged

Figure 6: Visualizing named entity recognition (left) and disfluencies in speech transcription (right).

with provided data in and out of the classroom. Student teams reported results orally to classmates in short presentations and in write-ups. The third case study in the English language history class was completed individually by fewer students.[8] Students were instructed to complete the case components and then answer an anonymous case satisfaction survey (Tables 1- 2). This provided a chance to self-report on the learning experience.

Instructor observations of class interactions suggest that several pedagogical benefits emerged. First, students engaged in increased critical thinking about analysis, data, and methods in class. Second, the reporting exercise nurtured co-learning, as students could observe how others approach a problem and choose to visualize, summarize, and present results. Third, the case approach offered a structured framework for teamwork.

Figure 7 (p. 6) shows that a majority of students evaluated the activity positively on all measures, agreeing that the experience was engaging, educational, interesting, and that it stimulated critical thinking and learning (Q1, Q5, Q9, Q14, Q15). Students reported that the activity and tool were clear and straightforward (Q2, Q11, Q12). Crucially, most students felt the experience was relevant to and practiced class material, enhanced their understanding of linguistics, and engaged them in such problem solving (Q3, Q6, Q7, Q8).

Students were also given the opportunity to provide qualitative feedback about their experience; examples are in Table 2 (p. 6). Nearly half the students reported that they particularly enjoyed learning about practical, real-world applications of linguistics. They recognized the links between the concepts seen in class and the case studies. Students found the texts in the second case study (from email data) to be particularly entertaining, and they appreciated the open-ended nature of that case study compared with the first case study.

The negative comments centered on three issues: (1) the modest amount of data provided for analysis; (2) the constraints of Linguine (e.g., allows downloading results as JSON, not csv); and (3) the reporting experience, which a few students found repetitive in the first case study. This feedback has been valuable for continuing to enhance Linguine and case-based instructional materials.

5 Conclusion

We presented the integration of the pedagogical web application Linguine and case studies using this tool in courses. We will continue to explore the system and its educational use and effectiveness in parallel. Developing a systematic process for preparing new case studies is left for future work. Planned expansions of the system and materials include increased focus on processing meaning, and expanding the analysis potential for transcribed speech to enable further pedagogical bridging of analyzing spoken and written language data in language science case studies.

Acknowledgments

The work was partially supported by an RIT PLIG grant. Many thanks to three senior project teams: ProNouns, Rigatoni, and Pastafarians helped develop Linguine's core functionality and interface.

References

Jason Baldridge and Katrin Erk. 2008. Teaching computational linguistics to a large, diverse student body: Courses, tools, and interdepartmental interaction. In *WS on Issues in Teaching CL.* pages 1–9.

James T Becker, François Boiler, Oscar L Lopez, Judith Saxton, and Karen L McGonigle. 1994. The natural history of Alzheimer's disease: Description of study cohort and accuracy of diagnosis. *Archives of Neurology* 51(6):585–594.

Steven Bird, Ewan Klein, and Edward Loper. 2009. *Natural language processing with Python: Analyzing text with the natural language toolkit.* O'Reilly.

---

[8] A co-author served as course instructor.

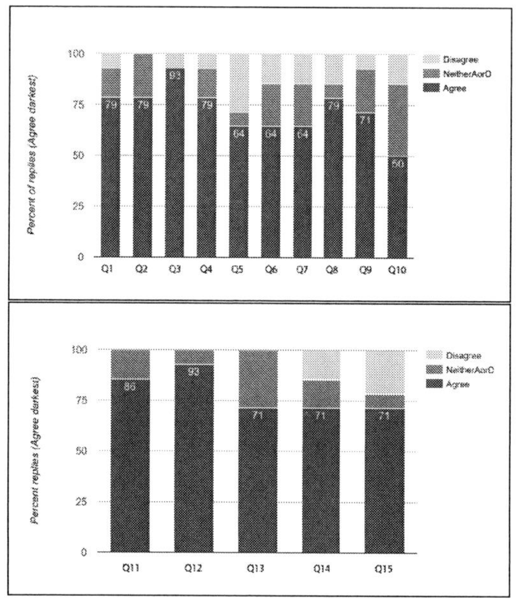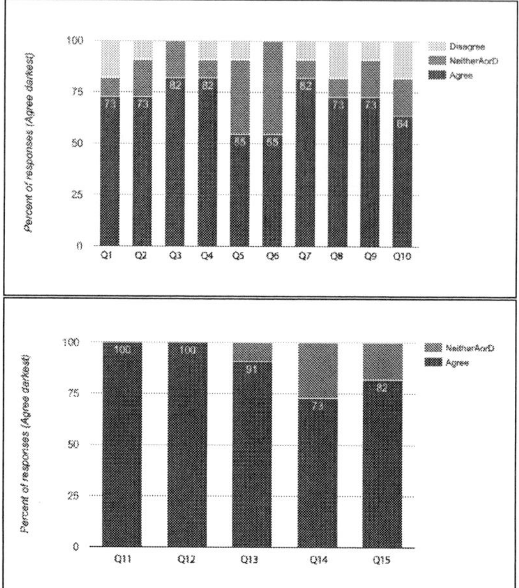

Figure 7: Percent replies for two cases in a class (N = 14 vs. 11 respondents). Top: Feedback on case study activities 1 and 2 shows that users mostly concur on statements in Table 1. Bottom: Feedback on the tool and its input suggest positive user experiences, increasing as tool familiarity grew.

Applications	• I learned that there are real world applications for what we learned in class. • got to work with real data on solving a real problem • I was able to come up with something that could prove to be useful in my life.
Engagement	• Interesting scenario, engaging • I really enjoyed using linguine, it's a great tool. • Keep the online tool, super fun.
Drawbacks	• n-grams could be downloadable as a csv for additional processing. • I wish there was a way to get quantitative data about the parse trees.
Presentations	• awkward having all of the groups present essentially the same information • the reporting part (in class) could use some modifications.

Table 2: Example open-ended feedback from the satisfaction survey.

Jessica Goldstein, Maggie Starbard, and Soren Wheeler (Prod). 2010. Agatha Christie and nuns tell a tale of Alzheimer's. *NPR* [June 1].

Bryan Klimt and Yiming Yang. 2004. The Enron corpus: A new dataset for email classification research. In *Europ Conf on Machine Learn.* pages 217–226.

Emanuele Lapponi, Erik Velldal, Nikolay A. Vazov, and Stephan Oepen. 2013. Towards large-scale language analysis in the cloud. In *WS on Nordic Lang. Research Infra. at NODALIDA.* pages 1–10.

Shana Lebowitz. 2015. Here's exactly how to write an email to your CEO. *Business Insid.* [Nov. 13].

Christopher D. Manning, Mihai Surdeanu, John Bauer, Jenny Finkel, Steven J. Bethard, and David McClosky. 2014. The Stanford CoreNLP Natural Language Processing Toolkit. In *ACL Systems Demonstrations.* pages 55–60.

W Detmar Meurers, Gerald Penn, and Frank Richter. 2002. A web-based instructional platform for constraint-based grammar formalisms and parsing. In *WS on Effective Tools and Methodologies for Teaching NLP and CL.* pages 19–26.

Ellie Pavlick and Joel Tetreault. 2016. An empirical analysis of formality in online communication. *TACL* 4:61–74.

Katharine Perera. 1980. The assessment of linguistic difficulty in reading material. *Ed R* 32(2):151–161.

Greta Szatloczki, Ildiko Hoffmann, Veronika Vincze, Janos Kalman, and Magdolna Pakaski. 2015. Speaking in Alzheimer's disease, is that an early sign? Importance of changes in language abilities in Alzheimer's disease. *Front in Aging Neurosci.* 7:195.

GraphDocExplore:
A Framework for the Experimental Comparison
of Graph-based Document Exploration Techniques

Tobias Falke and **Iryna Gurevych**

Research Training Group AIPHES and UKP Lab
Department of Computer Science, Technische Universität Darmstadt
`https://www.aiphes.tu-darmstadt.de`

Abstract

Graphs have long been proposed as a tool to browse and navigate in a collection of documents in order to support exploratory search. Many techniques to automatically extract different types of graphs, showing for example entities or concepts and different relationships between them, have been suggested. While experimental evidence that they are indeed helpful exists for some of them, it is largely unknown which type of graph is most helpful for a specific exploratory task. However, carrying out experimental comparisons with human subjects is challenging and time-consuming. Towards this end, we present the *Graph-DocExplore* framework. It provides an intuitive web interface for graph-based document exploration that is optimized for experimental user studies. Through a generic graph interface, different methods to extract graphs from text can be plugged into the system. Hence, they can be compared at minimal implementation effort in an environment that ensures controlled comparisons. The system is publicly available under an open-source license.[1]

1 Introduction

Structures that reveal relationships between different information units in a document collection, e.g. relations between mentioned organizations, have been proposed to support humans analyzing document collections. Especially in *exploratory search* scenarios, where the information need is complex and cannot be served by a simple keyword search (Marchionini, 2006), these structures

are deemed beneficial. Even without supporting software, humans were found to naturally create such structures for themselves (Chin et al., 2009).

Consequently, many types of structures and approaches to extract them from text have been proposed. These include concept hierarchies (Sanderson and Croft, 1999; Yang, 2012), concept maps (Briggs et al., 2004), predicate-argument networks (van Ham et al., 2009), entailment between propositions (Adler et al., 2012) or co-occurrences of named entities (Benikova et al., 2014). All of them can be seen as labeled graphs in which nodes and edges represent different information units extracted from a document collection.

However, what remains unclear is which of these graphs are most helpful for a specific document exploration task. Only few papers evaluate their proposed graphs in a user study and usually just compare it to baselines such as keyword-based search. Direct comparisons between different types of graphs are missing.

Carrying out such a comparative user study is a difficult endeavor. Typically, one would have different groups of subjects that work on a given task under different conditions, e.g. with graph A or B. The subjects' performance on the task, measured for example in completion time or result quality, would then be compared between the groups to draw conclusions on whether graph A or B is more helpful. The first challenge is that a full end-user application has to be built around a graph-extraction method for such an experiment, which usually involves a non-trivial amount of implementation work. Second, even if full systems are already available for comparison, they might not be usable: Every difference between two systems, as small as different font sizes or colors, can influence a subject's performance. As a result, observed performance differences cannot be directly attributed to the different graphs.

---

[1] `https://github.com/UKPLab/`
`emnlp2017-graphdocexplore`

19

Proceedings of the 2017 EMNLP System Demonstrations, pages 19–24
Copenhagen, Denmark, September 7–11, 2017. ©2017 Association for Computational Linguistics

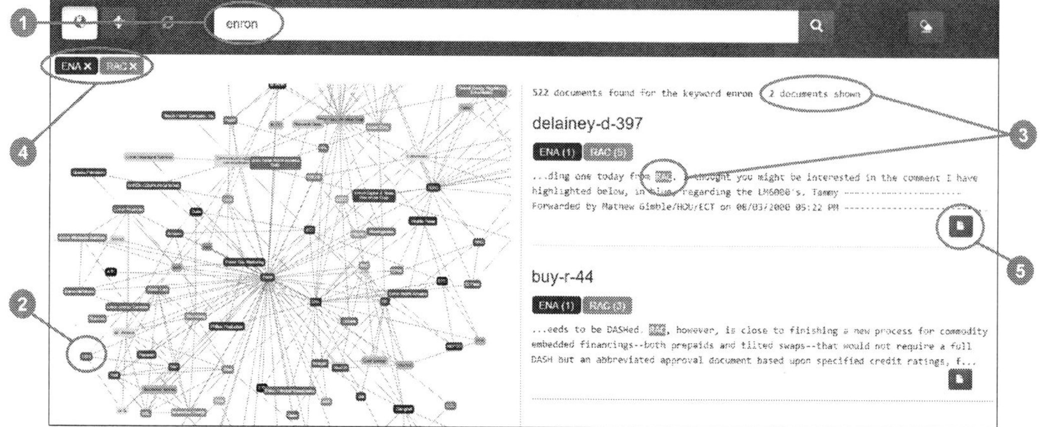

Figure 1: User interface: After entering a search term (1), the system displays retrieved documents (right) and a graph built from them (left). When clicking on a node or edge (2), documents are filtered and highlighted (3) according to the spans associated with the selected graph element. Active filters are shown at the top (4). Opening a document (5) shows its full text with all highlighted spans.

In this work, we present *GraphDocExplore*, a framework for graph-based document exploration. Due to the following properties, it is particularly useful to carry out user studies as described above:

User Interface The framework already contains a fully implemented, modern and intuitive web application for explorative search in documents that can be used for experimental studies.

Graph-Text-Integration Rather than showing the constructed graph independently, it is tightly integrated with the documents via navigation, filtering and highlighting features to ensure that a user can effectively make use of it (see Figure 1).

Logging All actions a user performs in the web application are captured in a detailed log for further analysis and reconstruction of user behavior.

Graph-Independence Different methods to extract graphs can be plugged into a generic interface, such that fair experimental comparisons that effectively control for all other confounding factors can be set up easily and quickly.

Dynamic Graphs Integrated methods for graph extraction are notified about all user actions and can dynamically modify their graph during a session, allowing to study the personalization of a graph based on the user actions.

The remainder of this paper is organized as follows: First, we review different types of graphs and corresponding systems proposed in the past

(§2). Then, we present our framework from a functional (§3) and technical perspective (§4). Finally, we report results of a first user study (§5).

2 Related Work

Many methods to structure document collections can be seen as different kinds of labeled graphs generated from the documents. Early work studied *concept hierarchies* which are graphs with concepts as nodes and edges representing hyponomy relations (Sanderson and Croft, 1999; Lawrie et al., 2001; Kummamuru et al., 2004). More recently, personalized versions were proposed (Yang, 2012, 2015). *Concept maps* are a more expressive variant of these graphs in which the edges have different labels defining their meaning rather than all being taxonomic (Novak and Gowin, 1984) and can be used for the same purpose (Briggs et al., 2004). Another popular type of graph shows *keywords* (Tixier et al., 2016) or *entities* (Benikova et al., 2014) as nodes with unlabeled edges between them depicting co-occurrences. Other graphs were suggested to depict entailment (Adler et al., 2012) or relations expressed by a specific predicate (van Ham et al., 2009). All of these structures can be captured with the abstract graph model in our framework.

In addition to specific graphs, more complex applications, such as *new/s/leak* (Yimam et al., 2016), *Jigsaw* (Görg et al., 2013) or *Overview*[2],

---

[2] https://www.overviewdocs.com

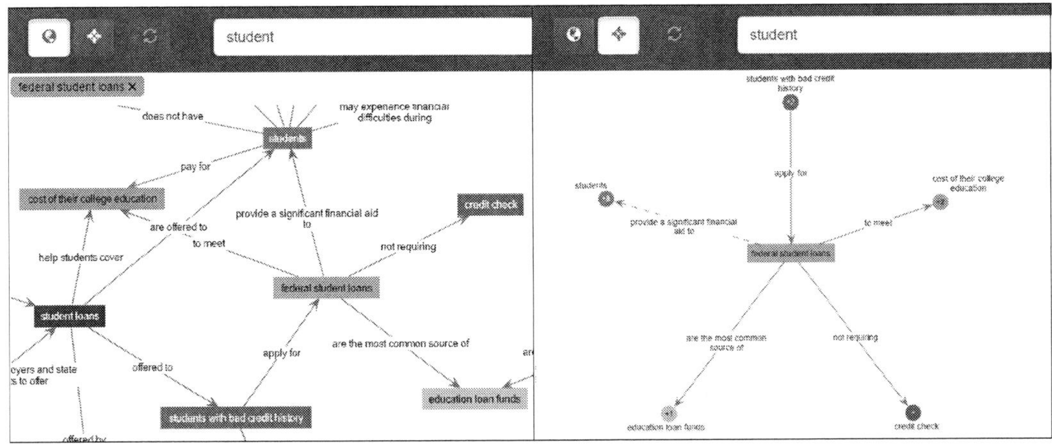

Figure 2: Layouts: *Full (left):* The graph is displayed completely and can be zoomed, panned and moved. *Focused (right):* A single focus node and its neighbors are visible. Selecting a neighbor moves the focus.

have been developed to support document exploration by integrating many different techniques, including graphs, in a single application. In contrast to our work, their focus is on productive use, while we are mainly interested in the experimental evaluation, requiring us to study the use of specific graphs in isolation. Moreover, note that graphs in which nodes represent full documents, as obtained by traditional document clustering or document chains (Shahaf and Guestrin, 2010), are less useful for our application because no fine-grained highlights can be provided for nodes and edges.

With regard to experimental evaluations, only few of the suggested graphs were extrinsically evaluated and proven to be helpful in an exploratory search scenario. Both Kummamuru et al. (2004) and Yang (2012) compare their approaches with previous work in user studies, but restrict the comparison to other methods producing concept hierarchies. Kang et al. (2011) compare the powerful Jigsaw system against simpler alternatives, including keyword-based search and pen and paper. To the best of our knowledge, no studies have been carried out for other types of graphs, e.g. for concept maps, and there are no studies comparing different types of graphs against each other. Thus, the framework presented in this work is highly needed to make such comparisons.

3 Functionality

The system for graph-based document exploration was designed in the style of well-known search engine interfaces. As shown in Figure 1, the list of search results is complemented by a visualization of the graph that has been extracted from the retrieved documents. This type of integration follows the popular paradigm of faceted search, in which different taxonomies, either predefined or extracted from the results (Hearst and Stoica, 2009), are offered along with the results to filter them. Instead of the typically small, single-level taxonomies, our application takes this idea further by offering a comprehensive graph.

User Interaction After executing a query, a user can both scroll through the list of retrieved documents or navigate through the generated graph. Every node and (optionally) edge in the graph is associated with at least one span in one of the retrieved documents (see Figure 5). Note that these spans must not match the label of the graph element, but can be other phrases referring to it. If a user selects an element in the graph, the corresponding spans are highlighted in the document snippets and the results are filtered to the subset of documents that contain at least one associated span. Filters can be combined, which reduces the documents to those containing spans for all, can be temporally deactivated and can also be removed completely. In the result list, the number of corresponding spans for each filter is displayed. Colors of nodes in the graph, filter tags and highlighted spans match. In the result list, a user can switch to the full text view of a document, which also contains highlights according to the current filters.

Graph Layouts The application currently provides two different graph visualizations that we found to yield useful renderings for graphs of different sizes. At any point, a user can switch between them using the buttons in the top left corner. The left part of Figure 2 gives an example of the *full* layout, which is a force-directed layout showing the complete graph. It allows the user to zoom in and out and pan to fully inspect the graph. While it has the advantage that it can provide an overview of the complete graph, the visualization can become complex for large graphs.

As an alternative, the application offers a *focused* layout, which is shown on the right side of Figure 2. It shows only one focus node and its direct neighbors at a time, while every neighbor node has a number indicating how many more edges are connected to it. Selecting one of the neighbors moves that node to the center and displays its neighbors. This allows to go through the graph step by step and it usually yields much cleaner visualizations, as the number of visible nodes is limited. Both visualizations support directed and undirected graphs. The modular design of the application allows to add alternative visualizations in the future.

Logging In order to be able to thoroughly study the behavior of users that are working with the application, it creates a comprehensive log of all actions that a user performed. Figure 3 illustrates how such a log looks like for a user session. The user, working on documents about student loans, starts by issuing the query *credit check*. The corresponding log entry lists the keyword and a list of the retrieved documents (1). Next, she scrolled through the result list and stopped with documents 3, 26 and 17 in the visible section of the list (2). Zooming the graph made a certain set of nodes visible (3). She then selected one of the nodes (4), which automatically created a filter (5) and reduced the result list correspondingly. From the filtered result list, she opened document 17 (6), scrolled to a certain position (7) and closed it afterwards (8). She then switches to the alternative graph layout (9) and continues her search. Note that the actual log also contains timestamps.

4 Architecture and Implementation

The framework has been implemented following a server-client-architecture and designed to be easily extensible in different regards. In the following, we provide an overview of the architecture and describe two aspects, the integration of graph

```
1 SEARCH "credit check" doc-0,doc-8,doc-3,...
2 RES_SCROLLED doc-3,doc-26,doc-17
3 ZOOMED 42,65,89,57,35,24
4 NODE_CLICKED 24
5 FILTER_ADDED 24
6 DOC_OPENED doc-17
7 DOC_SCROLLED [516-1468]
8 BACK_TO_RES
9 GRAPH_SWITCHED focused
...
```

Figure 3: Example for a user interaction log.

generators and dynamic graphs, in more detail.

Overview Figure 4 depicts the architecture of the framework. The server-side portion is realized in *Java*. To enable the keyword search, we integrated *Apache Solr*[3] to index the documents. Different graph generation modules can be plugged into the system and have access to the documents. Several document collections can be loaded into the framework and used with different graphs. User actions are logged in a text-based format. In addition to the graphs, the modular design also allows to easily change the search engine, e.g. to Lucene, or the logging mechanism, e.g. to a database. On the client-side, the user interface described in the previous section is realized with *AngularJS*.[4] The server exposes a *REST API* to handle all communication with the frontend.

Graph Interface As mentioned above, different graph generation modules can be used with the framework. A configuration file defines the active type of graph per document collection. When starting a new search, the framework instantiates the corresponding graph generator and provides the retrieved documents. The generator can then apply its custom processing logic to the documents and return the resulting graph. To offload expensive preprocessing work, a generator can also access precomputed data for each document. Figure 5 shows the data structure in which a graph is represented in the framework. Both a node and an edge have a label, containing a description string used in the visualization and a list of spans in the documents. Note that the latter is crucial for the interaction between the graph and the documents through filtering and highlighting. The sys-

---

[3]http://lucene.apache.org/solr/
[4]https://angularjs.org/

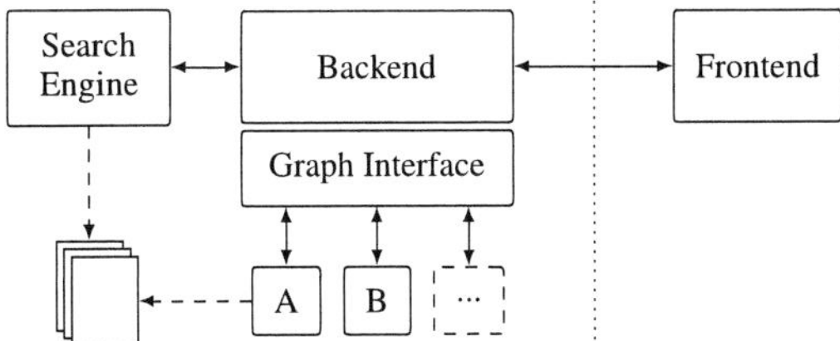

Figure 4: System architecture, enabling the integration of different graph generation models.

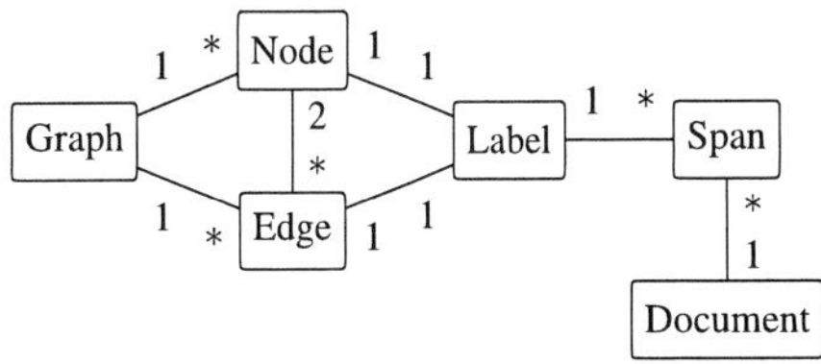

Figure 5: Data structure to capture different types of text graphs in UML-style class notation.

tem supports both labeled and unlabeled as well as directed and undirected graphs.

As examples, we created two graph generation modules for our framework. The first is a file-based generator that simply reads a static graph for a document collection from a file. The second integrates DKPro Core (Eckart de Castilho and Gurevych, 2014) to create co-occurrence graphs of automatically recognized entities. It demonstrates how a broad range of linguistic preprocessing tools can be easily made available and utilized in our framework. Similarly, many other graph generation methods can be used with the framework. When comparing them against each other in a user study, the common web application ensures a controlled experimental setting.

Dynamic Graphs As part of the graph generation interface, implementations are also notified about the actions that a user performs in the application. All events that are documented in the interaction log (see Figure 3) are provided through the interface. Further, a graph generator can modify its generated graph after the initial creation. In case of a change to the graph, the user is notified and can trigger an update of the visualization in the frontend. This setup makes it possible to create dynamic instead of static graphs and to use the framework to study their usefulness. While some work has been done in this direction (Yang, 2012; Shahaf and Guestrin, 2010), the development of methods that interactively adapt and personalize a graph for document exploration to a specific user has received only little attention. With our application, we provide an important evaluation framework that is needed to move further into this interesting direction of research.

5 User Study

To verify whether the user interface and interaction of the presented application is in line with user expectations, we conducted a first preliminary user study. Since the focus was on usability, all subjects worked with the same graph rather than comparing different graph types. 20 researchers from our lab and students from the university participated. They used the application to explore a collection of web pages on student loans (as in Figure 2) and answered a questionnaire asking for feedback on different parts of the application.

The results showed that the application was perceived as being very intuitive. Subjects could easily interpret the meaning of the graph and how it can be used to filter and highlight the documents. With regard to the different layouts, 60% preferred the focused layout because it was "clearer" and "less cluttered", while only 15% preferred the full layout, the rest being undecided. However, several subjects noted that the full layout is still useful to get the big picture, advocating to offer both options in the tool. In addition, the participants provided many useful suggestions to improve the application, e.g. adding tooltips, which have been incorporated into the current version.

6 Conclusion

In this paper, we presented *GraphDocExplore*, a framework for graph-based document exploration. Its web application augments a traditional keyword-search interface with a graph extracted from the search results. The graph can be used to navigate, filter and explore a collection of documents in an intuitive way. With its generic graph generator interface, different approaches to extract graphs from text can be plugged into the framework, providing an ideal environment to compare these approaches in controlled experimental evaluations with users. Further, the framework supports graphs that are dynamically altered based on user interactions, allowing to study methods for the interactive personalization of navigation graphs. The framework and its source code are publicly available at `https://github.com/UKPLab/emnlp2017-graphdocexplore`.

Acknowledgments

We would like to thank Alexander Gerhard Gössl, Arwed Gölz, Ramy Hcini and Christoph Sebastian Vollbrecht for their help with the implementation and all participants of the user study for their feedback. This work has been supported by the DFG as part of the Research Training Group "Adaptive Preparation of Information from Heterogeneous Sources" (AIPHES) under grant No. GRK 1994/1.

References

Meni Adler, Jonathan Berant, and Ido Dagan. 2012. Entailment-based Text Exploration with Application to the Health-care Domain. In *Proceedings of the 50th Annual Meeting of the ACL*, pages 79–84, Jeju, Republic of Korea.

Darina Benikova, Uli Fahrer, Alexander Gabriel, Manuel Kaufmann, Seid Muhie Yimam, Tatiana von Landesberger, and Chris Biemann. 2014. Network of the Day: Aggregating and Visualizing Entity Networks from Online Sources. In *Workshop Proceedings KONVENS 2014*, Hildesheim, Germany.

Geoffrey Briggs, David A. Shamma, Alberto J. Cañas, Roger Carff, Jeffrey Scargle, and Joseph D. Novak. 2004. Concept Maps Applied to Mars Exploration Public Outreach. In *Concept Maps: Theory, Methodology, Technology. Proceedings of the First International Conference on Concept Mapping*, pages 109–116, Pamplona, Spain.

George Chin, Olga A. Kuchar, and Katherine E. Wolf. 2009. Exploring the analytical processes of intelligence analysts. In *Proceedings of the SIGCHI Conference on Human Factors in Computing Systems*, pages 11–20, Boston, MA, USA.

Richard Eckart de Castilho and Iryna Gurevych. 2014. A broad-coverage collection of portable NLP components for building shareable analysis pipelines. In *Proceedings of the Workshop on Open Infrastructures and Analysis Frameworks for HLT*, pages 1–11, Dublin, Ireland.

Carsten Görg, Zhicheng Liu, Jaeyeon Kihm, Jaegul Choo, Haesun Park, and John T. Stasko. 2013. Combining Computational Analyses and Interactive Visualization for Document Exploration and Sensemaking in Jigsaw. *IEEE Transactions on Visualization and Computer Graphics*, 19(10):1646–1663.

Marti A. Hearst and Emilia Stoica. 2009. NLP support for faceted navigation in scholarly collections. In *Proceedings of the 2009 Workshop on Text and Citation Analysis for Scholarly Digital Librarie*, pages 62–70, Singapore.

Youn-Ah Kang, Carsten Görg, and John T. Stasko. 2011. How Can Visual Analytics Assist Investigative Analysis? Design Implications from an Evaluation. *IEEE Transactions on Visualization and Computer Graphics*, 17(5):570–583.

Krishna Kummamuru, Rohit Lotlikar, Shourya Roy, Karan Singal, and Raghu Krishnapuram. 2004. A hierarchical monothetic document clustering algorithm for summarization and browsing search results. In *Proceedings of the 13th International Conference on WWW*, pages 658–665, New York, USA.

Dawn Lawrie, W. Bruce Croft, and Arnold Rosenberg. 2001. Finding topic words for hierarchical summarization. In *Proceedings of the 24th Annual International ACM SIGIR Conference*, pages 349–357, New Orleans, LA, USA.

Gary Marchionini. 2006. Exploratory Search. *Communications of the ACM*, 49(4):41–46.

Joseph D. Novak and D. Bob Gowin. 1984. *Learning How to Learn*. Cambridge University Press, Cambridge.

Mark Sanderson and Bruce Croft. 1999. Deriving concept hierarchies from text. In *Proceedings of the 22nd Annual International ACM SIGIR Conference*, pages 206–213, Berkeley, CA, USA.

Dafna Shahaf and Carlos Guestrin. 2010. Connecting the Dots Between News Articles. In *Proceedings of the 16th ACM SIGKDD International Conference on Knowledge Discovery and Data Mining*, pages 623–632, Washington, DC, USA.

Antoine Tixier, Konstantinos Skianis, and Michalis Vazirgiannis. 2016. GoWvis: A Web Application for Graph-of-Words-based Text Visualization and Summarization. In *Proceedings of ACL-2016 System Demonstrations*, pages 151–156, Berlin, Germany.

Frank van Ham, Martin Wattenberg, and Fernanda B. Viegas. 2009. Mapping Text with Phrase Nets. *IEEE Transactions on Visualization and Computer Graphics*, 15(6):1169–1176.

Hui Yang. 2012. Constructing Task-Specific Taxonomies for Document Collection Browsing. In *Proceedings of the 2012 Joint Conference on EMNLP and CoNLL*, pages 1278–1289, Jeju Island, Korea.

Hui Yang. 2015. Browsing Hierarchy Construction by Minimum Evolution. *ACM Transactions on Information Systems*, 33(3):1–33.

Seid Muhie Yimam, Heiner Ulrich, Tatiana von Landesberger, Marcel Rosenbach, Michaela Regneri, Alexander Panchenko, Franziska Lehmann, Uli Fahrer, Chris Biemann, and Kathrin Ballweg. 2016. new/s/leak – Information Extraction and Visualization for Investigative Data Journalists. In *Proceedings of the 54th Annual Meeting of the ACL*, pages 163–168, Berlin, Germany.

SGNMT – A Flexible NMT Decoding Platform for Quick Prototyping of New Models and Search Strategies

Felix Stahlberg[†] and **Eva Hasler[‡]** and **Danielle Saunders[†]** and **Bill Byrne[‡†]**

[†]Department of Engineering, University of Cambridge, UK

[‡]SDL Research, Cambridge, UK

Abstract

This paper introduces SGNMT, our experimental platform for machine translation research. SGNMT provides a generic interface to neural and symbolic scoring modules (*predictors*) with left-to-right semantic such as translation models like NMT, language models, translation lattices, n-best lists or other kinds of scores and constraints. Predictors can be combined with other predictors to form complex decoding tasks. SGNMT implements a number of search strategies for traversing the space spanned by the predictors which are appropriate for different predictor constellations. Adding new predictors or decoding strategies is particularly easy, making it a very efficient tool for prototyping new research ideas. SGNMT is actively being used by students in the MPhil program in Machine Learning, Speech and Language Technology at the University of Cambridge for course work and theses, as well as for most of the research work in our group.

1 Introduction

We are developing an open source decoding framework called SGNMT, short for Syntactically Guided Neural Machine Translation.[1] The software package supports a number of well-known frameworks, including TensorFlow[2] (Abadi et al., 2016), OpenFST (Allauzen et al., 2007), Blocks/Theano (Bastien et al., 2012; van Merriënboer et al., 2015), and NPLM (Vaswani et al., 2013). The two central concepts in the

SGNMT tool are *predictors* and *decoders*. Predictors are scoring modules which define scores over the target language vocabulary given the current internal predictor state, the history, the source sentence, and external side information. Scores from multiple, diverse predictors can be combined for use in decoding.

Decoders are search strategies which traverse the space spanned by the predictors. SGNMT provides implementations of common search tree traversal algorithms like beam search. Since decoders differ in runtime complexity and the kind of search errors they make, different decoders are appropriate for different predictor constellations.

The strict separation of scoring module and search strategy and the decoupling of scoring modules from each other makes SGNMT a very flexible decoding tool for neural and symbolic models which is applicable not only to machine translation. SGNMT is based on the OpenFST-based Cambridge SMT system (Allauzen et al., 2014). Although the system is less than a year old, we have found it to be very flexible and easy for new researchers to adopt. Our group has already integrated SGNMT into most of its research work.

We also find that SGNMT is very well-suited for teaching and student research projects. In the 2015-16 academic year, two students on the Cambridge MPhil in Machine Learning, Speech and Language Technology used SGNMT for their dissertation projects.[3] The first project involved using SGNMT with OpenFST for applying subword models in SMT (Gao, 2016). The second project developed automatic music composition by LSTMs where WFSAs were used to define the space of allowable chord progressions in 'Bach' chorales (Tomczak, 2016). The LSTM provides the 'creativity' and the WFSA enforces constraints

---

[1]`http://ucam-smt.github.io/sgnmt/html/`
[2]SGNMT relies on the TensorFlow fork available at `https://github.com/ehasler/tensorflow`

[3]`http://www.mlsalt.eng.cam.ac.uk/Main/CurrentMPhils`

25

Proceedings of the 2017 EMNLP System Demonstrations, pages 25–30
Copenhagen, Denmark, September 7–11, 2017. ©2017 Association for Computational Linguistics

Predictor	Predictor state	`initialize(·)`	`predict_next()`	`consume(token)`
NMT	State vector in the GRU or LSTM layer of the decoder network and current context vector.	Run encoder network to compute annotations.	Forward pass through the decoder to compute the posterior given the current decoder GRU or LSTM state and the context vector.	Feed back `token` to the NMT network and update the decoder state and the context vector.
FST	ID of the current node in the FST.	Load FST from the file system, set the predictor state to the FST start node.	Explore all outgoing edges of the current node and use arc weights as scores.	Traverse the outgoing edge from the current node labelled with `token` and update the predictor state to the target node.
n-gram	Current n-gram history	Set the current n-gram history to the begin-of-sentence symbol.	Return the LM scores for the current n-gram history.	Add `token` to the current n-gram history.
Word count	None	Empty	Return a cost of 1 for all tokens except `</s>`.	Empty
UNK count	Number of consumed UNK tokens.	Set UNK counter to 0, estimate the λ parameter of the Poisson distribution based on source sentence features.	For `</s>` use the log-probability of the current number of UNKs given λ. Use zero for all other tokens.	Increase internal counter by 1 if `token` is UNK.

Table 1: Predictor operations for the NMT, FST, n-gram LM, and counting modules.

that the chorales must obey. This second project in particular demonstrates the versatility of the approach. For the current, 2016-17 academic year, SGNMT is being used heavily in two courses.

2 Predictors

SGNMT consequently emphasizes flexibility and extensibility by providing a common interface to a wide range of constraints or models used in MT research. The concept facilitates quick prototyping of new research ideas. Our platform aims to minimize the effort required for implementation; decoding speed is secondary as optimized code for production systems can be produced once an idea has been proven successful in the SGNMT framework. In SGNMT, scores are assigned to partial hypotheses via one or many predictors. One predictor usually has a single responsibility as it represents a single model or type of constraint. Predictors need to implement the following methods:

- `initialize(src_sentence)` Initialize the predictor state using the source sentence.

- `get_state()` Get the internal predictor state.

- `set_state(state)` Set the internal predictor state.

- `predict_next()` Given the internal predictor state, produce the posterior over target tokens for the next position.

Predictor	Description
nmt	Attention-based neural machine translation following Bahdanau et al. (2015). Supports Blocks/Theano (Bastien et al., 2012; van Merriënboer et al., 2015) and TensorFlow (Abadi et al., 2016).
fst	Predictor for rescoring deterministic lattices (Stahlberg et al., 2016).
nfst	Predictor for rescoring non-deterministic lattices.
rtn	Rescoring recurrent transition networks (RTNs) as created by HiFST (Allauzen et al., 2014) with late expansion.
srilm	n-gram Kneser-Ney language model using the SRILM (Heafield et al., 2013; Stolcke et al., 2002) toolkit.
nplm	Neural n-gram language models based on NPLM (Vaswani et al., 2013).
rnnlm	Integrates RNN language models with TensorFlow as described by Zaremba et al. (2014).
forced	Forced decoding with a single reference.
forcedlst	n-best list rescoring.
bow	Restricts the search space to a bag of words with or without repetition (Hasler et al., 2017).
lrhiero	Experimental implementation of left-to-right Hiero (Siahbani et al., 2013) for small grammars.
wc	Number of words feature.
unkc	Applies a Poisson model for the number of UNKs in the output.
ngramc	Integrates external n-gram posteriors, e.g. for MBR-based NMT according Stahlberg et al. (2017).
length	Target sentence length model using simple source sentence features.

Table 2: Currently implemented predictors.

- `consume(token)` Update the internal predictor state by adding `token` to the current history.

The structure of the predictor state and the implementations of these methods differ substantially between predictors. Tab. 2 lists all predictors which are currently implemented. Tab. 1 summarizes the semantics of this interface for three very common predictors: the neural machine translation (NMT) predictor, the (deterministic) finite state transducer (FST) predictor for lattice rescoring, and the n-gram predictor for applying n-gram language models. We also included two examples (word count and UNK count) which do not have a natural left-to-right semantic but can still be represented as predictors.

2.1 Example Predictor Constellations

SGNMT allows combining any number of predictors and even multiple instances of the same predictor type. In case of multiple predictors we combine the predictor scores in a linear model. The following list illustrates that various interesting decoding tasks can be formulated as predictor combinations.

- `nmt`: A single NMT predictor represents pure NMT decoding.

- `nmt,nmt,nmt`: Using multiple NMT predictors is a natural way to represent ensemble decoding (Hansen and Salamon, 1990; Sutskever et al., 2014) in our framework.

- `fst,nmt`: NMT decoding constrained to an FST. This can be used for neural lattice rescoring (Stahlberg et al., 2016) or other kinds of constraints, for example in the context of source side simplification in MT (Hasler et al., 2016) or chord progressions in 'Bach' (Tomczak, 2016). The *fst* predictor can also be used to restrict the output of character-based or subword-unit-based NMT to a large word-level vocabulary encoded as FSA.

- `nmt,rnnlm,srilm,nplm`: Combining NMT with three kinds of language models: An RNNLM (Zaremba et al., 2014), a Kneser-Ney n-gram LM (Heafield et al., 2013; Stolcke et al., 2002), and a feedforward neural network LM (Vaswani et al., 2013).

Decoder	Description
greedy	Greedy decoding.
beam	Beam search as described in Bahdanau et al. (Bahdanau et al., 2015).
dfs	Depth-first search. Efficiently enumerates the complete search space, e.g. for exhaustive FST-based rescoring.
restarting	Similar to DFS but with better admissible pruning behaviour.
astar	A* search (Russell and Norvig, 2003). The heuristic function can be defined via predictors.
sepbeam	Associates hypotheses in the beam with only one predictor. Efficiently approximates system-level combination.
syncbeam	Beam search which compares hypotheses after consuming a special synchronization symbol rather than after each iteration.
bucket	Multiple beam search passes with small beam size. Can have better pruning behaviour than standard beam search.
vanilla	Fast beam search decoder for (ensembled) NMT. This implementation is similar to the decoder in Blocks (van Merriënboer et al., 2015) but can only be used for NMT as it bypasses the predictor framework.

Table 3: Currently implemented decoders.

- `nmt,ngramc,wc`: MBR-based NMT following Stahlberg et al. (2017) with n-gram posteriors extracted from an SMT lattice (`ngramc`) and a simple word penalty (`wc`).

3 Decoders

Decoders are algorithms to search for the highest scoring hypothesis. The list of predictors determines how (partial) hypotheses are scored by implementing the methods `initialize(·)`, `get_state()`, `set_state(·)`, `predict_next()`, and `consume(·)`. The *Decoder* class implements versions of these methods which apply to all predictors in the list. `initialize(·)` is always called prior to decoding a new sentence. Many popular search strategies can be described via the remaining methods `get_state()`, `set_state(·)`, `predict_next()`, and `consume(·)`. Algs. 1 and 2 show how to define greedy and beam decoding in this way.[4][5]

Tab. 3 contains a list of currently implemented decoders. The UML diagram in Fig. 1 illustrates the relation between decoders and predictors.

---

[4]Formally, `predict_next()` in Algs. 1 and 2 returns pairs of tokens and their costs.

[5]String concatenation is denoted with ·.

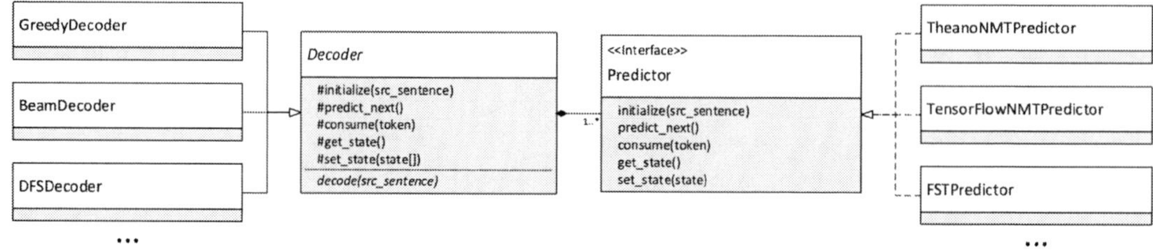

Figure 1: Reduced UML class diagram.

Algorithm 1 Greedy(src_sen)

1: `initialize`(src_sen)
2: $h \leftarrow \langle \texttt{<s>} \rangle$
3: **repeat**
4:    $P \leftarrow$`predict_next`()
5:    $(t, c) \leftarrow \arg\max_{(t', c') \in P} c'$
6:    $h \leftarrow h \cdot t$
7:    `consume`(t)
8: **until** $t = \texttt{</s>}$
9: **return** h

Algorithm 2 Beam(n, src_sen)

1: `initialize`(src_sen)
2: $H \leftarrow \{(\langle \texttt{<s>} \rangle, 0.0, \texttt{get\_state}())\}$
3: **repeat**
4:    $H_{next} \leftarrow \emptyset$
5:    **for all** $(h, c, s) \in H$ **do**
6:      `set_state`(s)
7:      $P \leftarrow$`predict_next`()
8:      $H_{next} \leftarrow H_{next} \cup$
$$\bigcup\nolimits_{(t', c') \in P} (h \cdot t', c + c', s)$$
9:    **end for**
10:   $H \leftarrow \emptyset$
11:   **for all** $(h, c, s) \in n\text{-best}(H_{next})$ **do**
12:     `set_state`(s)
13:     `consume`($h_{|h|}$)
14:     $H \leftarrow H \cup \{(h, c, \texttt{get\_state}())\}$
15:   **end for**
16: **until** Best hypothesis in H ends with $\texttt{</s>}$
17: **return** Best hypothesis in H

NMT batch decoding The flexibility of the predictor framework comes with degradation in decoding time. SGNMT provides two ways of speeding up pure NMT decoding, especially on the GPU. The *vanilla* decoding strategy exposes the beam search implementation in Blocks (van Merriënboer et al., 2015) which processes all active hypotheses in the beam in parallel. We also implemented a beam decoder version which decodes multiple sentences at once (batch decoding) rather than in a sequential order. Batch decoding is potentially more efficient since larger batches can make better use of GPU parallelism. The key concepts of our batch decoder implementation are:

- We use a scheduler running on a separate CPU thread to construct large batches of computation (GPU jobs) from multiple sentences and feeding them to the *jobs* queue.

- The GPU is operated by a single thread which communicates with the CPU scheduler thread via queues containing jobs. This thread is only responsible for retrieving jobs in the *jobs* queue, computing them, and putting them in the *jobs_results* queue, minimizing the down-time of GPU computation.

- Yet another CPU thread is responsible for processing the results computed on the GPU

in the *job_results* queue, e.g. by getting the n-best words from the posteriors. Processed jobs are sent back to the CPU scheduler where they are reassembled into new jobs.

This decoder is able to translate the WMT English-French test sets *news-test2012* to *news-test2014* on a Titan X GPU with 911.6 words per second with the word-based NMT model described in Stahlberg et al. (2016).[6] This decoding speed seems to be slightly faster than sequential decoding with high-performance NMT decoders like Marian-NMT (Junczys-Dowmunt et al., 2016) with reported decoding speeds of 865 words per second.[7] However, batch decoding with Marian-NMT is much faster reaching over 4,500 words

---

[6] Theano 0.9.0, cuDNN 5.1, Cuda 8 with CNMeM, Intel® Core i7-6700 CPU

[7] Note that the comparability is rather limited since even though we use the same beam size (5) and vocabulary sizes (30k), we use (a) a slightly slower GPU (Titan X vs. GTX

per second.[8] We think that these differences are mainly due to the limited multithreading support and performance in Python especially when using external libraries as opposed to the highly optimized C++ code in Marian-NMT. We did not push for even faster decoding as speed is not a major design goal of SGNMT. Note that batch decoding bypasses the predictor framework and can only be used for pure NMT decoding.

Ensembling with models at multiple tokenization levels SGNMT allows masking predictors with alternative sets of modelling units. The conversion between the tokenization schemes of different predictors is defined with FSTs. This makes it possible to decode by combining scores from both a subword-unit (BPE) based NMT (Sennrich et al., 2016) and a word-based NMT model with character-based NMT, masking the BPE-based and word-based NMT predictors with FSTs which transduce character sequences to BPE or word sequences. Masking is transparent to the decoding strategy as predictors are replaced by a special wrapper (*fsttok*) that uses the masking FST to translate `predict_next()` and `consume()` calls to (a series of) predictor calls with alternative tokens. The *syncbeam* variation of beam search compares competing hypotheses only after consuming a special word boundary symbol rather than after each token. This allows combining scores at the word level even when using models with multiple levels of tokenization. Joint decoding with different tokenization schemes has the potential of combining the benefits of the different schemes: character- and BPE-based models are able to address rare words, but word-based NMT can model long-range dependencies more efficiently.

System-level combination We showed in Sec. 2.1 how to formulate NMT ensembling as a set of NMT predictors. Ensembling averages the individual model scores in each decoding step. Alternatively, system-level combination decodes the entire sentence with each model separately, and selects the best scoring complete hypothesis over all models. In our experiments, system-level combination is not as effective as en-

sembling but still leads to moderate gains for pure NMT. However, a trivial implementation which selects the best translation in a postprocessing step after separate decoding runs is slow. The *sepbeam* decoding strategy reduces the runtime of system-level combination to the single system level. The strategy applies only one predictor rather than a linear combination of all predictors to expand a hypothesis. The single predictor is linked by the parent hypothesis. The initial stack in *sepbeam* contains hypotheses for each predictor (i.e. system) rather than only one as in normal beam search. We report a moderate gain of 0.5 BLEU over a single system on the Japanese-English ASPEC test set (Nakazawa et al., 2016) by combining three BPE-based NMT models from Stahlberg et al. (2017) using the *sepbeam* decoder.

Iterative beam search Normal beam search is difficult to use in a time-constrained setting since the runtime depends on the *target* sentence length which is a priori not known, and it is therefore hard to choose the right beam size beforehand. The *bucket* search algorithm sidesteps the problem of setting the beam size by repeatedly performing small beam search passes until a fixed computational budget is exhausted. Bucket search produces an initial hypothesis very quickly, and keeps the partial hypotheses for each length in buckets. Subsequent beam search passes refine the initial hypothesis by iteratively updating these buckets. Our initial experiments suggest that bucket search often performs on a similar level as standard beam search with the benefit of being able to support hard time constraints. Unlike beam search, bucket search lends itself to risk-free (i.e. admissible) pruning since all partial hypotheses worse than the current best complete hypothesis can be discarded.

4 Conclusion

This paper presented our SGNMT platform for prototyping new approaches to MT which involve both neural and symbolic models. SGNMT supports a number of different models and constraints via a common interface (*predictors*), and various search strategies (*decoders*). Furthermore, SGNMT focuses on minimizing the implementation effort for adding new predictors and decoders by decoupling scoring modules from each other and from the search algorithm. SGNMT is actively being used for teaching and research and we

---

1080), (b) a different training and test set, (c) a slightly different network architecture, and (d) words rather than subword units.

[8]`https://marian-nmt.github.io/features/`

welcome contributions to its development, for example by implementing new predictors for using models trained with other frameworks and tools.

Acknowledgments

This work was supported by the U.K. Engineering and Physical Sciences Research Council (EPSRC grant EP/L027623/1).

References

Martın Abadi, Ashish Agarwal, Paul Barham, Eugene Brevdo, Zhifeng Chen, Craig Citro, Greg S Corrado, Andy Davis, Jeffrey Dean, Matthieu Devin, et al. 2016. Tensorflow: Large-scale machine learning on heterogeneous distributed systems. *arXiv preprint arXiv:1603.04467*.

Cyril Allauzen, Bill Byrne, Adrià de Gispert, Gonzalo Iglesias, and Michael Riley. 2014. Pushdown automata in statistical machine translation. *Computational Linguistics*, 40(3):687–723.

Cyril Allauzen, Michael Riley, Johan Schalkwyk, Wojciech Skut, and Mehryar Mohri. 2007. OpenFst: A general and efficient weighted finite-state transducer library. In *International Conference on Implementation and Application of Automata*, pages 11–23. Springer.

Dzmitry Bahdanau, Kyunghyun Cho, and Yoshua Bengio. 2015. Neural machine translation by jointly learning to align and translate. In *ICLR*.

Frédéric Bastien, Pascal Lamblin, Razvan Pascanu, James Bergstra, Ian Goodfellow, Arnaud Bergeron, Nicolas Bouchard, David Warde-Farley, and Yoshua Bengio. 2012. Theano: New features and speed improvements. In *NIPS*.

Jiameng Gao. 2016. Variable length word encodings for neural translation models. MPhil dissertation, University of Cambridge.

Lars Kai Hansen and Peter Salamon. 1990. Neural network ensembles. *IEEE transactions on pattern analysis and machine intelligence*, 12(10):993–1001.

Eva Hasler, Adrià de Gispert, Felix Stahlberg, Aurelien Waite, and Bill Byrne. 2016. Source sentence simplification for statistical machine translation. *Computer Speech & Language*.

Eva Hasler, Felix Stahlberg, Marcus Tomalin, Adrià de Gispert, and Bill Byrne. 2017. A comparison of neural models for word ordering. In *INLG*, Santiago de Compostela, Spain.

Kenneth Heafield, Ivan Pouzyrevsky, Jonathan H. Clark, and Philipp Koehn. 2013. Scalable modified Kneser-Ney language model estimation. In *ACL*, pages 690–696, Sofia, Bulgaria.

Marcin Junczys-Dowmunt, Tomasz Dwojak, and Hieu Hoang. 2016. Is neural machine translation ready for deployment? a case study on 30 translation directions. *arXiv preprint arXiv:1610.01108*.

Bart van Merriënboer, Dzmitry Bahdanau, Vincent Dumoulin, Dmitriy Serdyuk, David Warde-Farley, Jan Chorowski, and Yoshua Bengio. 2015. Blocks and fuel: Frameworks for deep learning. *arXiv preprint arXiv:1506.00619*.

Toshiaki Nakazawa, Manabu Yaguchi, Kiyotaka Uchimoto, Masao Utiyama, Eiichiro Sumita, Sadao Kurohashi, and Hitoshi Isahara. 2016. ASPEC: Asian scientific paper excerpt corpus. In *LREC*, pages 2204–2208, Portoroz, Slovenia.

Stuart J. Russell and Peter Norvig. 2003. *Artificial Intelligence: A Modern Approach*, 2 edition. Pearson Education.

Rico Sennrich, Barry Haddow, and Alexandra Birch. 2016. Neural machine translation of rare words with subword units. In *ACL*, pages 1715–1725, Berlin, Germany.

Maryam Siahbani, Baskaran Sankaran, and Anoop Sarkar. 2013. Efficient left-to-right hierarchical phrase-based translation with improved reordering. In *EMNLP*, pages 1089–1099, Seattle, Washington, USA.

Felix Stahlberg, Adrià de Gispert, Eva Hasler, and Bill Byrne. 2017. Neural machine translation by minimising the Bayes-risk with respect to syntactic translation lattices. In *EACL*, pages 362–368, Valencia, Spain.

Felix Stahlberg, Eva Hasler, Aurelien Waite, and Bill Byrne. 2016. Syntactically guided neural machine translation. In *ACL*, pages 299–305, Berlin, Germany.

Andreas Stolcke et al. 2002. SRILM – an extensible language modeling toolkit. In *Interspeech*, volume 2002, page 2002.

Ilya Sutskever, Oriol Vinyals, and Quoc V. Le. 2014. Sequence to sequence learning with neural networks. In *NIPS*, pages 3104–3112. MIT Press.

Marcin Tomczak. 2016. Bachbot. MPhil dissertation, University of Cambridge.

Ashish Vaswani, Yinggong Zhao, Victoria Fossum, and David Chiang. 2013. Decoding with large-scale neural language models improves translation. In *EMNLP*, pages 1387–1392, Seattle, Washington, USA.

Wojciech Zaremba, Ilya Sutskever, and Oriol Vinyals. 2014. Recurrent neural network regularization. *arXiv preprint arXiv:1409.2329*.

StruAP: A Tool for Bundling Linguistic Trees through Structure-based Abstract Pattern

Kohsuke Yanai, Misa Sato, Toshihiko Yanase, Kenzo Kurotsuchi,
Yuta Koreeda, and **Yoshiki Niwa**
Research & Development Group, Hitachi, Ltd.

Abstract

We present a tool for developing tree structure patterns that makes it easy to define the relations among textual phrases and create a search index for these newly defined relations. By using the proposed tool, users develop tree structure patterns through abstracting syntax trees. The tool features (1) intuitive pattern syntax, (2) unique functions such as recursive call of patterns and lexicon reference, and (3) whole workflow support for relation development and validation. We report the current implementation of the tool and its effectiveness.

1 Introduction

This paper describes a tool that helps users semantically bundle linguistic trees such as a constituency tree and a dependency tree. We refer to the tool as StruAP (<u>Stru</u>cture-based <u>A</u>bsract <u>P</u>attern). By using the proposed tool, the user can easily define relations that are specific to a given business use case and create a search index for the newly defined relations. The search index allows the user to retrieve sentences that include the defined relations. For instance, we can interpret the following sentence as including a *spin-off* relation between *Japanese electronics maker Hitachi* and *home appliance and industrial equipment divisions*.

> *Japanese electronics maker Hitachi will spin off its home appliance and industrial equipment divisions by April to become quicker in decision-making to respond to market changes.* [1]

If we define a *spin-off* relation and extract textual phrases consisting of the relation from large amounts of documents, we can investigate which companies spin off a given business segment, such as *home appliance*, by using standard information retrieval techniques.

By using the proposed tool StruAP, users develop tree structure patterns of the relations through abstracting syntax trees. We assume that in most practical use cases, newly defining relations specific to the use case and developing the corresponding relation extraction modules, instead of use of a universal relation taxonomy and a general extraction algorithm, are required. For example, in a use case of investment decisions, more than ten relations, such as "acquire", "sue", and "penalize", are important to investigate companies. However, it is difficult to develop and maintain a relation extraction module based on linguistic trees because implementation of the logics for traversing trees tends to be complicated. Thus, a tool to help develop and maintain structural patterns of relations would be useful.

The proposed tool is related to semantic role labelling. There are several tools available (Punyakanok et al., 2008; Collobert et al., 2011; Kshirsagar et al., 2015) . However, these tools implicitly assume a kind of general relation taxonomy. When adding new relations in these tools, users need to prepare a certain amount of training data for each relation. The proposed tool aims to help the user to newly define relations for each use case and develop extraction modules within several hours.

The features of the proposed tool are as follows:

1. Intuitive pattern syntax, which is an abstracted representation of outputs of syntax parsers,

2. Unique functions such as recursive call of

Proceedings of the 2017 EMNLP System Demonstrations, pages 31–36
Copenhagen, Denmark, September 7–11, 2017. ©2017 Association for Computational Linguistics

patterns and lexicon reference for word level pattern matching,

3. Whole workflow support for relation development and validation.

This paper is structured as follows. We describe related work in Section 2 and the proposed tool in Section 3. We explain the implementation of the tool in Section 4. Section 5 discusses the effectiveness of the tool and Section 6 concludes this paper.

2 Related Work

Tgrep2 is a grep-like tool for tree expressions (Rohde, 2005). The tool allows users to search tree expressions with a given tree query. The expressivity of Tgrep2 has been expanded and a tree query tool Tregex has been developed (Levy and Andrew, 2006). Besides these tools, several tools for tree queries are already available, such as TIGERSearch (Brants et al., 2002), NiteQL (Heid et al., 2004), LPath+ (Lai and Bird, 2005), and a query language for threaded trees (Singh, 2012). However, all these tools are for grep-like purposes but do not support the whole workflow of the relation development. Although Odin's Runes (Valenzuela-Escárcega et al., 2016) provides an information extraction framework, it does not cover the whole workflow. In addition, their pattern languages are path-based and difficult to intuitively understand. For example, a Tregex tree query for the *spin-off* relation can be written as follows:

```
(VP<(VB<<#spin)<(PRT(RP<<#off)))
  $--MD>VP$--NP>S
```

Please refer to (Levy and Andrew, 2006) for the detailed pattern syntax of Tregex. The above pattern expression is different from that of the usual parser outputs. Our proposed tool allows users to easily create a structure-based pattern by directly editing a constituency tree or a dependency tree generated by syntax parsers.

3 Proposed Model

Table 1 illustrates the concept of our proposed model. First, we get a syntax tree by using a parser, such as Stanford's CoreNLP (Manning et al., 2014). The left column shows the syntax tree obtained by parsing the sample text shown in Section 1. We change the

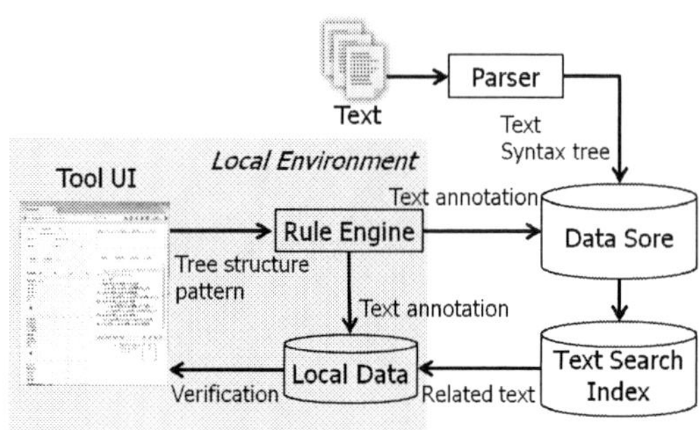

Figure 1: Architecture

expression a little from the original output of Stanford's CoreNLP by adding `lemma=`, `POS=`, and so on. The bold face parts indicate important structures to represent the *spin-off* relation. Thus, we can obtain the generalized structure of the *spin-off* relation by removing non-essential subtrees and lemma information. The right column shows an example of generalized structure. This paper refers to the generalized structure as a structure-based pattern, in contrast to a path-based pattern. Here, $\star$ means a repeat of any subtree, while `#a[0-2]` means target subtrees to be extracted as elements of the relation. Table 2 shows examples of extracted relations by applying the pattern shown in the right column of Table 1. From a computational point of view, the proposed tool bundles multiple tree instances based on abstract structure, and gives an index for retrieval of the tree instances. In the context of NLP (natural language processing), the main application is relation extraction.

3.1 Architecture and Workflow

Figure 1 describes the architecture of the proposed tool. We parse texts that are utilized for a target application and store the generated linguistic trees in a data store in advance. Then, we prepare a text search index for full text search, which is also used later to retrieve relations extracted by the tool. The data store and text search index are running on the server side. If users want to, they can use the proposed tool in only a local environment without server side settings.

Figure 2 shows snapshots of the web-based user interface of the proposed tool. There are 4 tabs: SAMPLE, VALIDATE, EDIT, and INDEX. The procedure to develop a pattern of the *spin-off* relation is as follows:

```
(.POS=ROOT&.lemma=will
 (.POS=S&.lemma=will
  (.POS=NP&.lemma=Hitachi
   (.POS=JJ&.lemma=japanese _)
   (.POS=NNS&.lemma=electronics _)
   (.POS=NN&.lemma=maker _)
   (.POS=NNP&.lemma=Hitachi _))
  (.POS=VP&.lemma=will
   (.POS=MD&.lemma=will _)
   (.POS=VP&.lemma=spin
    (.POS=VB&.lemma=spin _)
    (.POS=PRT&.lemma=off
     (.POS=RP&.lemma=off _))
    (.POS=NP&.lemma=division
     (.POS=PRP$&.lemma=its _)
     (.POS=NN&.lemma=home _)
     (.POS=NN&.lemma=appliance _)
     (.POS=CC&.lemma=and _)
     (.POS=JJ&.lemma=industrial _)
     (.POS=NN&.lemma=equipment _)
     (.POS=NNS&.lemma=division _))
    (.POS=PP&.lemma=by
     ...
```

```
(.POS=S
 *
 (#a1.POS=NP *)
 (.POS=VP
  (*.POS=MD _)
  *
  (.POS=VP
   (#a0.POS=VB&.lemma=spin _)
   (.POS=PRT
    (.POS=RP&.lemma=off _))
   (#a2.POS=NP *) *) *) *)
```

Table 1: Syntax tree (left) and structure-based pattern (right).

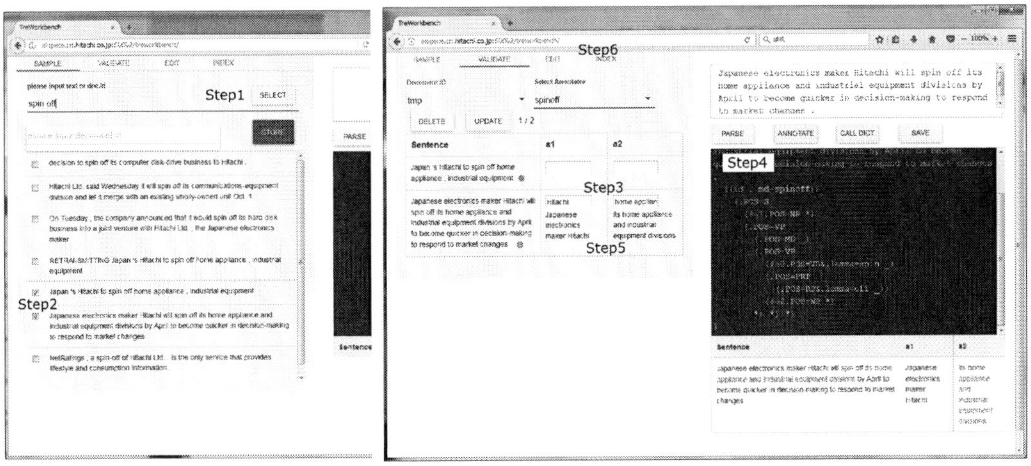

Figure 2: Snapshots of StruAP.

Step 1 In the SAMPLE tab, find several texts of a basis of a tree structure pattern by keyword search. The keyword "spin off" draws relevant sentences from the data store by using the text search index.

Step 2 Choose proper sentences and click the STORE button to save the sentences into the local data store.

Step 3 In the VALIDATE tab, prepare a validation dataset before developing a tree structure pattern. In Figure 2, we decode *Hitachi* for a1 as a subject phrase, and *home appliance* for a2 as a object phrase. Fill out the a[1-2] text fields with the corresponding words.

Step 4 Click the "c" button to parse the sentence and generate its syntax tree in the text area of the right pane. Change the syntax tree to a tree structure pattern through abstraction as shown in Table 1, and click the ANNOTATE button (or Ctrl-Shift-o) to confirm if the pattern works well. A user can see the respective phrases of a[1-2] in the table area below. Although no syntactic error correction is available, frequent use of the shortcut key is helpful to avoid syntactic errors.

Step 5 Click the SAVE button to add the edited pattern into the corresponding pattern file. The rule engine generates text annotations by applying the tree structure pattern, and writes the annotations into the local data store. In the VALIDATE tab, the user can check the differences of a[1-2] between the validation dataset written in Step 3 and the generated annotations. The differences are highlighted in red.

Step 6 Click the UPDATE button in the INDEX tab to write the annotations for all of the stored documents into the data store on the server side, and update the text search index for extracted relations.

By following the above steps, a text search index for relations is ready for an external application. The CALL DICT button and EDIT tab are related to the lexicon reference explained in Section 3.2.

3.2 Detailed Pattern Specifications

Table 3 lists a sample of pattern expressions of the proposed model. Our model permits leaf node match (_), alternatives (|), subtree retrieval (#), negation (!), and quantification (*, ?, +). In addition, the user can use two unique functions: lexicon reference and subpattern call.

Lexicon Reference The following pattern is a simple one representing a causal relation between subtree a1 and subtree a2.

```
(.POS=S *
 (#a1.POS=NP *)
 (.POS=VP * (.lemma=increase|cause _)
  (#a2.POS=NP) *) *)
```

Here, the pattern (.lemma=increase|... would be long because many words can be used as a lemma for the leaf node. In this case, users can use word lists described in separate files, instead of writing down all of the words in the pattern subtree. A pattern using lexicon reference is as follows:

```
(.POS=S *
 (#a1.POS=NP *)
 (.POS=VP * (.lemma=\dic.affect _)
  (#a2.POS=NP) *) *)
```

The affect represents the name of a word list containing the words *increase* and *cause*. Users can also define a list of words for a1 and a2.

Subpattern Call It is useful to partially refer to pre-defined subpatterns because the same subpatterns occur repeatedly in different tree structure patterns. The following is an example of a subpattern definition.

```
(
 ((ref . (leaf pos)))
 (.POS=VP *
  (.POS=\arg.pos&.lemma=\dic.spinoff *)
  (#a2.POS=NP *) *)
)
```

Here, ref is a reserved word meaning subpattern definition, leaf is the name of the subpattern, pos is the name of the argument variable. \arg.pos is expanded to a given argument. The user can call the subpattern as follows:

```
(.POS=S *
 (#a1.POS=NP *)
 (.POS=VP *
  (\ref.leaf VB|VBZ) *) *)
```

Here, \ref.leaf means the call of the subpattern whose name is leaf. VB|VBZ is the argument of the subpattern and is substituted for \arg.pos in the subpattern. When creating a pattern for a sentence with a complicated syntax structure, the recursive call of a subpattern is useful. An example of a recursive call is as follows:

```
(
 ((ref . (lib.vp_loop leaf_pattern pos)))
 (.POS=VP *
  (\ref.vp_loop \arg.leaf_pattern VB) *)
)
(
 ((ref . (lib.vp_loop leaf_pattern pos)))
 (\ref.\arg.leaf_pattern \arg.pos)
)

(.POS=S *
 (#a1.POS=NP *)
 (\ref.vp_loop leaf VB|VBZ)
 *)
```

This pattern partially corresponds to the pattern syntax A .+(VP) B of Tregex.

4 Implementation

The proposed tool StruAP is implemented in Python. Syntax trees are expanded on python data structures and tree structure patterns are directly applied on the data structure. This means we do not use translation from our model to existing query lauguage, such as SQL. In the current implementation, we use Cassandra[2] as a data store and Solr[3] as a text search index. We also use Hadoop[4] for parallel processing of the rule engine. While the tool comes with the web-based user interface shown in Figure 2, command line tools for the Linux environment are also available. Users can easily start up the web version of the tool by using a docker image [5] with several configurations for the data store and the text search index. For the command line version, users edit files for tree patterns and lexicon reference with their

---

[2] Cassandra, http://cassandra.apache.org

[3] Apache Solr, http://lucene.apache.org/solr

[4] Hadoop, http://hadoop.apache.org

[5] docker, https://www.docker.com/

a1	a2	text
Pepsi	the restaurant unit	Pepsi will spin off the restaurant unit by the end of the year .
Mannesmann	its Internet business	The chairman also said Mannesmann might spin off its Internet business .
Rhone-Poulenc	part of its chemicals activities	As part of the plan Rhone-Poulenc would spin off part of its chemicals activities to focus on healthcare , in a bid to boost its share price and earnings .

Table 2: Examples of extracted relations. ©1994–2010 New York Times.

Pattern	Subtree to be matched
`(.POS=PRT *)`	Subtree whose POS is PRT.
`(.POS=VB|VBD _)`	Leaf node whose POS is VB or VBD.
`(.POS=VB&.lemma=spin _)`	Leaf node POS of which is VB, and the lemma of which is *spin*.
`(#a0.POS=VB _)`	Leaf node whose POS is VB. Retrieve the matched node with the name of a0.
`(.POS=NP&.type!=tmod *)`	Subtree POS of which is NP, the dependency type of which is not *tmod*.
`*`	Zero or more occurrences of any subtree.
`(*.POS!=NP|NN|NNS *)`	Zero or more occurrences of the subtree whose POS is not NP, NN, nor NNS.
`(?.POS=MD|CC|VP *)`	Zero or one occurrences of the subtree whose POS is MD, CC or VP.
`(+.POS=NN|NP *)`	One or more occurrences of the subtree whose POS is NN or NP.

Table 3: Sample of pattern expressions.

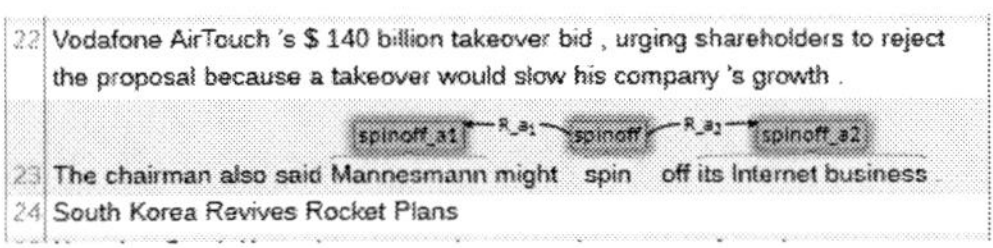

Figure 3: brat view of generated annotations.

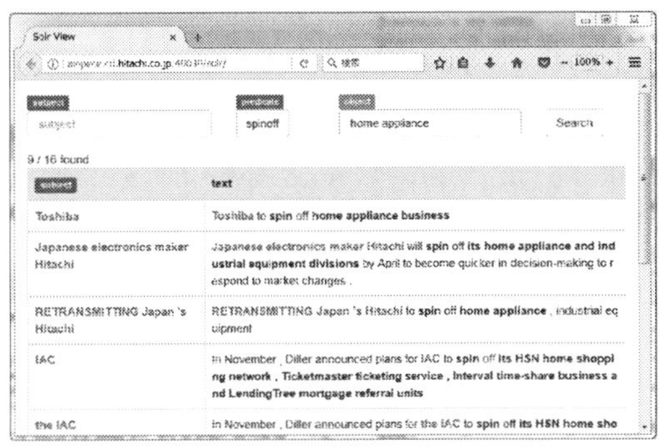

Figure 4: Example of application using extracted relations.

favorite editors and run the rule engine from the Linux command line. We implemented the tool for the English language and Japanese language. Stanford's CoreNLP (Manning et al., 2014) and CaboCha (Kudo and Matsumoto, 2002) are used for the English language and Japanese language, respectively. For the English version, the user can use both constituent trees and dependency trees as the basis of the tree structure patterns. On the other hand, only dependency trees are available for the Japanese version because CaboCha does not output constituent trees.

We can easily integrate the annotation tool brat [6] into the proposed tool via the data store. Figure 3 visualizes the generated annotations in the data store with brat view.

Figure 4 shows a simple example of an application that uses extracted relations. This application uses the same text search index as that of the proposed tool. For example, we can retrieve sentences that include the *spin-off* relation with the object phrase of *home appliance* by entering *home appliance* in the object phrase text field. The highlighted text fragments correspond to the subject phrases. By using the same search index,

the tool can be used to directly maintain and update the relation data for the application. Similarly, we can implement various applications using case-specific relations through the index of the proposed tool.

5 Discussion

We roughly investigated the efficiency of the proposed tool in an actual relation development task. Table 4 shows the number of tree structure patterns and the lines of the word lists for lexicon reference, which are developed by two non-researchers in an hour. Although developing tree structure patterns is generally difficult, more than 54 patterns were developed within an hour. We consider that the proposed tool is easy to use and very effectively identifies essential structures for target relations because the tool provides intuitive pattern

[6] brat, http://brat.nlplab.org

relation	Developer A	Developer B
spin-off		
# of patterns	8	12
# of words	3	2
sue		
# of patterns	7	10
# of words	5	4
penalize		
# of patterns	8	9
# of words	8	4

Table 4: Efficiency investigation. Developer A is translator, but not researcher; Developer B is software engineer, but not researcher.

syntax and whole workflow support. The use of a bracketed syntax to define patterns is arguable. However, we suppose users can develop lots of patterns faster by editting bracketed patterns in a text-based editor, than by use of a graphical tree editor.

On the other hand, there are not enough words for lexicon reference for an actual application. Although the function of the lexicon reference is useful, the current tool is not helpful to increase the variety of predicate words and clue words.

We have already used the tool in several cases. We have developed 657 patterns in total, and the number of words in the lexicons used for the patterns is 6406. Especially, our development of end-to-end argument generation system in debating (Sato et al., 2015) relied on the proposed tool. We conclude that the proposed model is effective when it is necessary to newly define case-specific relations and non-researchers are involved in development of the relation extraction.

6 Conclusion

This paper describes a tool for developing tree structure patterns, which makes it easy to define relations among textual phrases, and creates a search index for these newly defined relations. The tool assumes that in most practical use cases, newly defining relations specific to the use cases is required. In such cases, the proposed tool is effective to identify essential tree structure patterns.

Future work includes developing semi-automatic abstraction using frequent subtree mining and integrating techniques to collect clue words for lexicon reference. Another direction is to support collaboration between users. Similar subpattern search helps users to avoid duplicating a pattern created by another user.

References

Sabine Brants, Stefanie Dipper, Silvia Hansen, Wolfgang Lezius, and George Smith. 2002. The TIGER treebank. In *Proceedings of the Workshop on Treebanks and Linguistic Theories*.

Ronan Collobert, Jason Weston, Léon Bottou, Michael Karlen, Koray Kavukcuoglu, and Pavel Kuksa. 2011. Natural language processing (almost) from scratch. *J. Mach. Learn. Res.*, 12:2493–2537.

Ulrich Heid, Holger Voormann, Jan-Torsten Milde, Ulrike Gut, Katrin Erk, and Sebastian Padó. 2004. Querying both time-aligned and hierarchical corpora with NXT search. In *Proceedings of LREC-2004*, pages 1455 – 1459.

Meghana Kshirsagar, Sam Thomson, Nathan Schneider, Jaime Carbonell, Noah A. Smith, and Chris Dyer. 2015. Frame-semantic role labeling with heterogeneous annotations. In *Proceedings of ACL-IJCNLP 2015 Short Papers*, pages 218–224.

Taku Kudo and Yuji Matsumoto. 2002. Japanese dependency analysis using cascaded chunking. In *Proceedings of CoNLL 2002 Post-Conference Workshops*, pages 63–69.

Catherine Lai and Steven Bird. 2005. Lpath+: A first-order complete language for linguistic tree query. In *Proceedings of the 19st Pacific Asia Conference on Language, Information and Computation, PACLIC*.

R. Levy and G. Andrew. 2006. Tregex and tsurgeon: tools for querying and manipulating tree data structures. In *Proceedings of LREC-2006*.

Christopher D. Manning, Mihai Surdeanu, John Bauer, Jenny Finkel, Steven J. Bethard, and David McClosky. 2014. The Stanford CoreNLP natural language processing toolkit. In *ACL System Demonstrations*, pages 55–60.

Vasin Punyakanok, Dan Roth, and Wen-tau Yih. 2008. The importance of syntactic parsing and inference in semantic role labeling. *Comput. Linguist.*, 34(2):257–287.

Douglas L. T. Rohde. 2005. Tgrep2 user manual version 1.15.

Misa Sato, Kohsuke Yanai, Toshinori Miyoshi, Toshihiko Yanase, Makoto Iwayama, Qinghua Sun, and Yoshiki Niwa. 2015. End-to-end argument generation system in debating. In *Proceedings of ACL-IJCNLP 2015 System Demonstrations*.

Anil Kumar Singh. 2012. A concise query language with search and transform operations for corpora with multiple levels of annotation. In *Proceedings of LREC-2012*.

Marco A. Valenzuela-Escárcega, Gus Hahn-Powell, and Mihai Surdeanu. 2016. Odin's runes: A rule language for information extraction. In *Proceedings of LREC-2016*.

KnowYourNyms? A Game of Semantic Relationships

Ross Mechanic, Dean Fulgoni, Hannah Cutler, Sneha Rajana,
Zheyuan Liu, Bradley Jackson, Anne Cocos,
Chris Callison-Burch and **Marianna Apidianaki***
Computer and Information Science Department, University of Pennsylvania
* LIMSI, CNRS, Université Paris-Saclay, 91403 Orsay
{rmechanic,dfulgoni,hcutler,srajana,zheyuan,jacbrad
acocos,ccb,marapi}@seas.upenn.edu

Abstract

Semantic relation knowledge is crucial for
natural language understanding. We introduce *KnowYourNyms?*, a web-based game
for learning semantic relations. While providing users with an engaging experience,
the application collects large amounts of
data that can be used to improve semantic
relation classifiers. The data also broadly
informs us of how people perceive the relationships between words, providing useful insights for research in psychology and
linguistics.

1 Introduction

Knowledge of semantic relationships can help numerous NLP tasks that need to infer meaning from
text, such as text classification, content analysis
and query answering. We apply the "games with
a purpose" methodology (von Ahn and Dabbish,
2004) to the task of discovering semantic relationships between words. Our aim is to collect a large
volume of accurately labeled lexical relationships
through this type of crowdsourcing. Gamification
offers several advantages compared to a fully automatic or manual relation identification process
since it enables acquiring considerable amounts of
high quality data at no cost.

We have created a simple game called
KnowYourNyms? with the tag line *Keep your brain
on its toes*. It asks players to list word for a prompt
in a short amount of time. As the seconds tick
down, they type as many answers as they can for
prompts like "What are kinds of seafood?" or
"What are the parts of a volcano?" or "What's the
opposite of fat?". Table 1 shows the hyponyms,
meronyms and antonyms that our players provided
in response to these questions. Their answers are
useful as training data for natural language under-

hyponyms of seafood: fish (54), shrimp (53), lobster (38),
crab (36), clams (24), salmon (17), oysters (12), scallops
(12), shellfish (10), mussels (10), cod (7), tuna (7), tilapia (5),
whale (4), trout (4), octopus (4), shark (4), squid (3), prawn
(3), haddock (3), flounder (2), catfish (2), swordfish (2), eel
(2), sushi (2), bass (2), calamari (2), mussles (2).
Words suggested once: muss-, pearls, suslhi, prawns,
schrimp, seal, hadsoxk, crab", sepia, scampi, scalop, sea-
weed, dolphin, fi-, seaww-, snapper, s-, pr-, seabass, jelly-
fish, cra-, muscles, oy-, soup, sardine, mahi, herrin, mussells,
tipica, tun-, lob-, sa-, osyter, crawdad, roe, swai-, cram-, pa-,
caviar, seewee-, carp, oyste-, sw-, musse-.
meronyms of volcano: lava (32), rock (12), magma (10),
mountain (9), crater (9), smoke (7), eruption (7), ash (6), fire
(6), vent (4), heat (4), mouth (3), steam (2), danger (2), dust
(2), volcano (2), cone (2), core (2), geodes (2).
Words suggested once: crust, energy, moutain, hot, village,
sulfur, mount-, caldera, throat, pummice, gas, top, side, sill,
stones, sparks, motlen, lawa, japan, opening, soil, head, earth,
metal, op-, cliff, cond-, cr-, pl-, flow, pressure, spout, clay,
pollution, sediment, rim
antonyms of fat: thin (15), skinny (13), slender (5), slim (4),
small (4), tiny (3), fit (3), trim (2), lean (2).
Words suggested once: delgado, svelt, narrow, bare, attrac-
tive, anorexic, teeny, underweight, bulemic, in shape, under-,
wispy, healthy, light, smal-, little

Table 1: Example relationships provided by
KnowYourNyms? players (with frequency counts).

standing applications and may provide useful insights for psycholinguistics research.

Go to www.know-your-nyms.com to play
KnowYourNyms?.

2 Related Work

Several games with a purpose (GWAPs) have
been developed for gathering linguistic annotations for building resources and training systems
(Chamberlain et al., 2013). Lafourcade (2007)
and Fort et al. (2014) developed games for defining semantic relations and dependency relations
in French. Chamberlain et al. (2008) created
Phrase Detectives to annotate and validate things
like co-reference. Jurgens and Navigli (2014) recently proposed using video games to link Word-

Proceedings of the 2017 EMNLP System Demonstrations, pages 37–42
Copenhagen, Denmark, September 7–11, 2017. ©2017 Association for Computational Linguistics

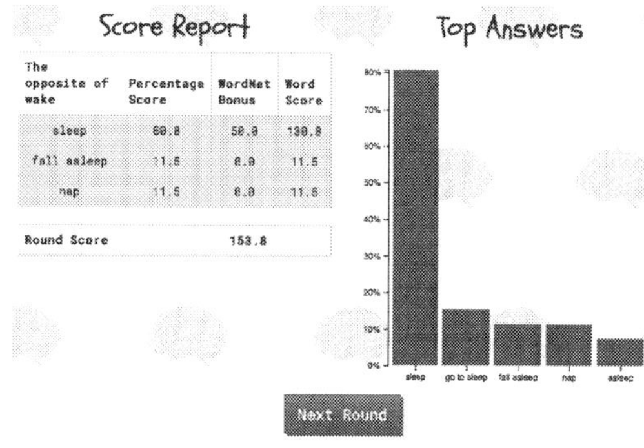

Figure 1: This example scoring page shows the scores for the player's words, and the top answers.

Net senses to images and perform word sense disambiguation. *KnowYourNyms?* gathers high quality semantic relationships between English words to increase the coverage of resources like Word-Net and assign a taxonomic structure to the Paraphrase Database (Ganitkevitch et al., 2013). Additionally, it provides rich data for training relation detection systems like LexNET (Shwartz and Dagan, 2016), up to now trained on small training datasets (BLESS (Baroni and Lenci, 2011), EVA-Lution (Santus et al., 2015), ROOT9 (Santus et al., 2016) and K&H+N (Necsulescu et al., 2015)).

3 System Overview

KnowYourNyms? is modeled after GWAPs like the ESP game or the Google Image Labeler, which use human-based computation to gather metadata to improve image recognition classifiers (von Ahn and Dabbish, 2004). At a high level, the application is simple. Once a user creates an account, she may start a round of the game. For each round, the system selects a specific word (called the "base word") and asks the user to name as many semantic relationship pairs for that word as possible in a set time limit. After the allotted time expires, these named pairs are recorded in our database and serve as data points for possible semantic relationships. The user then sees a display of her scoring performance, which is primarily based on how many other users named the same relationships for the given base word. In this way, the scoring is reminiscent of Family Feud, a popular game show that incentivizes answering questions in a way most similar to your peers. The scoring screen also shows the most popular answers to the question,

in their appropriate distribution. Once completed, another round begins. The rounds are short (5-20 seconds, depending on the relation type), which makes the game fun and easy to play in short periods of time.

4 System Implementation

4.1 Architecture

The web application was built with the Django framework, using Python for all backend and database interaction and standard JavaScript, HTML, and CSS for the frontend, including the jQuery, d3.js, and Bootstrap JavaScript/CSS libraries. We used AWS Elastic Beanstalk, which deploys our Django web application to an AWS EC2 server. The application has multiple components that are important to the user experience, which are separated into three main views.

Welcome Screen This screen gives information about the purpose of the game, what semantic relationships are, how to play, and a little about our team. When a user is signed in this screen displays some statistics about the player, including number of completed rounds, total score, and average score per round. Four checkboxes are displayed, one for each playable semantic relationship type (synonyms, antonyms, hyponyms, and meronyms). These allow the user to select which relations to play. All are selected by default.

Game Play A timer begins immediately as the round starts. To answer the question prompt, the user may type as many semantic relationships as possible into text forms. Each discrete answer is known as an input word. Forms are dynamically generated upon pressing tab or enter, for however many input words are necessary during that round. At the end of 20 seconds, the round immediately ends and the user is directed to the scoring page.

Scoring Page Figure 1 shows what a player sees after the time elapses for a round. This scoring page displays two items to the player. The first is a table breakdown of all input words during the round, mapping each to a score for that word. It also includes the total round score. The second is a bar graph showing the top answers for that question. Here, users can observe which relations they identified or missed compared to the entire population.

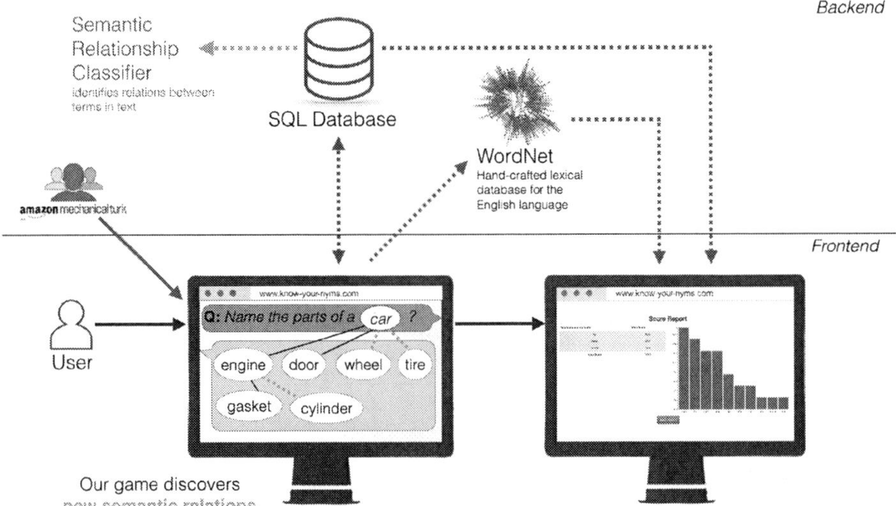

Figure 2: The application flow of the *KnowYourNyms?* game. The bottom half of the figure depicts the application functionality from the user's perspective (frontend). The top half of the figure shows the components of the system backend. Note that the "Semantic Relationship Classifier" is faded because we trained and tested the Classifier on the players' data in an offline setting (see Section 6.2).

4.2 Base Word Selection

Base words are those used for each round's question; they are the 'X' in a potential (X,Y) semantic relationship pair. Good base words are essential for good questions, as there aren't necessarily good synonyms for 'triceratops' or many parts of a 'sphere'. To address these issues, we build four separate vocabulary lists for the base words, one for each allowed semantic relationship type extracted from WordNet. We select base words that have at least one synonym or antonym, and at least three hyponyms or meronyms in WordNet. To make sure we don't ask users about rare words, which might discourage the users from continuing playing, we only retain unigrams and bigrams that occur at least 1,000,000 times in the Google n-grams corpus. Table 2 shows the number of base words retained from WordNet for each relation type. Finally, we have integrated a "skip" button which allows the users to skip queries for which they cannot think of any good relations.

4.3 Scoring

We incentivize players to generate many answers to each prompt by giving them a score at the end of each round. The score is based on the percentage of other users who named a word when they were given the same base word and relationship type.

Relation	Base Words
Synonyms	9,172
Antonyms	2,016
Hyponyms	4,107
Meronyms	678

Table 2: # of base words for each relation type.

Finally, the score is also potentially augmented by a WordNet bonus, which is a simple boolean check of whether the word pair is linked by this specific relation in WordNet. The total score for each word is the sum of these values, sorted in descending order in the final score table.

4.4 Data Visualization

In order for users to see the most common responses for each round, a bar graph is included on the scoring page that shows the top 5 responses and the percentage of previous users who gave them. The percentages for scoring are calculated on the backend. On the frontend, we use the data visualization library d3.js, in order to dynamically create a bar graph that is scaled to the appropriate size for the window. This allows the graph to be seen on mobile devices, or to be dynamically resized as the user changes the size of a desktop window.

5 Design Decisions

5.1 User Identification

We require users to create an account. This design decision was mainly driven by quality control concerns. Since we don't expect all users to provide good answers, it is important that we be able to filter out malicious users, so that we can gather data that has sufficiently high quality for research purposes. An additional benefit of user identification is that it allows to not present a user with the same query several times, since this could skew the data.

5.2 Vocabulary Selection

The list of base words is traversed in a specific order by each user. Compared to fully random selection, this has the advantage of not repeating words until all have been played by the user. Presenting the user with the same words a few rounds apart is unacceptable from a user experience standpoint. Furthermore, having different users play the same words is important since it leads to better scoring and percentage visualization. Finally, this traversal is beneficial for learning high confidence relationships, as we collect data on fewer base words in a more concentrated way. To cover more words, we decided to allow a small amount of randomness which consists in drawing a word randomly from the whole vocabulary list every five items.

6 Evaluation

6.1 Crowdsourced Approach

To evaluate our game, we asked 160 crowdworkers to play *KnowYourNyms?* on Amazon Mechanical Turk for ten rounds each. Our intention was to seed the game with data so that normal users would receive scores based on words suggested by previous players. Although these workers were only asked to play ten rounds, many went on to play thirty, forty, or even a hundred rounds of the game. From these workers, we received over 15,000 user inputs. Table 3 gives a breakdown of the relations that we have collected so far. Here are some examples of the most frequently suggested word pairs for our relation types. Synonyms include **pony-horse**, woods-forest, **woods-trees**, **marching-walking**, **electricity-power**, **four-quad**, **looking-seeing**, **frequent-often**, **woody-forest**, and **pester-annoy**. Antonyms include **sleep-awake**, limited-unlimited, prefix-suffix,

Users (n)	Rels	Rels not in WordNet	Rels in WordNet
all	17,603	16,813	790
n<=3	15,895	15,265 (96%)	630
3<n<=5	724	672 (93%)	52
5<n<=15	794	723 (91%)	71
15<n<=30	153	126 (82%)	27
n>30	37	27 (73%)	10

Table 3: The number of relations (rels) learned at different confidence levels, where confidence is measured by the number of users (n) who named the relation. We compare this to the number of relations found in WordNet for the same base words.

desirable-undesirable, **similarity-difference**, **similarity-different**, hitch-unhitch, immature-mature, wake-sleep, and **sterile-dirty**. Meronyms include **knife-handle**, knife-blade, chain-link, **woods-trees**, book-cover, **writings-words**, **ice-water**, **month-days**, **aquarium-fish**, and **chain-metal**. Hyponyms include **seafood-fish**, seafood-shrimp, **seafood-lobster**, **sleep-deep**, **similarity-same**, seafood-crab, **plaster-paris**, Asian-Chinese, Asian-Japanese, and **hitch-trailer** Bold items are relations that are **not present** in WordNet.

We surveyed the crowd workers about their feelings about the game and whether or not they would play again. The first 30 crowd workers played the game before anyone else had played, so many of their scores were empty (the game relies on previous players). Those workers rated the game on average 3.9/5 on experience and 3.8/5 on likelihood of playing again. However, our second group of crowd workers was given the game with many more of the rounds already played, which improved scoring. These workers rated the experience 4.46/5 on average, and 4.43/5 for likelihood of playing again. Moreover, many of the second round of workers left comments stating that they "loved this addicting game", that the game "is fun", "makes you think fast" and "really wakes up the brain", and made useful suggestions for improvement. The positive reaction about playing the game (especially the shift in positivity as the scoring became more clear) is evidence that this game may work on a larger scale, and may allow us to gather important word relationship data from players for free.

6.2 Classifier Evaluation

To demonstrate how this game could be used to collect training data for semantic relation classi-

	Count Train/ Val	Count Test	P	R	F
meronyms	1162	248	0.44	0.91	0.59
hyponyms	337	313	0.50	0.01	0.01
antonyms	1279	22	0.25	0.77	0.38
synonyms	859	14	0.02	0.14	0.03
random	1038	354	0.58	0.40	0.47
total / avg	4675	951	0.50	0.41	0.34

Table 4: **P**recision, **R**ecall, and **F**-Score of the LexNET semantic relation classifier, when trained and evaluated on data collected by *KnowYourNyms?*.

fiers, we used our players' data to train and evaluate a state-of-the-art semantic relationship classifier, LexNET (Shwartz and Dagan, 2016). Our dataset consisted of 8613 meronym, antonym, hyponym and synonym pairs proposed by at least five users, and 6228 random word pairs. From these 14,841 pairs, we extracted a subset of 951 pairs for testing and used the remaining 4675 pairs whose constituent words did not overlap with the test set for training and validation. The classifier achieved an overall weighted average F-Score of 0.34 over the test set. The full results of this experiment are given in Table 4.

7 Discussion

One of the challenging aspects of making this game fun to play is selecting words and relation types that are easy for people to think of answers for. Despite our attempts to filter the vocabulary sets drawn from WordNet to be high frequent words with several WordNet relations, we found that many players were stumped by some of our questions. Here are examples of the questions that most users pressed the "Pass" button for:

- What are kinds of geology? (71% passed)
- What are kinds of a saver? (70%)
- What is the opposite of conception? (67%)
- What is the opposite of differentiated? (67%)
- What are kinds of hormones? (67%)
- What is another word for notorious? (60%)
- What are kinds of sinking? (56%)
- What are kinds of barley? (56%)

Some prompts are clearly more difficult for users to answer than others. We hypothesized that abstract words (e.g. *geology*, *sinking*, *dissolution*) are more difficult to provide relations for than concrete words. An indicator of annotation difficulty for a word is the number of times users choose to skip it: if they cannot think of any good relationships, users can choose to pass to the next round. We calculate the correlation between word difficulty – measured as the ratio of the number of times the word was skipped to the number of times it was seen – and concreteness scores in the dataset built by Brysbaert et al. (2014) (hereafter CON-CRETE) which contains ratings for 37,058 English words and 2,896 two-word expressions. Words are ranked on a 5-point rating scale going from abstract words (low values) to words with concrete meaning (high values). We expect abstract words to be more difficult to handle and more frequently skipped by our users compared to concrete words.

We perform the correlation calculation on 412 lemma-relation pairs extracted from *KnowYourNyms?*. From these, 40 correspond to specific terms and named entities (e.g. *cytochrome, methyl, Utah, Mexico, etiology, flora, Maryland*) that are not in CONCRETE (it only includes words known to 85% of the annotators and excludes proper names). We intend to use existence in CONCRETE as a criterion for identifying words that would be too difficult for the annotators and should be excluded from our game.

The Pearson correlation results for the remaining 372 words indicate a negative correlation of -0.2007 between word difficulty and concreteness ($p < 0.001$), confirming our assumption that more abstract words are more difficult to handle. Correlation for the 99 lemmas in CONCRETE that were seen at least 10 times by our crowdworkers is even higher, - 0.3851 ($p < 0.001$),

Finally, we intend to analyze the collected relations in the light of typicality and gradual semantic category membership, as proposed in (Vulić et al., 2016), to make them more useful for textual entailment tasks.

8 Conclusions and Future Work

KnowYourNyms? gamifies the process of gathering pairs of words holding specific semantic relationships that are not found in existing resources. While providing users with an entertaining experience, our application enables collection of large amounts of data that can be used to improve semantic relation classifiers and content analysis tools. This application offers exciting possibilities for further development. As the number of players grow, our lexical relation dataset will keep expanding. This will provide new opportunities for evaluation in full-blown applications and will richen our understanding of how people perceive word relations.

9   Software and Data

We release the software that underlies our game under the BSD open source license. We provide instructions on how to set up your own instance of the game and populate it with your own base words and semantic relationship types. The software is available at `https://github.com/rossmechanic/know_your_nyms/`. A file containing the semantic relations collected during our initial testing of the game is also included in the repository.

Acknowledgments

We would like to thank Ani Nenkova and Jonathan Smith for the discussions and useful feedback on this project, and the Mechanical Turk workers who did the play testing.

This material is based in part on research sponsored by DARPA under grant number FA8750-13-2-0017 (the DEFT program). The U.S. Government is authorized to reproduce and distribute reprints for Governmental purposes. The views and conclusions contained in this publication are those of the authors and should not be interpreted as representing official policies or endorsements of DARPA and the U.S. Government. This work has also been supported by the French National Research Agency under project ANR-16-CE33-0013.

References

Marco Baroni and Alessandro Lenci. 2011. How we BLESSed distributional semantic evaluation. In *Proceedings of GEMS*. Edinburgh, UK, pages 1–10.

Marc Brysbaert, Amy Beth Warriner, and Victor Kuperman. 2014. Concreteness ratings for 40 thousand generally known English word lemmas. *Behavior Research Methods* 46(3):904–911.

Jon Chamberlain, Karën Fort, Udo Kruschwitz, Mathieu Lafourcade, and Massimo Poesio. 2013. Using games to create language resources: Successes and limitations of the approach. In *The Peoples Web Meets NLP*, Springer, pages 3–44.

Jon Chamberlain, Massimo Poesio, and Udo Kruschwitz. 2008. Phrase detectives: A web-based collaborative annotation game. In *Proceedings of I-Semantics 08*. pages 42–49.

Karën Fort, Bruno Guillaume, and Hadrien Chastant. 2014. Creating Zombilingo, a Game With A Purpose for dependency syntax annotation. In *Proceedings of GamifIR '14*. Amsterdam, The Netherlands, pages 2–6.

Juri Ganitkevitch, Benjamin Van Durme, and Chris Callison-Burch. 2013. PPDB: The Paraphrase Database. In *Proceedings of NAACL/HLT*. Atlanta, Georgia, pages 758–764.

David Jurgens and Roberto Navigli. 2014. It's All Fun and Games until Someone Annotates: Video Games with a Purpose for Linguistic Annotation. *TACL* 2:449–464.

Mathieu Lafourcade. 2007. Making people play for Lexical Acquisition with the JeuxDeMots prototype. In *Proceedings of SNLP'07*, Pattaya, Thailand.

Silvia Necsulescu, Sara Mendes, David Jurgens, Núria Bel, and Roberto Navigli. 2015. Reading Between the Lines: Overcoming Data Sparsity for Accurate Classification of Lexical Relationships. In *Proceedings of *SEM*. Denver, Colorado, pages 182–192.

Enrico Santus, Alessandro Lenci, Tin-Shing Chiu, Qin Lu, and Chu-Ren Huang. 2016. Nine features in a random forest to learn taxonomical semantic relations. In *Proceedings of LREC*. Portoroz, Slovenia.

Enrico Santus, Frances Yung, Alessandro Lenci, and Chu-Ren Huang. 2015. EVALution 1.0: an Evolving Semantic Dataset for Training and Evaluation of Distributional Semantic Models. In *Proceedings of Linked Data in Linguistics: Resources and Applications*. Beijing, China, pages 64–69.

Vered Shwartz and Ido Dagan. 2016. CogALex-V Shared Task: LexNET - Integrated Path-based and Distributional Method for the Identification of Semantic Relations. In *Proceedings of CogALex-V*. Osaka, Japan, pages 80–85.

Luis von Ahn and Laura Dabbish. 2004. Labeling images with a computer game. In *Proceedings of the SIGCHI Conference on Human Factors in Computing Systems*. Vienna, Austria, pages 319–326.

Ivan Vulić, Daniela Gerz, Douwe Kiela, Felix Hill, and Anna Korhonen. 2016. HyperLex: A Large-Scale Evaluation of Graded Lexical Entailment. *CoRR* abs/1608.02117.

The Projector: An Interactive Annotation Projection Visualization Tool

Alan Akbik and **Roland Vollgraf**
Zalando Research
Charlottenstraße 4, 10969 Berlin
`firstname.lastname@zalando.de`

Abstract

Previous works proposed *annotation projection* in parallel corpora to inexpensively generate treebanks or propbanks for new languages. In this approach, linguistic annotation is automatically transferred from a resource-rich source language (SL) to translations in a target language (TL). However, annotation projection may be adversely affected by *translational divergences* between specific language pairs. For this reason, previous work often required careful qualitative analysis of projectability of specific annotation in order to define strategies to address quality and coverage issues. In this demonstration, we present THE PROJECTOR, an interactive GUI designed to assist researchers in such analysis: it allows users to execute and visually inspect annotation projection in a range of different settings. We give an overview of the GUI, discuss use cases and illustrate how the tool can facilitate discussions with the research community.

1 Introduction

Natural language processing research relies heavily on the availability of textual corpora annotated with various levels of syntactic and semantic information such as *treebanks* (Marcus et al., 1993) or *propbanks* (Palmer et al., 2005). However, the manual creation of such resources is known to be highly costly and therefore difficult to scale across languages and domains (Hovy et al., 2006).

Annotation Projection. As a cost-effective alternative, previous work suggested the use of *annotation projection* (Yarowsky et al., 2001) in parallel corpora to automatically create NLP resources for new languages. This approach requires only a par-

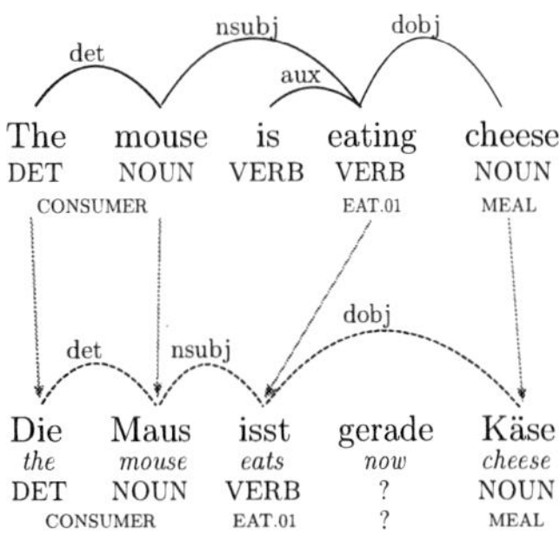

Figure 1: An English sentence with syntactic and semantic annotations predicted by a parser, and a German translation. These annotations are transferred onto aligned German words, thus automatically labeling the German sentence (with exception of the unaligned German word *gerade*).

allel corpus consisting of sentences in a resource-rich source language (SL) and their translations in a target language (TL), as well as existing parsers for the SL. It leverages the hypothesis that translated sentences will share a degree of syntactic and, in particular, semantic parallelism (Padó and Lapata, 2009), thus allowing us to automatically transfer linguistic annotations from SL to TL.

For example, consider Figure 1 which shows an English SL sentence and its German TL translation, with word-level alignments indicated as lines between the sentences. State-of-the-art parsers and semantic role labelers (SRL) are used to predict labels for the English sentence. Following the word alignments, this annotation is then transferred onto the German sentence. The English word *cheese*, for instance, is aligned to the German *Käse* (cheese). We therefore learn that *Käse* is also a noun (NOUN), that in this sentence it is a direct object (dobj) and that it takes the semantic role of MEAL. Following this process, we can thus automatically annotate the German sentence with (partial) syntactic and semantic labels.

A Need for Qualitative Analysis. However,

Proceedings of the 2017 EMNLP System Demonstrations, pages 43–48
Copenhagen, Denmark, September 7–11, 2017. ©2017 Association for Computational Linguistics

while annotation projection has been successfully employed to transfer various types of annotation (Yarowsky et al., 2001; Hwa et al., 2005; Padó and Lapata, 2009; Van der Plas et al., 2011; Akbik et al., 2015), it is not always clear how well specific annotation can be transferred to a specific TL. Previous work noted a range of issues including non-literal translations and general *translational divergences* (Dorr, 1994) between languages which cause incorrect annotation to be projected. For this reason, previous work often included qualitative analyses and carefully defined heuristics to address these problems.

Contributions. To facilitate such analysis and discussion, we present THE PROJECTOR, a web-based UI that visualizes the projection of syntactic and shallow semantic annotation in parallel sentences[1]. Our tool enables researchers to execute annotation projection for manually created examples or pre-loaded corpora, and allows researchers to visually inspect individual sentence pairs and types of linguistic annotation.

This paper is structured as follows: we first review relevant related work in annotation projection. We then give an overview of THE PROJECTOR, briefly sketch use cases for this tool and discuss directions for future research.

2 Previous Work

Syntactic Annotation Projection. Early work proposed the projection of shallow and deep syntactic information in parallel corpora, including part-of-speech tags (Yarowsky et al., 2001), syntactic chunks (Yarowsky and Ngai, 2001) and dependency trees (Hwa et al., 2005). However, these works also noted problems stemming from *translational divergences* (Dorr, 1994; Van Leuven-Zwart, 1989), i.e. systematic differences between languages on the structural and semantic realization levels. This may cause incorrect labels to be projected, or annotation gaps in the TL corpus. For instance, as Figure 1 shows, while a continuous process may be expressed in English using *gerunds* (the word *eating*), the continuous verb aspect generally does not exist in German which instead uses an adverbial construction (the word *gerade*, meaning *now*, which is unaligned and therefore remains unlabeled in Figure 1).

To filter out and correct such errors, previ-

ous work defined various heuristics such as filtering of infrequent alignments (Yarowsky et al., 2001), transformation rules that encode linguistic knowledge (Hwa et al., 2005) and the use of cross-lingual word clusters as constraints in projection (Täckström et al., 2012). More recently, Tiedemann (2014) argued that the ongoing harmonization of linguistic annotation across languages as pursued by the *universal dependencies* project (Nivre et al., 2016) has produced tagsets without language-specific syntax that can more easily be projected[2].

Semantic Annotation Projection. Previous work also investigated the applicability of annotation projection to shallow semantic annotation such as semantic role labels (SRL). Padó and Lapata (2009) first analyzed the viability of transferring SRL in the FRAMENET-formalism (Baker et al., 1998) and found a greater degree of parallelism for semantic than syntactic annotation. Van der Plas et al. (2011) applied this approach to the verb-centric PROPBANK-formalism of SRL (Palmer et al., 2005).

In our previous work, we defined a two-step process of filtering and semi-supervised learning to address problems caused by non-literal translations and coverage gaps (Akbik et al., 2015). We applied our approach to generate propbanks for 7 languages from 3 language groups (Akbik et al., 2015), and experimented with projecting both syntactic and semantic annotation to three low-resource languages (Akbik et al., 2016b). Qualitative analysis revealed propositions evoked by complex predication (Bonial et al., 2014) to be a major source of translational divergences of shallow semantics (Akbik et al., 2016a).

Qualitative Analysis. Previous works illustrated the need for qualitative analysis to identify error sources and define strategies to address translational divergences. However, to the best of our knowledge, no visualization tool is available that specifically addresses this task. While there exist tools that focus on inspecting and correcting word alignments (Gilmanov et al., 2014) as well as frameworks for visualization of various layers of linguistic annotation (Krause and Zeldes, 2016), THE PROJECTOR differs in that it specializes in the projection of various types of linguistic annotation in parallel corpora and interactive analysis.

---

[1] A screencast is available at https://vimeo.com/ 217035646

[2] The *gerund* verb type, for instance, is abstracted away from in universal PoS tags to a general VERB class.

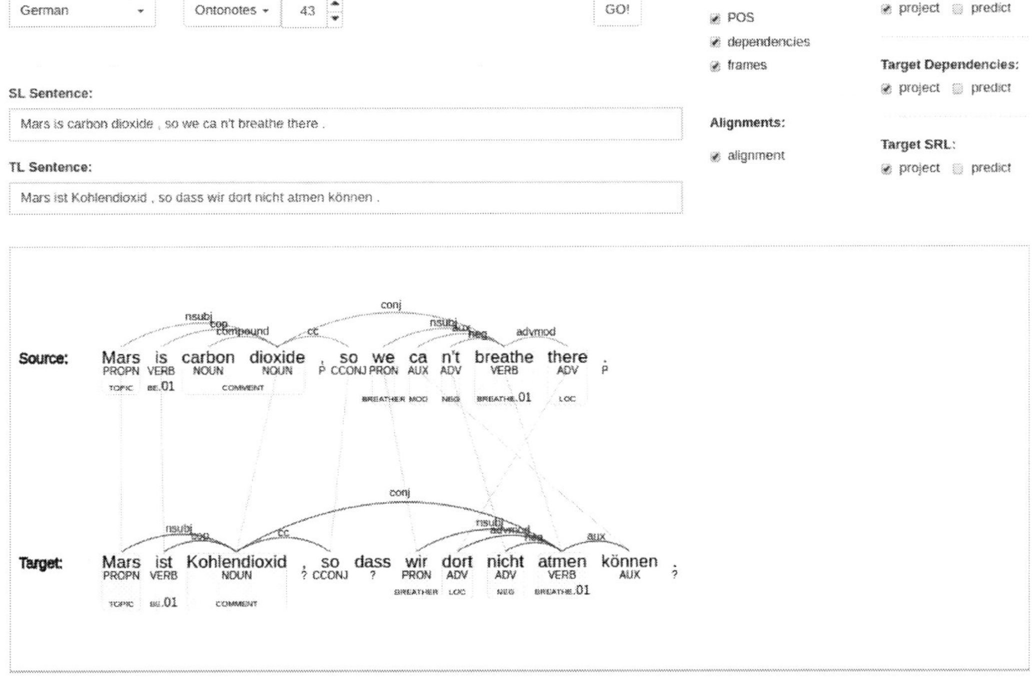

Figure 2: THE PROJECTOR's main view showing a gold-labeled English sentence from ONTONOTES and a word-aligned German translation. The German sentence is labeled using annotation projection.

3 THE PROJECTOR User Interface

THE PROJECTOR is a Web-based GUI that allows users to inspect alignments and projected annotation. We give an overview of the layout, input fields and visualization options (sec. 3.1) discuss the two main usage modes (sec. 3.2), and illustrate two example usage scenarios (sec. 3.3).

3.1 Layout

Figure 2 illustrates THE PROJECTOR's main view. It is divided into input fields (top right), visualization options (top left) and the visualization pane (bottom half).

3.1.1 Input Fields

The input fields are grouped to the top left of the main screen. Two selection options are mandatory: the first is the **target language** dropdown option to indicate the TL of the annotation projection approach[3]. The second is the **input** option that can either be set to *manual* (users manually supply a sentence or sentence pair) or used to select a pre-loaded monolingual corpus in CoNLL-U

format. At time of writing, we pre-loaded both the ONTONOTES (Hovy et al., 2006) and the *universal dependencies* corpora (Nivre et al., 2016).

There are two textual inputs, namely the **SL sentence** and the **TL sentence** fields. Users populate these fields with a translated sentence pair. At least one of the two fields must be populated - in this case, a translation is automatically generated using the Google Translate API (Wu et al., 2016). The fields can either be populated by manually entering a sentence, or - if a corpus is selected as input option - be populated by selecting a sentence using the **corpus navigator**. Once the selection is complete and at least one sentence field populated, users hit the **go** button to execute and visualize annotation projection.

3.1.2 Visualization Options

Visualization options are divided into options that pertain to the source or target sentence. On the source side, users can check which layers of visualization should be displayed. Options include PoS tags, dependency trees and semantic frames and roles.

On the target side, users choose between several options for each layer. PoS tags and dependency trees can be either *predicted* using a TL parser

---

[3]At time of writing, we tested setups with the following TLs: Chinese, French, German and Japanese - through there is no principal limitation on the scope of TLs

or *projected* using annotation projection. By toggling between these options, users compare between predicted and projected annotation. Since SRL information is projected onto entire TL constituents, users additionally specify whether they are identified using predicted or projected dependency tree information. In addition, users choose whether or not to show the word alignments.

3.1.3 Visualization Pane

The visualization pane displays annotation projection for a sentence pair according to the current settings. If activated, dependency trees are displayed above a sentence. PoS tags are placed directly beneath each word. SRL labels are displayed as boxes around constituents, where each layer corresponds to one semantic frame.

3.2 Modes

The tool supports two general modes of interaction: (1) an *interactive mode* in which users supply an example sentence (or sentence pair) and execute alignment, parsing and projection on-the-fly, and (2) a *corpus mode* in which a gold-labeled corpus is loaded that can be browsed and employed in annotation projection.

3.2.1 Interactive Mode

The first mode is intended for analysis of specific linguistic constructs in the source or target language. Researchers select "manual" as input option and create an example sentence for the construct of interest. To analyze how a SL construct transfers to a TL, users enter the example sentence in the source field. Similarly, to investigate a specific TL construct, they enter the example sentence in the target field. Users may supply the corresponding SL or TL translation themselves or simply leave the other field blank - if only one sentence is provided, our tool uses the Google Translate API to automatically retrieve a translation and fill in the missing field.

Parsing pipelines. Upon clicking **go**, the SL sentence is sent to a pipeline of NLP tools, namely the STANFORDNLP tools (Manning et al., 2014) to tokenize, lemmatize, PoS tag and dependency parse the sentence and MATEPLUS (Roth and Woodsend, 2014) to predict SRL annotation. We used the standard models provided for STANFORDNLP and trained MATEPLUS over the version 3 release of propbank annotations (Bonial et al., 2014) for the ONTONOTES corpus.

The target language sentence is parsed using the transition-based MATE parser (Bohnet and Nivre, 2012) which we trained for each TL over version 1.4 release of the universal dependency treebank.

Alignment and projection. Word alignments are heuristically detected on-the-fly using word co-occurrence weights as determined by the BerkeleyAligner (DeNero and Liang, 2007) over the 2016 release of the OPENSUBTITLES parallel corpus for all supported language pairs (Tiedemann, 2012). Using these alignments, we execute annotation projection of all syntactic and semantic information. Word-level PoS tags and semantic frames are simply transferred to aligned words in the target language, while dependencies are transferred to corresponding word pairs. For semantic roles (which label entire constituents), we identify the best matching TL constituent using the Jaccard distance as described in (Padó and Lapata, 2009).

Results. The GUI displays the sentence pair with all predicted and projected annotations. Users may change visualization options, and experiment with modifications to the sentence pair (for instance, chose a different translation).

3.2.2 Corpus Mode

The second mode is to enable qualitative analysis for cases in which a gold labeled corpus already exists either for the source or target language. This setting allows us to inspect annotation projection without interference from potentially incorrect parses[4]. Users select a corpus in the input field, and then browse sentences using the navigation field. Depending on whether the gold-labeled corpus is loaded for the SL or TL side, a different pipeline of tools is executed:

Gold-labeled SL corpus. If users select an English gold corpus (ONTONOTES in the current setup), no SL parsing pipeline is executed. Instead, the sentence is automatically translated into the selected TL and the alignment, TL parsing and projection pipeline executed. If the translation is incorrect or lacking, users may manually enter a better TL translation and re-execute the approach.

Gold-labeled TL corpus. If users select a TL gold corpus (the universal dependency treebanks in the current setup), the currently selected sentence is first translated into English and then parsed using the default English parsing pipeline

---

[4]In previous work, we showed that many TL annotation errors were caused by parsing errors on the SL side that were propagated during projection (Akbik et al., 2015).

and word-aligned. The annotation is then projected back onto the TL sentence where it can be compared to the original gold labels.

3.3 Example Scenarios

We now present two example usage scenarios.

3.3.1 Scenario 1: Study of Translational Divergences

In the first scenario, a user may be interested to study the effects of specific items of SL or TL syntax known to be divergent between languages. For instance, as previously discussed, one might study how continuous aspects in English verbs are transferred to a language that has no such verb aspect. German, for instance, expresses this information either implicitly or through a variety of more complex constructions.

To investigate this, the user may type in a number of sentences in both English and German that convey continuous information and investigate annotation projection. One example may be the sentence pair in Figure 1: Here, the user finds that (1) the continuous aspect does not introduce errors since universal PoS tags and dependencies do not reflect such information, but that (2) the adverbial construction in German remains unlabeled. Other examples (see the accompanying screencast) show that syntactic projection is sometimes affected, while semantic projection is more robust. Based on these investigations, the user may conclude that either heuristic rules or a semi-supervised learning approach are appropriate to close the quality and coverage gap.

3.3.2 Scenario 2: Adding A Layer of Annotation

A second example scenario is to investigate adding a layer of annotation to an already existing TL treebank. For instance, the universal dependencies treebanks are annotated with gold-standard PoS and dependency information for over 40 languages. However, there is as-yet no semantic layer of annotation. Previous work proposed to re-use English propositions as a layer of annotations for the universal treebanks (Akbik et al., 2015; Haverinen et al., 2015), but the applicability of these labels is a matter of ongoing discussion.

To investigate, a user may load a TL universal dependency corpus and browse example sentences. Each sentence is automatically translated into English, labeled with semantic roles which are then projected back onto the TL. Users qualitatively analyze whether the propositions are fitting and identify sources of errors such as suboptimal automatic translations, source language parsing errors and translational divergences.

4 Demonstration and Outlook

We present THE PROJECTOR as a hands-on demo where users can enter sentences or sentence pairs and request parsing and on-the-fly annotation projection. In order to enable the research community to quickly set up annotation projection experiments and discuss crosslingual syntax and semantics, we plan to make the toolkit publicly available, either through an online demo or in form of open source code. Our current work on THE PROJECTOR focuses on extending the functionality of the demo and the projection framework. This includes adding additional layers of annotation, such as named entities and word senses, into the parsing and projection pipeline. We also aim to enable more flexibility in choosing SL parsers and heuristics to address translational divergences, as proposed in previous work.

Acknowledgements

We would like to thank the anonymous reviewers for their helpful comments. This project has received funding from the European Union's Horizon 2020 research and innovation programme under grant agreement no 732328 ("FashionBrain").

References

Alan Akbik, Laura Chiticariu, Marina Danilevsky, Yunyao Li, Shivakumar Vaithyanathan, and Huaiyu Zhu. 2015. Generating high quality proposition banks for multilingual semantic role labeling. In *ACL 2015, 53rd Annual Meeting of the Association for Computational Linguistics*, pages 397–407.

Alan Akbik, Xinyu Guan, and Yunyao Li. 2016a. Multilingual aliasing for auto-generating proposition banks. In *COLING 2016, 26th International Conference on Computational Linguistics*, pages 3466–3474.

Alan Akbik, Kumar Vishwajeet, and Yunyao Li. 2016b. Towards semi-automatic generation of proposition banks for low-resource languages. In *EMNLP 2016, Conference on Empirical Methods on Natural Language Processing*, pages 993–998.

Collin F Baker, Charles J Fillmore, and John B Lowe. 1998. The berkeley framenet project. In *ACL 1998, 36th Annual Meeting of the Association for Computational Linguistics*, pages 86–90.

Bernd Bohnet and Joakim Nivre. 2012. A transition-based system for joint part-of-speech tagging and labeled non-projective dependency parsing. In *EMNLP-CoNLL 2012: Conference on Empirical Methods in Natural Language Processing and Computational Natural Language Learning*, pages 1455–1465.

Claire Bonial, Julia Bonn, Kathryn Conger, Jena D. Hwang, and Martha Palmer. 2014. Propbank: Semantics of new predicate types. In *LREC 2014, 9th International Conference on Language Resources and Evaluation*, pages 3013–3019.

John DeNero and Percy Liang. 2007. The berkeley aligner. http://code.google.com/p/berkeleyaligner/.

Bonnie J Dorr. 1994. Machine translation divergences: A formal description and proposed solution. *Computational Linguistics*, 20(4):597–633.

Timur Gilmanov, Olga Scrivner, and Sandra Kübler. 2014. Swift aligner, a multifunctional tool for parallel corpora: Visualization, word alignment, and (morpho)-syntactic cross-language transfer. In *LREC 2014, 9th International Conference on Language Resources and Evaluation*, pages 2913–2919.

Katri Haverinen, Jenna Kanerva, Samuel Kohonen, Anna Missilä, Stina Ojala, Timo Viljanen, Veronika Laippala, and Filip Ginter. 2015. The finnish proposition bank. *Language Resources and Evaluation*, 49(4):907–926.

Eduard Hovy, Mitchell Marcus, Martha Palmer, Lance Ramshaw, and Ralph Weischedel. 2006. Ontonotes: the 90% solution. In *Human Language Technology Conference of the NAACL*, pages 57–60.

Rebecca Hwa, Philip Resnik, Amy Weinberg, Clara Cabezas, and Okan Kolak. 2005. Bootstrapping parsers via syntactic projection across parallel texts. *Natural language engineering*, 11(03):311–325.

Thomas Krause and Amir Zeldes. 2016. Annis3: A new architecture for generic corpus query and visualization. *Digital Scholarship in the Humanities*, 31(1):118–139.

Christopher D. Manning, Mihai Surdeanu, John Bauer, Jenny Finkel, Steven J. Bethard, and David McClosky. 2014. The Stanford CoreNLP natural language processing toolkit. In *ACL 2014. 52nd Annual Meeting of the Association for Computational Linguistics: System Demonstrations*, pages 55–60.

Mitchell P Marcus, Mary Ann Marcinkiewicz, and Beatrice Santorini. 1993. Building a large annotated corpus of english: The penn treebank. *Computational linguistics*, 19(2):313–330.

Joakim Nivre, Marie-Catherine de Marneffe, Filip Ginter, Yoav Goldberg, Jan Hajic, Christopher D Manning, Ryan McDonald, Slav Petrov, Sampo Pyysalo, Natalia Silveira, et al. 2016. Universal dependencies v1: A multilingual treebank collection. In *LREC 2016, 10th International Conference on Language Resources and Evaluation*, pages 1659–1666.

Sebastian Padó and Mirella Lapata. 2009. Cross-lingual annotation projection for semantic roles. *Journal of Artificial Intelligence Research*, 36(1):307–340.

Martha Palmer, Daniel Gildea, and Paul Kingsbury. 2005. The proposition bank: An annotated corpus of semantic roles. *Computational linguistics*, 31(1):71–106.

Lonneke Van der Plas, Paola Merlo, and James Henderson. 2011. Scaling up automatic cross-lingual semantic role annotation. In *ACL 2011, 49th Annual Meeting of the Association for Computational Linguistics*, pages 299–304.

Michael Roth and Kristian Woodsend. 2014. Composition of word representations improves semantic role labelling. In *EMNLP 2014, Conference on Empirical Methods in Natural Language Processing*, pages 407–413.

Oscar Täckström, Ryan McDonald, and Jakob Uszkoreit. 2012. Cross-lingual word clusters for direct transfer of linguistic structure. In *NAACL 2012, Conference of the North American Chapter of the Association for Computational Linguistics: Human language technologies*, pages 477–487.

Jörg Tiedemann. 2012. Parallel data, tools and interfaces in opus. In *LREC 2012, 8th International Conference on Language Resources and Evaluation*, pages 2214–2218.

Jörg Tiedemann. 2014. Rediscovering annotation projection for cross-lingual parser induction. In *COLING 2014, 25th International Conference on Computational Linguistics*, pages 1854–1864.

Kitty Van Leuven-Zwart. 1989. Translation and original: Similarities and dissimilarities, i. *International Journal of Translation Studies*, 1(2):151–181.

Yonghui Wu, Mike Schuster, Zhifeng Chen, Quoc V Le, Mohammad Norouzi, Wolfgang Macherey, Maxim Krikun, Yuan Cao, Qin Gao, Klaus Macherey, et al. 2016. Google's neural machine translation system: Bridging the gap between human and machine translation. *arXiv preprint arXiv:1609.08144*.

David Yarowsky and Grace Ngai. 2001. Inducing multilingual pos taggers and np bracketers via robust projection across aligned corpora. In *NAACL 2001, 2nd Meeting of the North American Chapter of the Association for Computational Linguistics on Language Technologies*, pages 1–8.

David Yarowsky, Grace Ngai, and Richard Wicentowski. 2001. Inducing multilingual text analysis tools via robust projection across aligned corpora. In *HLT 2001, 1st International Conference on Human Language Technology Research*, pages 1–8.

Interactive Visualization for Linguistic Structure

Aaron Sarnat, Vidur Joshi, Cristian Petrescu-Prahova
Alvaro Herrasti, Brandon Stilson, and Mark Hopkins
Allen Institute for Artificial Intelligence
Seattle, WA

Abstract

We provide a visualization library and web interface for interactively exploring a parse tree or a forest of parses. The library is not tied to any particular linguistic representation, but provides a general-purpose API for the interactive exploration of hierarchical linguistic structure. To facilitate rapid understanding of a complex structure, the API offers several important features, including expand/collapse functionality, positional and color cues, explicit visual support for sequential structure, and dynamic highlighting to convey node-to-text correspondence.

1 Introduction

Interpreting visual representations of linguistic structure can be challenging and time-consuming. Consider the examples provided in Figure 1, which visualize syntactic parses of the sentence "Although some people have provided negative reviews, her restaurants have reliably great music, good food, and excellent service, and they deliver!" These representations can result in cognitive overload, due to several concrete issues:

- **The visualizations are static.** If one is using the visualization for debugging purposes, then typically one cares about only a part of the linguistic structure, not every last detail. Unfortunately, a static visualization must include all information that could possibly be relevant.

- **The visualizations are large.** The screen real estate in Figure 1 is dominated by arrows that must be carefully tracked by the eye, in order to understand the relationships between

nodes. Visualizations of long sentences often run off the side of the screen, requiring the user to scroll to discover the endpoints of these arrows.

- **All node relationships look identical.** Predicate-argument relationships (e.g. "restaurants" as the subject of "have") get the same visual treatment as modifier relationships (e.g. "good" as a modifier of "food") and sequence elements (e.g. "good food" as an element of the sequence "great music, good food, and excellent service").

In this work, we provide a library and web interface for the interactive visualization of linguistic structure, seeking to minimize the cognitive load required to understand syntactic and semantic parses. Figure 2 shows a screenshot of our web UI for the same sentence as Figure 1. It reflects several of our visualization strategies (described in more detail in Section 3):

- Instead of a static visualization, we provide an interactive visualization with an expand/collapse functionality that allows the user to focus on what is relevant to her. For instance, the subclause "although some people have provided negative reviews" is collapsed in Figure 2, but can be expanded by clicking on it.

- To reduce the size of the visualization, we use a box layout, and use badging to eliminate simple leaf nodes (e.g. instead of creating a separate node for the article "her", it is represented by a badge on the node "restaurant").

- We use positional cues to highlight predicate-argument relationships (subjects appear to the left, objects to the right, modifiers attach

49

Proceedings of the 2017 EMNLP System Demonstrations, pages 49–54
Copenhagen, Denmark, September 7–11, 2017. ©2017 Association for Computational Linguistics

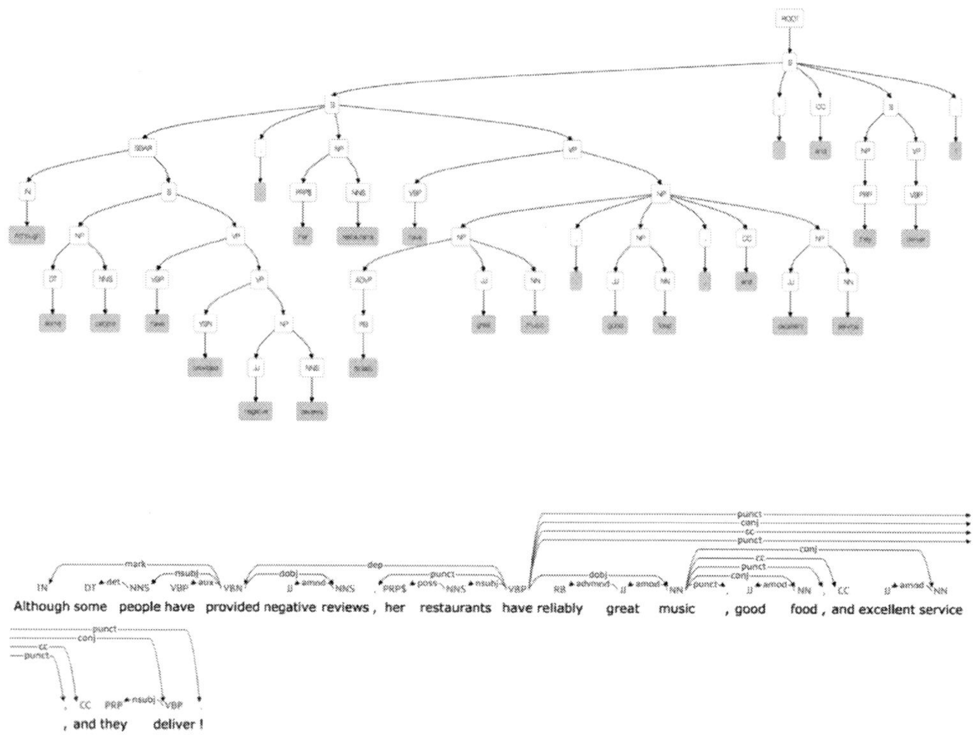

Figure 1: Typical visualizations of a constituency parse (top) and a dependency parse (bottom) for the sentence "Although some people have provided negative reviews, her restaurants have reliably great music, good food, and excellent service, and they deliver!"

to the bottom) and we provide specialized visualization for sequential structures (this occurs at two different levels in Figure 2, both for the clause sequence as well as the entity sequence "reliably great music, good food, and excellent service").

Our library is not tied to any particular linguistic formalism. In Section 4, we describe the flexible and configurable API. While our primary use case has been for creating custom grammars for mathematical language (Hopkins et al., 2017), we also provide a demonstration of how our API can be used to visualize output from the Stanford Parser (Socher et al., 2013).

2 Related Work

Most parse visualizations use the source sentence as an anchor, leaving it readable left-to-right. For constituency parses (where the words of the sentence are the leaves of the tree), this gives a representation like Figure 1 (top). For dependency parses (where the words of the sentences are the

nodes of the tree), this gives a representation like Figure 1 (bottom).

Figure 1 was generated from (Podgursky, 2015), which provides open-source code and a web interface for a static rendering of a constituency parse. There are a number of libraries (Stenetorp et al., 2012; Montani, 2016; Athar, 2010; Yimam et al., 2013) that provide static renderings of dependency parses similar to Figure 1 (bottom). Among these, Brat (Stenetorp et al., 2012) provides some interactive elements (like mouseover highlighting of subtrees, and the ability to add dependencies via drag-and-drop). Displacy (Montani, 2016) provides a general API for the static rendering of various dependency parsing schemes, e.g. Universal Dependencies (Nivre et al., 2016) and Stanford Dependencies (De Marneffe and Manning, 2008).

We are not aware of any recent tools for exploring parse forests. Historically, the REDWOODS annotation environment (Oepen et al., 2004) produced a static parse forest from a hand-built grammar, and then allowed users to select the best

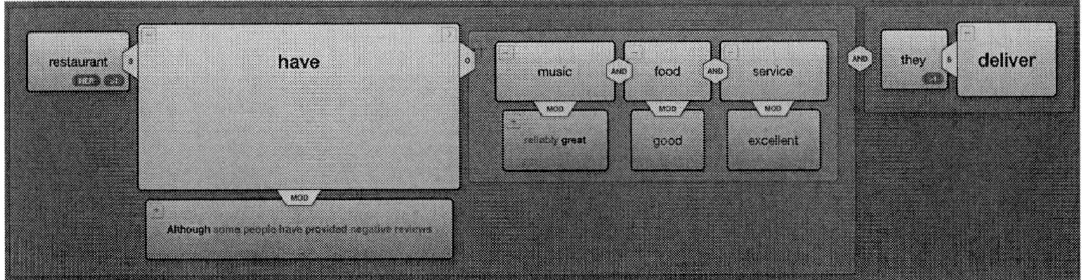

Figure 2: A screenshot of our parse visualization tool for the sentence "Although some people have provided negative reviews, her restaurants have reliably great music, good food, and excellent service, and they deliver!"

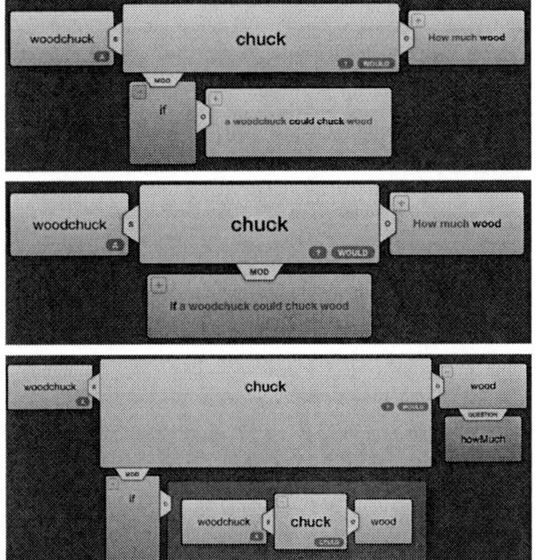

Figure 3: Three screenshots of our visualizer for the question "How much wood would a woodchuck chuck, if a woodchuck could chuck wood?": partially expanded (top), fully collapsed (middle), and fully expanded (bottom).

parse from this forest by repeatedly specifying constraints (called *discriminants* in the paper).

3 Key Features

In this section, we describe our key features for facilitating a rapid understanding of linguistic structure. As a companion to this section, we invite readers to use our web demonstration at http://hierplane.allenai.org/explain to interactively explore examples.[1]

---

[1] The user may experience some slowness when parsing certain sentences. This is due to the speed of the back-end parser, not the visualization library.

3.1 Expand/Collapse Functionality

Rather than a static rendering, our dynamic expand/collapse functionality allows the user to focus on relevant parts of the linguistic structure, while the rest is conveniently summarized at a coarser granularity. In Figure 3, the top screenshot shows a partially expanded structure that delves into the internal structure of the if-clause. The middle and bottom screenshots respectively show the fully collapsed and expanded visualizations.

3.2 Positional Cues to Distinguish Node Relations

Linguistic relationships can often be organized into intuitive clusters. For instance, subjects and objects can be roughly viewed as required arguments of a verb (exactly one per verb), while modifiers are optional (a verb can take any number of them, including zero). Our library allows the visual expression of these "relationship families" through positional cues. In Figure 3, the subject is attached to the left of its verb, the object is attached to the right of its verb, and all modifiers are attached beneath. For consistency, the object of the preposition "if" is also attached to its right. At a glance, this representation allows the user to read a gloss of the main clause by simply skimming the top line of the visualization (i.e. "a woodchuck would chuck how much wood?").

3.3 Color Cues to Distinguish Node Types

Our library provides support for using color to distinguish node types. In Figure 3, green represents events, blue represents entities, red represents modifiers, and gray is a catch-all for anything else.

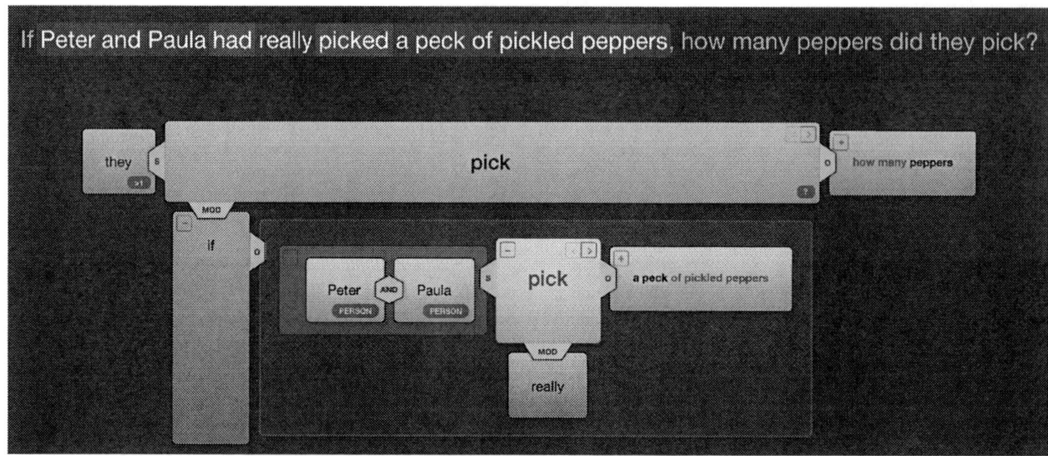

Figure 4: Dynamic highlighting of the correspondence between the linguistic structure and the source text: "If Peter and Paula had really picked a peck of pickled peppers, how many peppers did they pick?"

3.4 Badging

Some leaf nodes of linguistic structures convey very simple information about their parent node. We allow these nodes to be represented as badges rather than separate nodes. In Figure 3, the determiners ("a" for "a woodchuck") and modals ("would" for "would chuck") are represented as badges.

3.5 Sequence Support

Sequential structure is a fundamental linguistic element that is often difficult to access in a parse visualization. We make sequences visually explicit as a container of linked nodes. Examples include "Peter and Paula" in Figure 4 or the sequence of top-level clauses "her restaurants have...excellent service" and "they deliver" in Figure 2. Contrast this to the undistinguished representations of sequential structure found in Figure 1.

3.6 Dynamic Node-to-Text Highlighting

It can be difficult (particularly in semantic parses) to ascertain how the source text and the linguistic representation correspond. Upon mouse-over of a node, our visualizer highlights the part of the source text corresponding to the subtree rooted at that node. Parts that do not also correspond to some descendant node in the subtree are strongly highlighted. In Figure 4, upon mouse-over of the lower "pick" node, the corresponding segment "Peter and Paula had really picked a peck of pickled peppers" is weakly highlighted. The tokens "had" and "pecked" are strongly highlighted, be-

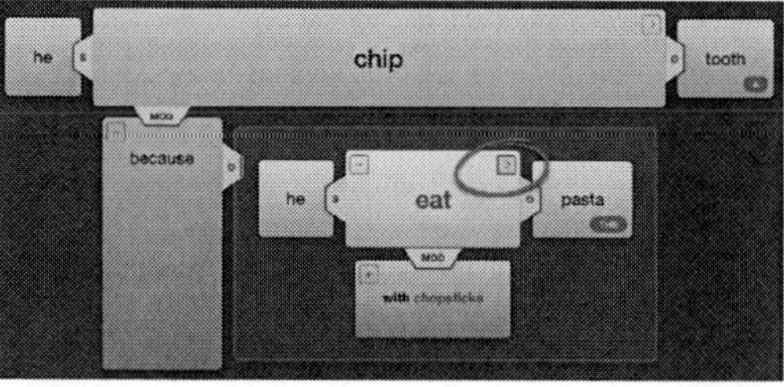

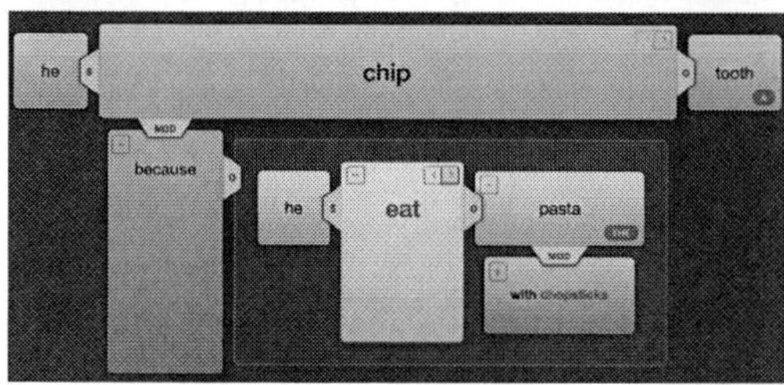

Figure 5: Before-and-after screenshots of forest exploration for the sentence "Because he ate the pasta with chopsticks, he chipped a tooth."

cause they do not correspond to any of the node's descendants.

3.7 Modular Forest Exploration

Our interactive setting permits a convenient exploration of parse forests. For instance, see Figure 5. The subtree rooted at "eat" has two interpretations, attaching "with chopsticks" to the verb or to the object. An indicator in the node's upper-right allows the user to browse these interpretations. We localize ambiguities to the lowest possible node to allow the user to explore the forest in a convenient, modular fashion (rather than cycling through an exponential number of parses at the root).

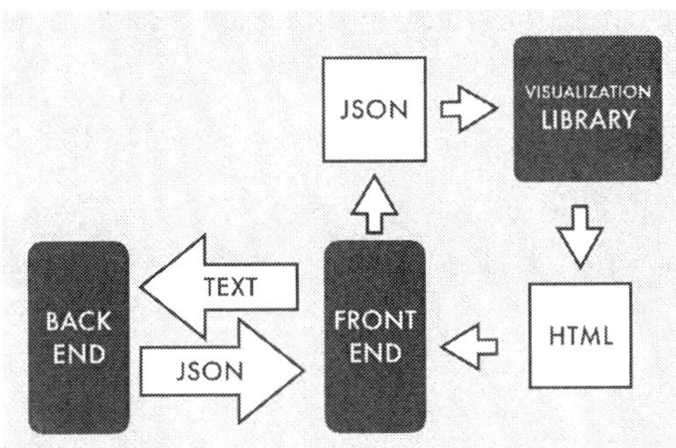

Figure 6: System architecture for our web interface. Similar architectures are employed by Brat and WebAnno.

4 APIs

Our web interface, hosted at `http://hierplane.allenai.org/explain,` has the architecture shown in Figure 6. The front-end accepts text input from the user. It forwards this text to the back-end and receives a JSON that contains an annotated tree and styling instructions. Figure 7 shows a simplified version of the JSON that renders the "He ate pasta with chopsticks" subtree in Figure 5. This JSON is passed to the visualization library, which renders it in HTML and returns this HTML to the front-end.

4.1 Basic Features

A key feature of our architecture is that the back-end is in charge of defining the node and edge types, and specifying how these should be displayed. This allows the visualization library to be independent of any particular linguistic annotation scheme. To demonstrate this flexibility, our demo provides two alternative back-ends. By default, it uses a custom grammar that we have been developing for parsing mathematical language (e.g.

```
http://hierplane.
allenai.org/explain/He%
20ate%20pasta%20with%
20chopsticks
```

utilizes the default back-end). However, we have also wrapped the Stanford Parser (Socher et al., 2013) as an alternative back-end. For any given sentence, one can try out this alternative by replacing the URL prefix

```
{
  "text": "He ate pasta with chopsticks.",
  "kindToStyle": [{
    "key": "event",
    "value": ["color1"]
  }, {
    "key": "entity",
    "value": ["color2"]
  }, {
    "key": "detail",
    "value": ["color3"]
  }],
  "linkToPosition": [{
    "key": "subj",
    "value": "left"
  }, {
    "key": "obj",
    "value": "right"
  }],
  "root": {
    "kind": "event",
    "word": "eat",
    "children": [{
      "kind": "entity",
      "word": "he",
      "link": "subj"
    }, {
      "kind": "entity",
      "word": "pasta",
      "link": "obj"
    }, {
      "kind": "detail",
      "word": "with",
      "link": "adv",
      "children": [{
        "kind": "entity",
        "word": "chopstick",
        "attributes": [">1"],
        "link": "parg"
      }]
    }]
  }
}
```

Figure 7: A simplified version of the JSON that describes the parse tree for "He ate pasta with chopsticks."

```
http://hierplane.allenai.
org/explain/
```

with

```
http://hierplane.allenai.
org/explain/stanford/
```

For instance:

```
http://hierplane.allenai.
org/explain/stanford/
```

```
He%20ate%20pasta%20with%
20chopsticks
```

will parse "He ate pasta with chopsticks" using the Stanford parser.

In the JSON returned by the back-end, each node in the tree is annotated with its kind and label ("word"), the type of edge ("link") connecting it to its parent, and its badges ("attributes"). The linkToPosition map allows each node to be positioned according to its relation to its parent (e.g. subjects are positioned to the left of their parents, according to the example JSON). The kindToStyle map specifies colors for the various node types.

4.2 Advanced Features

To enable interactive node-to-text highlighting, nodes in the input JSON tree can each be annotated with a span field that contains the indexes of the start and end characters of the substring corresponding to the node. To enable modular forest navigation, each node with a next or previous subtree can be annotated with codes identifying these subtrees. Navigation arrows are only rendered when they lead to another subtree. When a user clicks on one, the front-end sends the code identifying the desired subtree to the back-end, and expects the requested subtree as a response.

5 Conclusion

In this work, we have tried to rethink the visualization of hierarchical linguistic structure from the ground up, first identifying the problems that cause cognitive load (large, static visualizations with no cues to distinguish node or edge families), and then designing new tactics to counter these problems (e.g. expand/collapse functionality, positional cues to distinguish node relations, explicit sequence visualization, and dynamic node-to-text highlighting). We have also created the first tool to explore parse forests using modern web design. We plan to make our visualizer freely available as an open-source library and a web interface.

References

Awais Athar. 2010. Dependensee: A dependency parse visualization tool. http://chaoticity.com/dependensee-a-dependency-parse-visualisation-tool. Accessed: 2017-04-27.

Marie-Catherine De Marneffe and Christopher D Manning. 2008. Stanford typed dependencies manual. Technical report, Technical report, Stanford University.

Mark Hopkins, Cristian Petrescu-Prahova, Roie Levin, Ronan Le Bras, Alvaro Herrasti, and Vidur Joshi. 2017. Beyond sentential semantic parsing: Tackling the math sat with a cascade of tree transducers. In *EMNLP*.

Ines Montani. 2016. Displacy dependency visualizer. https://demos.explosion.ai/displacy. Accessed: 2017-04-27.

Joakim Nivre, Marie-Catherine de Marneffe, Filip Ginter, Yoav Goldberg, Jan Hajic, Christopher D Manning, Ryan McDonald, Slav Petrov, Sampo Pyysalo, Natalia Silveira, et al. 2016. Universal dependencies v1: A multilingual treebank collection. In *Proceedings of the 10th International Conference on Language Resources and Evaluation (LREC 2016)*, pages 1659–1666.

Stephan Oepen, Dan Flickinger, Kristina Toutanova, and Christopher D Manning. 2004. Lingo redwoods. *Research on Language and Computation*, 2(4):575–596.

Ben Podgursky. 2015. Nlpviz. http://nlpviz.bpodgursky.com. Accessed: 2017-04-27.

Richard Socher, John Bauer, Christopher D Manning, and Andrew Y Ng. 2013. Parsing with compositional vector grammars. In *ACL (1)*, pages 455–465.

Pontus Stenetorp, Sampo Pyysalo, Goran Topic, Tomoko Ohta, Sophia Ananiadou, and Jun'ichi Tsujii. 2012. brat: a web-based tool for nlp-assisted text annotation. In *EACL*.

Seid Muhie Yimam, Iryna Gurevych, Richard Eckart de Castilho, and Chris Biemann. 2013. Webanno: A flexible, web-based and visually supported system for distributed annotations. In *Proceedings of the 51st Annual Meeting of the Association for Computational Linguistics: System Demonstrations*, pages 1–6, Sofia, Bulgaria. Association for Computational Linguistics.

DLATK: Differential Language Analysis ToolKit

H. Andrew Schwartz[†] **Salvatore Giorgi**[‡] **Maarten Sap**[§]
Patrick Crutchley[‖] **Johannes C. Eichstaedt**[‡] **Lyle Ungar**[‡]

† Stony Brook University   ‡ University of Pennsylvania
§ University of Washington   ‖ Qntfy

`has@cs.stonybrook.edu, sgiorgi@sas.upenn.edu`

Abstract

We present *Differential Language Analysis Toolkit* (DLATK), an open-source python package and command-line tool developed for conducting social-scientific language analyses. While DLATK provides standard NLP pipeline steps such as tokenization or SVM-classification, its novel strengths lie in analyses useful for psychological, health, and social science: (1) incorporation of extra-linguistic structured information, (2) specified levels and units of analysis (e.g. document, user, community), (3) statistical metrics for continuous outcomes, and (4) robust, proven, and accurate pipelines for social-scientific prediction problems. DLATK integrates multiple popular packages (SKLearn, Mallet), enables interactive usage (Jupyter Notebooks), and generally follows object oriented principles to make it easy to tie in additional libraries or storage technologies.

1 Introduction

The growth of NLP for social and medical sciences has shifted attention in NLP research from understanding language itself (e.g. syntactic parsing or characterizing morphology) to understanding how language use characterizes people (e.g. by correlating language use characteristics with traits of the person producing the language). Much of this work has been done using Facebook and Twitter (Coppersmith et al., 2014).

Analyzing language for social science applications requires different tools and techniques than conventional NLP. Structured data are often beneficial to facilitate the use of the extensive extra-linguistic information such as the time and loca-tion of the post and author demographics (or even health or school records). Models can be made at multiple levels of analysis: documents, users, and different geographic (zip code, state or country) or temporal resolutions. Many of the outcomes (or dependent variables) are continuous (e.g. scores on personality tests), and researchers are often as interested in interpretable insights as they are with predictive accuracy (Kern et al., 2014a).

There are small "tricks" to obtain accurate predictive models or high correlations between language features and outcomes. Emoticon-aware tokenizers are needed, robust methods for creating LDA topics (different packages produce clusters of strikingly different quality), and subtle issues of regularization arise when combining demographic and language features in models. When these choices are combined with the complexity of the structured data, even NLP and data scientists can fail to produce high quality models. We therefore built a platform that integrates a variety of open-sourced tools, alongside our "tricks" and optimizations, to provide a well-documented, easy-to-use program for undertaking reproducible research in the area of NLP for the social sciences.

This software, which has now been used for the data analysis behind 32 papers in psychology, health care, and NLP, is now available under a GPLv3 software license.[1]

2 Overall Framework

The core of DLATK is a Python library depicted in Figure 1. The base class, DLAWorker, sits on top of a data engine (e.g. MySQL, HDFS/Spark) and is used to track corpus basics (corpus location, unit-of-analysis). The next level of classes acts on either: messages, features or outcomes. MessageAnnotator filters messages (removing du-

---

[1] http://dlatk.wwbp.org or http://github.com/dlatk/

55

Proceedings of the 2017 EMNLP System Demonstrations, pages 55–60
Copenhagen, Denmark, September 7–11, 2017. ©2017 Association for Computational Linguistics

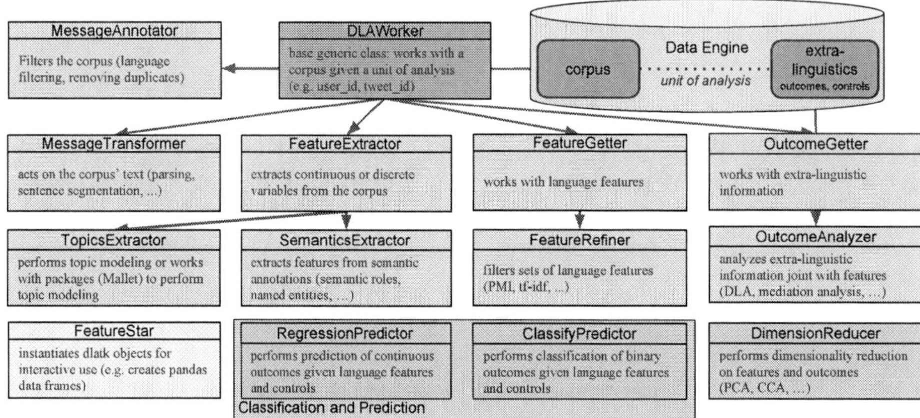

Figure 1: Basic DLATK package class structure.

plicate tweets, language filtering, etc.) while MessageTransformer acts on message text (tokenizing, part of speech tagging, etc.). FeatureExtractor converts document text to features (ngrams, character ngrams, etc.) and is responsible for writing while FeatureGetters read for downstream analysis or further refinement via FeatureRefiner. OutcomeGetter reads outcome tables (i.e., extra-linguistic information). Its child class OutcomeAnalyzer works with both linguistic and extra-linguistic information for statistical analyses (correlation, logistic regression, etc.) and various outputs (wordclouds, correlation matrices, etc.).

The bottom classes do not inherit but are utilizers of FeatureGetters and OutcomeGetters. This includes two classes for prediction, RegressionPredictor and ClassifyPredictor which carry out machine learning tasks: cross validation, feature selection, training models, building data-driven lexica, etc, while DimensionReducer provides unsupervised transformations on language and outcomes Finally, the FeatureStar class ("star" for wildcard) is used to interact with the other classes and transform important information into convenient data structures (e.g. Pandas dataframes).

3 Differential Language Analyses

The prototypical use of DLATK is to perform *differential language analysis* – the identification of linguistic features which either (a) independently explain the most variance for *continuous outcomes* or (b) are individually most predictive of *discrete outcomes* (Schwartz et al., 2013b). Unlike predictive techniques where one seeks to *produce outcome(s)* given language (discussed next), here, the goal is to *produce language* that is most related to or independently discriminant of outcomes.[2] DLATK supports several metrics for performing differential language analysis.

Continuous DLA Metrics. We support a variety of metrics for comparing language to continuous outcomes (e.g. age, degree of depression, personality factor scores, income). Primary metrics are based on **Pearson Product-Moment Correlation Coefficient** (Agresti and Finlay, 2008). When one requests control variables (e.g. finding the relationship with degree of depression, controlling for age and gender) then **ordinary least squares linear regression** is used (Rao, 2009) wherein the control variables are included alongside the linguistic variable as covariates and the outcome is the dependent variable.

Discrete DLA Metrics. While linear regression produces meaningful results for most situations, it is often ideal to use other metrics for discrete or Bernoulli outcomes. **Logistic regression** can be used in place of linear regression where, by assuming a dichotomous outcome, statistical significance tests are usually more accurate (Menard, 2002). Where controls are not needed, there are many other options, often less computationally complex, such as **TF-IDF, Informative Dirichlet Prior**,[3] or classification accuracy metrics like

---

[2] Even in basic prediction methods, like linear regression, the relationship between each linguistic feature and the outcome is complex – dependent on the covariance structure between all the variables. DLA works in a univariate, per-feature fashion or with a limited set of control variables (e.g. age and gender when discriminating personality).

[3] Bayesian approach to log-odds (Monroe et al., 2008).

Area Under the ROC Curve (Fawcett, 2006).

Multiple Hypothesis Testing. Most of the metrics have a corresponding standard significance test (e.g. Student's t-test for Pearson correlation and OLS regression), and most output confidence intervals by default. Permutation testing has been implemented for many of metrics without standard significance tests, such as AUC-ROC, with the linguistic feature vector shuffled relative to outcome (and controls, if applicable) multiple times to create a null distribution. Standard practice in differential language analysis (Schwartz et al., 2013b) is to correlate each of potentially thousands of single features (e.g., normalized usage of one single- or multi-word expression) with a given outcome. Thus, correcting for multiple comparisons is critical. When used through the interface script, DLATK by default corrects for multiple comparisons using the Benjamini-Hochberg method of FDR correction (Benjamini and Hochberg, 1995). Other options, such as the more conservative Bonferroni correction (Dunn, 1961) are also available.

4 Predictive Methods

As with traditional NLP, many social-scientific research objectives can be framed as *prediction* tasks, in which a model is fit to language features to predict an outcome. DLATK implements many available regression and classification tools, supplemented with feature selection functions for refining the feature space. A wide range of feature selection techniques have been empirically refined for accurate use in regression problems.

Feature selection. DLATK's ClassifyPredictor and RegressionPredictor classes include methods for feature selection, which is critical given what may be a very large space of linguistic features, e.g., 100s of thousands of 1- to 3-grams in a corpus. Both classes allow for pass-through of scikit-learn Pipelines (e.g. univariate feature selection based on feature correlation with outcome and family-wise error) and dimensionality reduction methods (e.g., PCA on feature matrix), including combination methods where FS and DR steps are applied to the original data in a serial manner.

Regression Models. DLATK supports a variety of regression models in order to take in features as well as extra-linguistic information and output a continuous value predictions. These include variants on penalized linear regression: **Ridge**,

Lasso, **Elastic-Net**, as well as non-linear techniques such as **Extremely Random Forests**. A common pipeline, referred to as "magic sauce" applies univariate feature selection and PCA to linguistic features independent of controls, and then uses ridge to fit a linear model from a combined reduced space to the outcomes.

Classification Models. DLATK implements a rich variety of classifiers, including **Logistic Regression** and **Support Vector Classifiers** with L_1 and L_2 regularization, as well ensemble and gradient boosting techniques such as **Extremely Randomized Trees**. As with regression, techniques have been setup so as to leverage extra-linguistic information effectively either as additional predictors or controls to try to "-out-predict".

5 Notable Functionality

Linguistic information Because DLATK was designed to exploit the full power of social media, a special emoticon-aware tokenizer is used while also leveraging Python's unicode capabilities. Though not specifically designed to be language independent, DLATK has been used in one non-English study (Smith et al., 2016).

Extra-linguistic information. Most functionality in DLATK is designed with extra-linguistic, also referred to as "outcomes", in mind. Such information ranges from meta-information of social media posts, such as time or location, to user attributes such as demographics or strong baselines one may wish to out-predict. For DLA, this means that one not only distinguishes target extra-linguistic information, but that controls are available. For prediction, extra-linguistic information can be incorporated as input to a model, taking into account the fact that such features are often less sparse and more reliable features of people than individual linguistic features.

Multiple Levels of Analysis. DLATK allows one to work with a single corpus at multiple levels of analysis, simply as a parameter to any action. For example, one may choose to analyze tweets themselves or group them by user_id, location, or even a combination of user and date. Extra-linguistic information often dictates particular levels of analyses (e.g. community level mortality rates or user-level personality questionnaire responses). Analysis setups are flexible for levels of analysis – for example, one can dynamically threshold which of the units of analyses are available (e.g. only include users with at least 1000 words or counties with 50,000 words).

Integration of Popular Packages. DLATK sits on top of many popular open source packages used for data analysis and machine learning (scikit-learn (Pedregosa et al., 2011) and statsmodels (Seabold and Perktold, 2010)) as well as NLP specific packages (Stanford parser (Chen and Manning, 2014), TweetNLP (Gimpel et al., 2011) and NLTK (Loper and Bird, 2002)). LDA topics can be created with the Mallet (McCallum, 2002) interface. After creation these topics can then be used downstream in any standard DLATK analysis pipeline. The *pip* and *conda* package management systems control python library dependencies.

Interactive Usage. The standard way to interact with DLATK is with the interface script through the command line. Often users will only see the two end points (the document input and the analysis output) and as a result this package is used as a "black box". In order to encourage data exploration the FeatureStar class converts the language features and extra-linguistic information into Pandas dataframes (McKinney, 2011) allowing users to import our methods into existing code. Sample use cases include opening up predictive models to explore feature coefficients and easily reading linguistic data into standard data visualization tools.

Visualization. When running DLA we often run separate correlations over tens of thousands of language features. While a single word might not give us considerable insight into our extra-linguistic information groups of words taken together can often tell a compelling story. To this end DLATK offers wordcloud output in the form of n-gram and topic clouds images. Figure 2 shows 1- to 3-grams significantly correlated with (a) age (positive; higher age), (b) age (negative; lower age), (c) educator occupation and (d) technology occupation. This was run over the Blog Authorship Corpus (Schler et al., 2006) packaged with DLATK. Here color represents the words frequency in the corpus (grey to red for infrequent to frequent) and size represents correlation strength.

Comparison to social-scientific tools. Traditional programs for text analysis in the social sciences are based on dictionaries (list of words associated with a particular psychological 'construct'

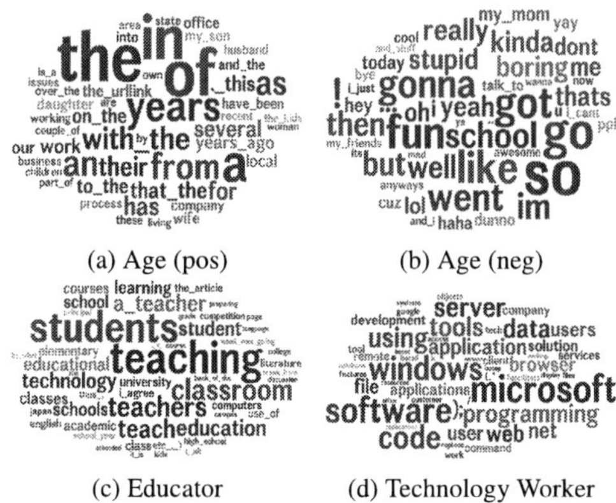

(a) Age (pos)   (b) Age (neg)

(c) Educator   (d) Technology Worker

Figure 2: 1- to 3-grams correlated with age and occupation class.

or language categories, such as 'positive emotion' or references to work and occupational terms). According to citations, the most popular tool is Linguistic Inquiry and Word Count (LIWC) (Pennebaker et al., 2015), followed by DICTION (Hart, 1984) and the General Inquirer (Stone et al., 1966). For a given document, these programs provide the relative frequency of occurrence of terms from the dictionaries. The use of dictionaries has the advantage that they provide relatively parsimonious language in a given text sample, and that the results are in principle comparable across studies. DLATK also reproduces the functionality of these dictionary-based approaches. Dictionaries, however, are often opaque units of analysis, as their overall frequency counts are determined by a few highly frequent words. If these words are ambiguous, interpretations of dictionary-based results can be misleading (Schwartz et al., 2013a). DLATK allows for the determination of words which drive a given dictionary category, and it can also produce data-driven lexica based on predictive models over ngrams, or even find, within a given dictionary category, the words most associated with.

DLATK can provide researchers with enough information to generate hypotheses and clarify the "nomological net" of a construct (Cronbach and Meehl, 1955); That is, help identify the psychological and social processes and constructs that relate to (are sufficiently correlated with) the outcome under investigation. Further, the fact that DLATK incorporates language features and controls in prediction tests allows the researcher to gauge how much construct-related variance is captured in language compared to meaningful demographic or socioeconomic baselines.

6 Evaluations

DLATK has been used as a data analysis platform in over 30 peer-reviewed publications, with venues ranging from general-interest (PLoS ONE: Schwartz et al., 2013b) to computer science methods proceedings (EMNLP: Sap et al., 2014) to psychology journals (JPSP: Park et al., 2015).

The most straightforward use for DLATK is to provide insight on linguistic features associated with a given outcome, the *differential language analyses* presented in Schwartz et al. (2013b). Other works to primarily use DLATK for correlation-type analyses examine outcomes like age (Kern et al., 2014b), gendered language and stereotypes (Park et al., 2016; Carpenter et al., 2016b), and efficacy of app-based well-being interventions (Carpenter et al., 2016a).

Another area one can evaluate the utility of DLATK is in building predictive models. Table 1 summarizes some predictive models reported in peer-reviewed publications. DLATK works to create models at multiple scales, i.e., for predicting aspects of single messages (e.g., tweet-wise temporal orientation; Schwartz et al., 2015), or predicting user-level attributes (e.g., severity of depression; Schwartz et al., 2014), or predicting community-level health outcomes (e.g., heart disease mortality; Eichstaedt et al., 2015).

7 Conclusion

DLATK has been under development for over five years. We have discussed some of its core functionality, including support for extra-linguistic features, multiple levels of analysis, and continuous variables. However, its biggest benefits may be flexibility and reliability due to many years of refinement over dozens of projects. We aspire for DLATK to serve as *a multipurpose Swiss Army Knife* for the researcher who is trying to understand the manifestations of social, psychological and health factors in the lives of language users.

Acknowledgments

This work was supported, in part, by the Templeton Religion Trust (grant TRT-0048). DLATK is an open-source project out of the University of Pennsylvania and Stony Brook University. We wish to thank all those who have contributed to its development, including, but not limited to: Youngseo Son, Mohammadzaman Zamani, Sneha Jha, Megha Agrawal, Margaret Kern, Gregory Park, Lukasz Dziuzinski, Phillip Lu,

Outcome	Score	Source
Demographic (user-level)		
Age	$R = 0.83$	Sap et al.
Gender	Acc $= 0.92$	(2014)
Big-Five Personality (user-level)		
Openness	$R = 0.43$	
Conscientiousness	$R = 0.37$	Park et al.
Extraversion	$R = 0.42$	(2015)
Agreeableness	$R = 0.35$	
Neuroticism	$R = 0.35$	
Temporal orientation (message-level)		
3-way classif	Acc $= 0.72$	Schwartz et al.
Intensity & affect (message-level)		(2015)
Intensity	$R = 0.85$	Preoţiuc-Pietro
Affect	$R = 0.65$	et al. (2016)
Mental health (user-level)		
PTSD	AUC $= 0.86$	Preoţiuc-Pietro
Depression	AUC $= 0.87$	et al. (2015)
Degree of dprssn	$R = 0.39$	Schwartz et al.
Physical health (US county-level)		(2014)
Heart disease mortality	$R = 0.42$	Eichstaedt et al. (2015)

Table 1: Survey of predictive model scores trained using DLATK in peer-reviewed publications. Scores reported are: R: Pearson correlation; Acc: accuracy; AUC: area under the ROC curve.

Thomas Apicella, Masoud Rouhizadeh, Daniel Rieman, Selah Lynch and Daniel Preoţiuc-Pietro.

References

Alan Agresti and Barbara Finlay. 2008. *Statistical Methods for the Social Sciences*. Allyn & Bacon, Incorporated.

Yoav Benjamini and Yosef Hochberg. 1995. Controlling the false discovery rate: a practical and powerful approach to multiple testing. *Journal of the royal statistical society. Series B (Methodological)*, pages 289–300.

Jordan Carpenter, P. Crutchley, R. D. Zilca, H. A. Schwartz, L. K. Smith, A. M. Cobb, and A. C. Parks. 2016a. Seeing the "big" picture: Big data methods for exploring relationships between usage, language, and outcome in internet intervention data. *Journal of Medical Internet Research*, 18(8).

Jordan Carpenter, D. Preoţiuc-Pietro, L. Flekova, S. Giorgi, C. Hagan, M. Kern, A. Buffone, L. Ungar, and M. Seligman. 2016b. Real Men don't say 'cute': Using Automatic Language Analysis to Isolate Inaccurate Aspects of Stereotypes. *Social Psychological and Personality Science*.

Danqi Chen and Christopher D Manning. 2014. A fast and accurate dependency parser using neural networks. In *EMNLP*.

Glen Coppersmith, Mark Dredze, and Craig Harman. 2014. Quantifying mental health signals in twitter. *ACL 2014*, 51.

Lee J Cronbach and Paul E Meehl. 1955. Construct validity in psychological tests. *Psychological bulletin*, 52(4):281.

Olive Jean Dunn. 1961. Multiple comparisons among

means. *Journal of the American Statistical Association*, 56(293):52–64.

Johannes C Eichstaedt, H. A. Schwartz, M. L. Kern, G. Park, D. R. Labarthe, R. M. Merchant, S. Jha, M. Agrawal, L. A. Dziurzynski, M. Sap, C. Weeg, E. E. Larson, L. H. Ungar, and M. Seligman. 2015. Psychological language on Twitter predicts county-level heart disease mortality. *Psychological Science*, 26:159–169.

Tom Fawcett. 2006. An introduction to ROC analysis. *Pattern recognition letters*, 27(8):861–874.

Kevin Gimpel, Nathan Schneider, Brendan O'Connor, Dipanjan Das, Daniel Mills, Jacob Eisenstein, Michael Heilman, Dani Yogatama, Jeffrey Flanigan, and Noah A Smith. 2011. Part-of-speech tagging for twitter: Annotation, features, and experiments. In *ACL*, pages 42–47.

Roderick P Hart. 1984. *Verbal style and the presidency: A computer-based analysis*. Academic Pr.

Margaret L Kern, J. C. Eichstaedt, H. A. Schwartz, L. Dziurzynski, L. H. Ungar, D. J. Stillwell, M. Kosinski, S. M. Ramones, and M. Seligman. 2014a. The online social self: An open vocabulary approach to personality. *Assessment*, 21:158–169.

Margaret L Kern, J. C. Eichstaedt, H. A. Schwartz, G. Park, L. H. Ungar, D. J. Stillwell, M. Kosinski, L. Dziurzynski, and M. Seligman. 2014b. From "sooo excited!!!" to "so proud": Using language to study development. *Developmental Psychology*, 50:178–188.

Edward Loper and Steven Bird. 2002. NLTK: The natural language toolkit. In *Proc. of the ACL-02 Workshop on Effective Tools and Methodologies for Teaching Natural Language Processing and Computational Linguistics - Volume 1*, ETMTNLP '02, pages 63–70, Stroudsburg, PA, USA. Association for Computational Linguistics.

Andrew Kachites McCallum. 2002. Mallet: A machine learning for language toolkit. Http://mallet.cs.umass.edu.

Wes McKinney. 2011. pandas: a foundational python library for data analysis and statistics.

Scott Menard. 2002. *Applied logistic regression analysis*. 106. Sage.

Burt L Monroe, Michael P Colaresi, and Kevin M Quinn. 2008. Fightin' words: Lexical feature selection and evaluation for identifying the content of political conflict. *Polit. Anal.*, 16(4):372–403.

Greg Park, H. A. Schwartz, J. C. Eichstaedt, M. L. Kern, D. J. Stillwell, M. Kosinski, L. H. Ungar, and M. Seligman. 2015. Automatic personality assessment through social media language. *Journal of Personality and Social Psychology*, 108:934–952.

Gregory Park, D. B. Yaden, H. A. Schwartz, M. L. Kern, J. C. Eichstaedt, M. Kosinski, D. Stillwell, L. H. Ungar, and M. Seligman. 2016. Women are warmer but no less assertive than men: Gender and language on facebook. *PloS one*, 11(5):e0155885.

F. Pedregosa, G. Varoquaux, A. Gramfort, V. Michel, B. Thirion, O. Grisel, M. Blondel, P. Prettenhofer, R. Weiss, V. Dubourg, J. Vanderplas, A. Passos, D. Cournapeau, M. Brucher, M. Perrot, and E. Duchesnay. 2011. Scikit-learn: Machine learning in Python. *JMLR*, 12:2825–2830.

James W Pennebaker, Ryan L Boyd, Kayla Jordan, and Kate Blackburn. 2015. The development and psychometric properties of LIWC2015. Technical report.

D. Preoţiuc-Pietro, H. A. Schwartz, G. Park, J. Eichstaedt, M. Kern, L. Ungar, and E. P. Shulman. 2016. Modelling valence and arousal in facebook posts. In *Proc. of the Workshop on Computational Approaches to Subjectivity, Sentiment and Social Media Analysis (WASSA)*, NAACL.

Daniel Preoţiuc-Pietro, M. Sap, H. A. Schwartz, and L. H. Ungar. 2015. Mental illness detection at the World Well-Being Project for the CLPsych 2015 Shared Task. In *Proc. of the Workshop on Computational Linguistics and Clinical Psychology: From Linguistic Signal to Clinical Reality*, NAACL.

C Radhakrishna Rao. 2009. *Linear statistical inference and its applications*, volume 22. John Wiley & Sons.

Maarten Sap, G. Park, J. C. Eichstaedt, M. L. Kern, D. J. Stillwell, M. Kosinski, L. H. Ungar, and H. A. Schwartz. 2014. Developing age and gender predictive lexica over social media. In *EMNLP*.

Jonathan Schler, Moshe Koppel, Shlomo Argamon, and James W Pennebaker. 2006. Effects of age and gender on blogging. In *AAAI spring symposium*.

H Andrew Schwartz, J. Eichstaedt, M. L. Kern, G. Park, M. Sap, D. Stillwell, M. Kosinski, and L. Ungar. 2014. Towards assessing changes in degree of depression through Facebook. In *Proc. of the Workshop on Computational Linguistics and Clinical Psychology: From Linguistic Signal to Clinical Reality*, ACL, pages 118–125.

H Andrew Schwartz, J. C. Eichstaedt, L. Dziurzynski, M. L. Kern, E. Blanco, S. Ramones, M. Seligman, and L. H. Ungar. 2013a. Choosing the right words: Characterizing and reducing error of the word count approach. In **SEM: Conf on Lex and Comp Semantics*, pages 296–305.

H Andrew Schwartz, J. C. Eichstaedt, M. L. Kern, L. Dziurzynski, S. M. Ramones, M. Agrawal, A. Shah, M. Kosinski, D. Stillwell, M. Seligman, and L. H. Ungar. 2013b. Personality, gender, and age in the language of social media: The Open-Vocabulary approach. *PLoS ONE*.

H Andrew Schwartz, G. Park, M. Sap, E. Weingarten, J. Eichstaedt, M. Kern, D. Stillwell, M. Kosinski, J. Berger, M. Seligman, and L. Ungar. 2015. Extracting human temporal orientation from Facebook language. In *NAACL*.

Skipper Seabold and Josef Perktold. 2010. Statsmodels: Econometric and statistical modeling with python. In *9th Python in Science Conference*.

Laura Smith, S. Giorgi, R. Solanki, J. C. Eichstaedt, H. A. Schwartz, M. Abdul-Mageed, A. Buffone, and Lyle H. Ungar. 2016. Does 'well-being' translate on twitter? In *EMNLP*.

Philip J Stone, Dexter C Dunphy, and Marshall S Smith. 1966. The general inquirer: A computer approach to content analysis.

QUINT: Interpretable Question Answering over Knowledge Bases

Abdalghani Abujabal[1], Rishiraj Saha Roy[1], Mohamed Yahya[2] and Gerhard Weikum[1]
[1]Max Planck Institute for Informatics, Saarland Informatics Campus, Germany
`{abujabal, rishiraj, weikum}@mpi-inf.mpg.de`
[2]Bloomberg L.P., London, United Kingdom
`myahya6@bloomberg.net`

Abstract

We present QUINT, a live system for question answering over knowledge bases. QUINT automatically learns role-aligned utterance-query templates from user questions paired with their answers. When QUINT answers a question, it visualizes the complete derivation sequence from the natural language utterance to the final answer. The derivation provides an explanation of how the syntactic structure of the question was used to derive the structure of a SPARQL query, and how the phrases in the question were used to instantiate different parts of the query. When an answer seems unsatisfactory, the derivation provides valuable insights towards reformulating the question.

1 Introduction

Motivation. A KB-QA system takes a natural language utterance as input and produces one or more crisp answers as output (Bast and Haussmann, 2015; Berant et al., 2013; Reddy et al., 2014; Yih et al., 2015). This is usually done through semantic parsing: translating the utterance to a formal query in a language such as SPARQL, and executing this query over a KB like Freebase (Bollacker et al., 2008) or YAGO (Suchanek et al., 2007) to return one or more answer entities.

In addition to answering questions, a KB-QA system should ideally be able to explain how an answer was derived i.e., how the system understood the users' questions. While rapid progress is being made on the KB-QA task, the quality of answers obtained from KB-QA systems are far from

perfect. This is due to a combination of factors related to the ambiguity of natural language, the underlying data (e.g., KB incompleteness, gaps in lexicon coverage) and the KB-QA systems themselves (e.g., errors in named entity recognition and disambiguation, query ranking). Explanations help address this gap in two ways: (i) helping users gain confidence when correct answers are returned, and (ii) making sense of the limitations of the system by looking at explanations for wrong answers, possibly providing cues to work around them. For an expert user, explanations also contribute to *traceability*: identifying the exact point of failure in the KB-QA system pipeline, which can be used for subsequent debugging.

In this work, we demonstrate QUINT (Abujabal et al., 2017), a state-of-the-art KB-QA system that gives step-by-step explanations of how it derives answers for questions. Furthermore, when QUINT is unable to link a specific phrase in the question to a KB item, it asks the user to reformulate the phrase. Such reformulations can be used to improve various components in the KB-QA pipeline such as underlying lexicons. QUINT takes the first step towards enabling interactive QA in the future, where the system can ask the user about parts of the question that it is unsure about.

Example. Take the question *"Where was Martin Luther raised?"*: QUINT returns `Eisleben` in Germany as the top answer. A quick look by the user at the derivation reveals that (i) *'Martin Luther'* was mapped to the KB entity `MartinLuther`, the theologist, and (ii) *'raised'* was interpreted as the KB predicate `placeOfBirth`. For (i), if the user had intended the US activist `MartinLutherKing` instead, a simple reformulation with *"martin luther king"* in the input returns `Atlanta`, the US city where Luther King was born. On the other hand, for (ii), if the birthplace was not the specific intent, a quick

[2]Work done while at the Max Planck Institute for Informatics

Proceedings of the 2017 EMNLP System Demonstrations, pages 61–66
Copenhagen, Denmark, September 7–11, 2017. ©2017 Association for Computational Linguistics

rephrasing of the question to *"Where did Martin Luther live?"* results in `Saxony-Anhalt`, which is derived from the predicate `placesLived`.

Motivated by the need for interpretable question answering, QUINT's approach to KB-QA relies on *role-aligned templates*, where each template consists of an *utterance template* based on a dependency parse pattern and a corresponding *query template* based on the SPARQL query language. The template (i) specifies how to chunk an utterance into phrases, (ii) guides how these phrases map to KB primitives by specifying their semantic roles as predicates, entities, or types, and (iii) aligns syntactic structure in the utterance to the semantic predicate-argument structure of the query.

Limitations of past work. Prior template-based approaches rely on a set of *manually* defined rules or templates to handle user questions (Berant et al., 2013; Fader et al., 2013, 2014; Unger et al., 2012; Yahya et al., 2013; Yao and Durme, 2014; Zou et al., 2014). The main drawback of these approaches is the limited coverage of templates, making them brittle when it comes to unconventional question formulations. In contrast, QUINT automatically learns templates from question-answer pairs.

Embedding-based methods (Bordes et al., 2014; Dong et al., 2015; Yang et al., 2014; Xu et al., 2016) map questions, KB entities, and subgraphs to a shared space for KB-QA without explicitly generating a semantic representation. This makes it difficult for such systems to generate fine-grained explanations to users.

Other approaches to KB-QA (Bast and Haussmann, 2015; Yih et al., 2015) over-generate query candidates for a given utterance with no fine-grained alignments to map natural language phrases in a question onto different KB items, making explainability challenging.

Contribution. The key contribution of this demo paper is a live online KB-QA system that visualizes the derivation steps for generating an answer, and thus takes the first steps towards explainable question-answering. The demo is available at the following URL: `https://gate.d5.mpi-inf.mpg.de/quint/quint`.

2 QUINT

We now give a brief overview of QUINT (Abujabal et al., 2017), the KB-QA system driving our demonstration. QUINT has a training phase

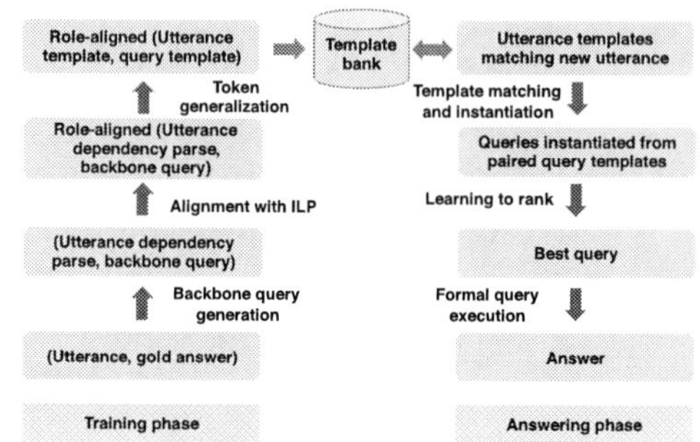

Figure 1: Overview of QUINT.

for automatically learning templates and a query ranking function, and an answering phase where templates are used to instantiate queries that are ranked by the learned function. Figure 1 shows a block diagram for QUINT.

2.1 Training phase

The input to QUINT's training phase is a set of natural language utterances $u \in U$ and the corresponding gold answer set A_u from a KB such as the one shown in Figure 2. An example of a training utterance is $u = $*"Where was Obama educated?"*, which is paired with the answer set $A_u = \{$`ColumbiaUniversity`, `HarvardUniversity`, `PunahouSchool`$\}$. First, entity mentions in each utterance u are detected and disambiguated to Freebase entities using the AIDA system (Hoffart et al., 2011).

Next, QUINT heuristically constructs a query to capture the question, the guiding intuition being that the correct query connects entities in a question u to an answer entity $a \in A_u$. To do this, QUINT starts by finding, for each answer entity $a \in A_u$, the smallest subgraph in the KB that contains all the entities detected in u and a (black nodes in Fig. 2 for $a = $`ColumbiaUniversity`). This subgraph is then extended by augmenting it with all *type nodes* connected to a (gray nodes `Organization` and `EducationalInstitution` in Fig. 2). This subgraph is transformed into a *backbone query* $\hat{q}$ by replacing the answer node (a) and any `cvt` nodes with distinct variables (`cvt` nodes are used to represent n-ary relations in Freebase). The resulting $\hat{q}$ is shown in Figure 3. This is followed by aligning the components of $\hat{q}$ and the dependency parse of u. The alignment problem is formulated as a constrained optimization and the best alignment m is obtained using Integer Linear Programming (ILP).

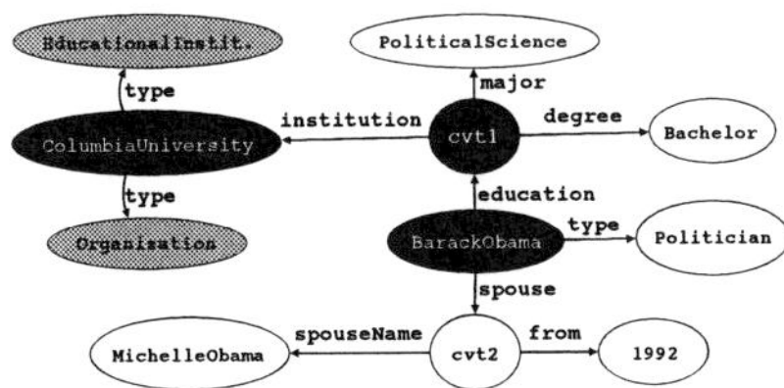

Figure 2: An example KB fragment.

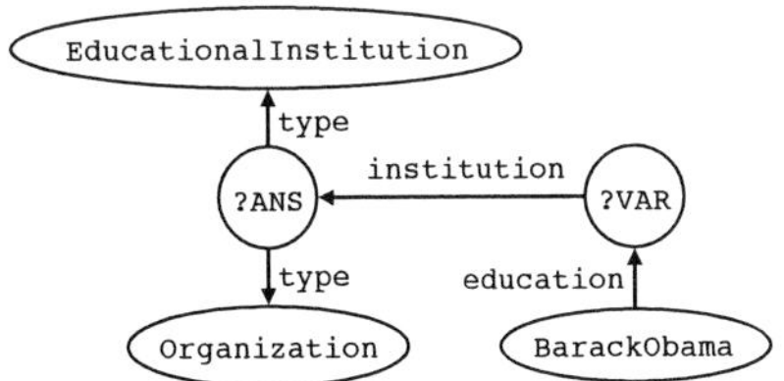

Figure 3: Backbone query $\hat{q}$ generated from the utterance *"Where was Obama educated?"* and the answer entity `ColumbiaUniversity`.

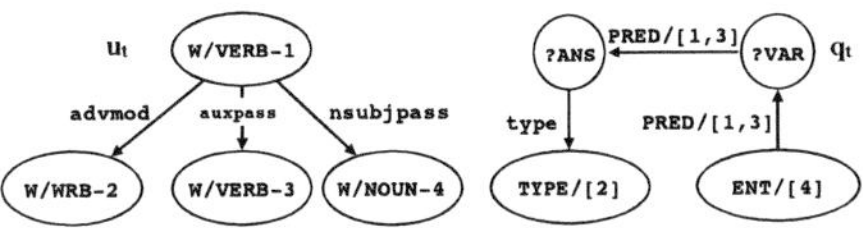

Figure 4: A pair of (utterance, query) templates. Shared numbers indicate alignment. W is a placeholder for any word. $ENT/PRED/TYPE$ are the semantic roles of nodes and edges.

To connect natural language phrases in a question to KB items, QUINT uses two kinds of weighted lexicons, a predicate lexicon $\mathcal{L}_P$ and a type lexicon $\mathcal{L}_C$. Entities, as mentioned above, are dealt with using an off-the-shelf named entity recognition and disambiguation system. The output of the ILP solver tells us which tokens in u are used to instantiate which KB items in the backbone query $\hat{q}$. Nodes in the dependency parse of u as well as nodes and edges in $\hat{q}$ that are not part of the alignment m are removed from the dependency parse of u and $\hat{q}$, respectively. In our running example, this results in dropping the node `EducationalInstitution` from $\hat{q}$ (Fig. 3). The obtained alignment is then generalized by dropping concrete values in both u and $\hat{q}$, which are referred to as an utterance template u_t and a query template q_t, respectively. This role-aligned template pair of (u_t, q_t) is added to a template repository T. The process is repeated for each training instance (u, A_u). However, since several utterances are likely to have similar syntactic structure, the number of templates $|T| \ll |U|$. Figure 4 shows the generated template from this instance.

Finally, as part of the training phase, QUINT trains a ranking function to rank the queries generated from matching a question against the template repository T. A learning-to-rank framework with a random forest classifier (Bast and Haussmann, 2015) is used to model a preference function for a pair of queries, given an input utterance.

2.2 Answering phase

When the trained system receives a new utterance u' from the user, the dependency parse of u' is matched against the utterance templates in T. For every match, the paired query template is instantiated using the alignment information together with the underlying lexicons. Thus, a set of candidate queries are obtained which are then ranked using the learning-to-rank framework. Finally, the answer of the top-ranked query is shown to the user.

3 Demonstration

We now give a walkthrough of our demonstration which shows QUINT's ability to explain its answers to both normal and technically proficient users through brief and detailed explanations, respectively. We use the question *"Where was Martin Luther raised?"* to drive this section.

3.1 Question and Answers

Figure 5 shows the main window of QUINT where the starting point for a user is the question box or one of the sample questions provided. An expert user can make several configuration choices (Fig. 5, bottom right):

- Model to load: a model includes a set of templates learned offline, and a corresponding learned query ranking function. The choices correspond to the training part of the WebQuestions (Berant et al., 2013) and Free917 (Cai and Yates, 2013) datasets.

- Whether to add answer type to queries: most KB-QA systems do not capture fine-grained types, while QUINT does so by design.

- The number of top-ranked queries to show answers for.

- The number of decision trees for the learning-to-rank module: this is used for query ranking during the answering phase (Sec. 2.2).

The answers to each of the top-k ranked queries

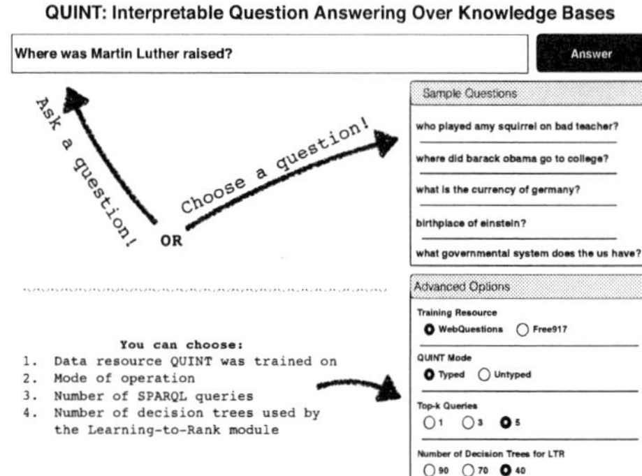

Figure 5: User input.

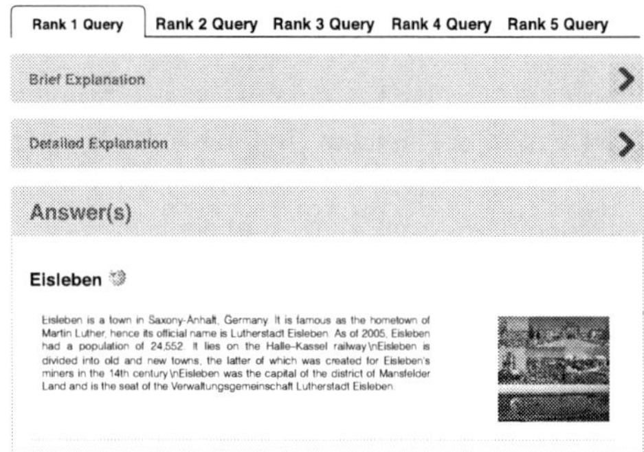

Figure 6: Retrieved answers from the KB.

in response to a question are given in individual tabs, as shown in Figure 6. To give more context to the user, wherever applicable, each answer is accompanied by a picture, a Wikipedia link and a short description from Freebase. For our running example question, the answer is `Eisleben`, where Martin Luther was born, for the best query. If we explore the rank-2 query, the answer is `Saxony-Anhalt`, which is the province in Germany where he lived.

3.2 Explanations

Explanations show how the given answers were derived. The ability to generate and display explanations is the core contribution of this system demonstration. QUINT generates two types of explanations: (i) a brief explanation geared towards non-technical users and (ii) a detailed explanation geared towards more advanced users.

Brief explanations provide an accessible and quick way for users to see how QUINT understood various parts of the question, resulting in the given set of answers. Figure 7 shows such an explanation for our running example. Brief explanations

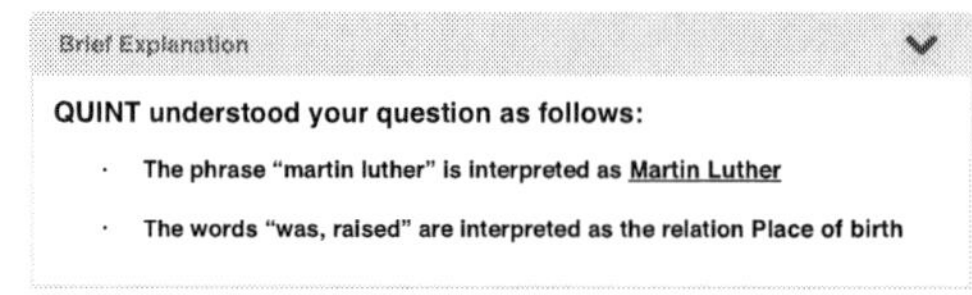

Figure 7: QUINT's brief explanation.

are particularly useful for normal users who are interested in confirming whether a given answer comes from interpreting the question as they intended. Where this is not the case, such an explanation guides users in reformulating their question to allow QUINT to better understand it.

Detailed explanations are geared towards advanced users who are familiar with dependency parses and SPARQL queries. A detailed explanation shows the derivation steps which roughly correspond to the right hand side of the diagram in Figure 1. First, the dependency parse of the input question is shown (Fig. 8). Below that is the *matching template* consisting of an utterance template that fits the utterance, and the corresponding query template that will be instantiated to generate a query. Shared numbers between the utterance template and the query template indicate alignment, i.e., which tokens in the utterance are used to instantiate which KB items in the query. In this example, we can see that the verb phrase *'was raised'* and the noun phrase *'Martin Luther'* are used to instantiate the KB-predicate and the KB-entity, respectively.

For a user to understand why QUINT maps a certain syntactic structure to a certain semantic form in a template, the user can view some training instances that produced the template. This is achieved by clicking *Template Provenance* (Fig. 9). For our example, two such instances are the questions *"Where was Obama educated?"* and *"Where are Riddell Helmets manufactured?"*.

Finally, the user is shown the SPARQL query that was executed to retrieve the shown answers (Fig. 10). The node labeled `?ANS` is the target answer node, and nodes marked as `?VAR` are intermediate join variables. Additionally, an alignment table with KB items is shown based on the alignments induced from the template (lower part of Fig. 10). For KB items, we find that *'Martin Luther'* was mapped to the theologist `MartinLuther` (other possibilities include the German diplomat with the same name

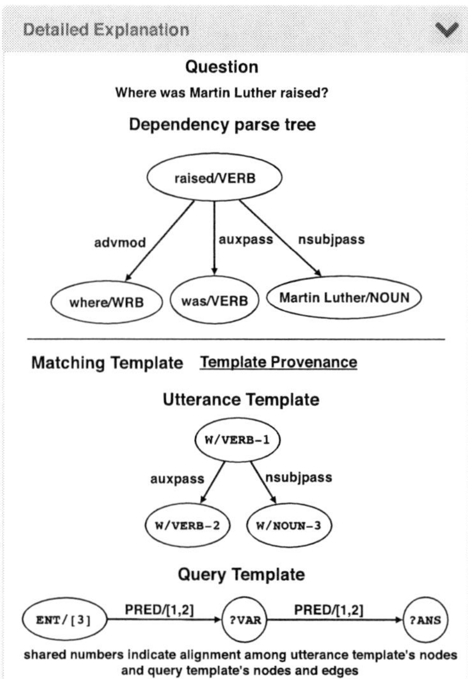

Figure 8: Question dependency parse and matched utterance and query template.

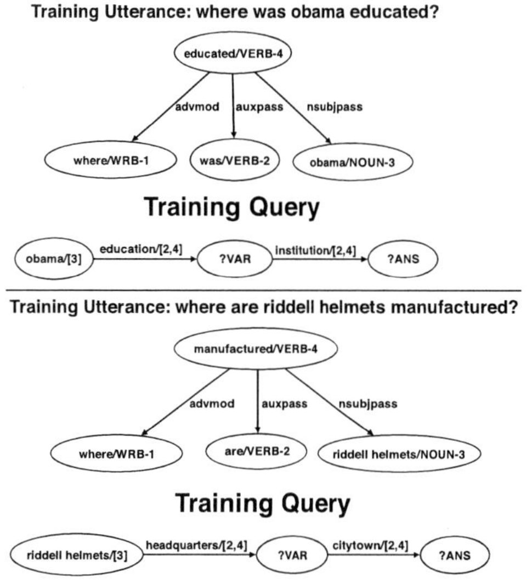

Figure 9: Structurally similar training instances to *"Where was Martin Luther raised?"*.

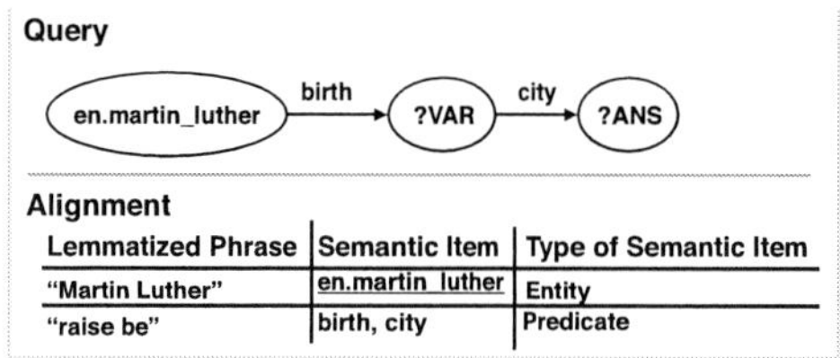

Figure 10: SPARQL KB-query and KB items.

and `MartinLutherKing`), and the lemmatized phrase *'be raise'* was mapped to the KB-predicate `placeOfBirth`. Looking at the rank-2 query, we find that *'raise'* was interpreted as `placesLived` in the KB. This is an alternative intention when the slightly ambiguous phrase *'raised'* is used.

4 Use Cases

When QUINT returns the correct answer, explanations allow the user to confirm its correctness by seeing how it was derived. When, on the other hand, things go wrong and an answer seems incorrect, explanations can give the user a better understanding of the limitations of the system (e.g., data incompleteness), and insights into overcoming these limitations (e.g., question rephrasing). We discuss some of these possible scenarios below, accompanied by real examples.

Incomplete lexicon. QUINT uses different lexicons to map the phrases in an utterance onto KB items (Sec. 2). These lexicons are inherently incomplete. For example, QUINT could not correctly answer the utterance *"countries of euro-union"* (implying the European Union) since the phrase *'euro-union'* does not have an entry in QUINT's lexicons. Therefore it shows the following message urging the user to reformulate the phrase: *The phrase* euro-union *in your input question could not be interpreted. Please reformulate the phrase.*

Incorrect query ranking. QUINT uses a learning-to-rank framework for ranking SPARQL queries. Sometimes, the most appropriate query is not ranked at the top. For example, for the utterance *"What is the former currency of Germany?"*, the top answer is `Euro`, which is incorrect. This is because the alignment information in the matching template fails to capture *'former'*. However, if the user explores the top-5 SPARQL queries, she finds that a query with the correct predicate `currencyFormerlyUsed` (as opposed to the incorrect `currencyUsed`) is indeed there and retrieves the desired answers `DeutscheMark`, `GermanRentenmark` and `GermanPapiermark`.

Incorrect disambiguation to KB items. Sometimes, the phrases in the input utterance are linked to wrong KB items as originally intended by the user. For example, for the utterance *"What* *language group does English belong to?"*, *'English'* gets mapped to the wrong entity `England`, resulting in an unexpected answer. When the user sees the brief explanation (Fig. 7), she can immediately observe this incorrect mapping. Subsequently, she may rephrase it as *'English language'* which may produce the desired answer.

Missed answer type constraints. Answer typing plays an important role in ensuring precise QA. For example, in *"Which college did Michelle Obama go to?"*, the user explicitly specifies that she is looking for *colleges*, as opposed to *"Where did Michelle Obama study?"*, which, for example, could include her high school as well. Here *'college'* is mapped to the KB type `University` and only when this constraint is added to the SPARQL query do we get the desired answer set `HarvardLawSchool` and `PrincetonUniversity`.

No matching templates. Sometimes an utterance is syntactically out of scope for QUINT: it has never seen similar instances during training. For example: *"Germany's capital during the forties?"*. In such cases, QUINT raises the message *We could not find any matching templates. Please reformulate your question.*

5   Conclusion

We presented a demonstration of QUINT, a system that uses automatically learned templates to provide interpretable answers to natural language questions over knowledge bases. When a user gets an answer to her question, our demonstration allows her to view the details of how the answer was derived. This improves her confidence in case of correct answers, while giving her a better understanding of the limitations of the QA system in case of mistakes, and how to work around them.

References

Abdalghani Abujabal, Mohamed Yahya, Mirek Riedewald, and Gerhard Weikum. 2017. Automated template generation for question answering over knowledge graphs. In *WWW*.

Hannah Bast and Elmar Haussmann. 2015. More accurate question answering on freebase. In *CIKM*.

Jonathan Berant, Andrew Chou, Roy Frostig, and Percy Liang. 2013. Semantic parsing on Freebase from question-answer pairs. In *EMNLP*.

Kurt Bollacker, Colin Evans, Praveen Paritosh, Tim Sturge, and Jamie Taylor. 2008. Freebase: A collaboratively created graph database for structuring human knowledge. In *SIGMOD*.

Antoine Bordes, Sumit Chopra, and Jason Weston. 2014. Question answering with subgraph embeddings. In *EMNLP*.

Qingqing Cai and Alexander Yates. 2013. Large-scale semantic parsing via schema matching and lexicon extension. In *ACL*.

Li Dong, Furu Wei, Ming Zhou, and Ke Xu. 2015. Question answering over freebase with multicolumn convolutional neural networks. In *ACL*.

Anthony Fader, Luke Zettlemoyer, and Oren Etzioni. 2013. Paraphrase-driven learning for open question answering. In *ACL*.

Anthony Fader, Luke Zettlemoyer, and Oren Etzioni. 2014. Open Question Answering over Curated and Extracted Knowledge Bases. In *KDD*.

Johannes Hoffart, Mohamed Amir Yosef, Ilaria Bordino, Hagen Fürstenau, Manfred Pinkal, Marc Spaniol, Bilyana Taneva, Stefan Thater, and Gerhard Weikum. 2011. Robust disambiguation of named entities in text. In *EMNLP*.

Siva Reddy, Mirella Lapata, and Mark Steedman. 2014. Large-scale semantic parsing without question-answer pairs. *TACL*.

Fabian M. Suchanek, Gjergji Kasneci, and Gerhard Weikum. 2007. Yago: A core of semantic knowledge. In *WWW*.

Christina Unger, Lorenz Bühmann, Jens Lehmann, Axel-Cyrille Ngonga Ngomo, Daniel Gerber, and Philipp Cimiano. 2012. Template-based question answering over RDF data. In *WWW*.

Kun Xu, Siva Reddy, Yansong Feng, Songfang Huang, and Dongyan Zhao. 2016. Question Answering on Freebase via Relation Extraction and Textual Evidence. In *ACL*.

Mohamed Yahya, Klaus Berberich, Shady Elbassuoni, and Gerhard Weikum. 2013. Robust question answering over the web of linked data. In *CIKM*.

Min-Chul Yang, Nan Duan, Ming Zhou, and Hae-Chang Rim. 2014. Joint relational embeddings for knowledge-based question answering. In *EMNLP*.

Xuchen Yao and Benjamin Van Durme. 2014. Information extraction over structured data: Question answering with freebase. In *ACL*.

Wen-tau Yih, Ming-Wei Chang, Xiaodong He, and Jianfeng Gao. 2015. Semantic parsing via staged query graph generation: Question answering with knowledge base. In *ACL*.

Lei Zou, Ruizhe Huang, Haixun Wang, Jeffrey Xu Yu, Wenqiang He, and Dongyan Zhao. 2014. Natural language question answering over RDF: a graph data driven approach. In *SIGMOD*.

Function Assistant: A Tool for NL Querying of APIs

Kyle Richardson and **Jonas Kuhn**
Institute for Natural Language Processing
University of Stuttgart
`kyle@ims.uni-stuttgart.de`

Abstract

In this paper, we describe **Function Assistant**, a lightweight Python-based toolkit for querying and exploring source code repositories using natural language. The toolkit is designed to help end-users of a target API quickly find information about functions through high-level natural language queries and descriptions. For a given text query and background API, the tool finds candidate functions by performing a translation from the text to known representations in the API using the semantic parsing approach of Richardson and Kuhn (2017). Translations are automatically learned from example text-code pairs in example APIs. The toolkit includes features for building translation pipelines and query engines for arbitrary source code projects. To explore this last feature, we perform new experiments on 27 well-known Python projects hosted on Github.

1 Introduction

Software developers frequently shift between using different third-party software libraries, or APIs, when developing new applications. Much of the development time is dedicated to understanding the structure of these APIs, figuring out where the target functionality lies, and learning about the peculiarities of how such software is structured or how naming conventions work. When the target API is large, finding the desired functionality can be a formidable and time consuming task. Often developers resort to resources like Google or StackOverflow to find (usually indirect) answers to questions.

We illustrate these issues in Figure 1 using two

```
## from nltk.parse.dependencygraph.py

class DependencyGraph(object):
    """A container ....for  a dependency structure"""

    def remove_by_address(self, address):
        """
        Removes the node with the given address.
        """

        # => implementation

    def add_arc(self, head_address, mod_address):
        """Adds an arc from the node specified by
        head_address to the node specified by
        the mod address....
        """
```

Figure 1: Example function documentation in Python NLTK about dependency graphs.

example functions from the well-known NLTK toolkit. Each function is paired with a short *docstring*, i.e., the quoted description under each function, which provides a user of the software a description of what the function does. While understanding the documentation and code requires technical knowledge of dependency parsing and graphs, even with such knowledge, the function naming conventions are rather arbitrary. The function `add_arc` could just as well be called `create_arc`. An end-user expecting another naming convention might be left astray when searching for this functionality. Similarly, the available description might deviate from how an end-user would describe such functionality.

Understanding the `remove_by_address` function, in contrast, requires knowing the details of the particular `DependencyGraph` implementation being used. Nonetheless, the function corresponds to the standard operation of *removing a node* from a dependency graph. Here, the technical details about how this removal is specific to a *given address* might obfuscate the overall purpose of the function, making it hard to find or understand.

Proceedings of the 2017 EMNLP System Demonstrations, pages 67–72
Copenhagen, Denmark, September 7–11, 2017. ©2017 Association for Computational Linguistics

At a first approximation, navigating a given API requires knowing *correspondences* between textual descriptions and source code representations. For example, knowing that the English expression *Adds an arc* in Figure 1 translates (somewhat arbitrarily) to `add_arc`, or that *given address* translates to `address`. One must also know how to detect paraphrases of certain target entities or actions, for example that *adding an arc* means the same as *creating an arc* in this context. Other technical correspondences, such as the relation between an `address` and the target dependency graph implementation, must be learned.

In our previous work (Richardson and Kuhn (2017), henceforth RK), we look at learning these types of correspondences from example API collections in a variety of programming languages and source natural languages. We treat each given API, consisting of text and function representation pairs, as a parallel corpus for training a simple semantic parsing model. In addition to learning translational correspondences, of the type described above, we achieve improvements by adding document-level features that help to learn other technical correspondences.

In this paper, we focus on using our models as a tool for querying API collections. Given a target API, our model learns an MT-based semantic parser that translates text to code representations in the API. End-users can formulate natural language queries to the background API, which our model will translate into candidate function representations with the goal of finding the desired functionality. Our tool, called **Function Assistant** can be used in two ways: as a black-box pipeline for building models directly from arbitrary API collections. As well, it can be customized and integrated with other outside components or models using the tool's flexible internal Python API.

In this paper, we focus on the first usage of our tool. To explore building models for new API collections, we run our pipeline on 27 open source Python projects from the well-known *Awesome Python* project list.[1] As in previous work, we perform synthetic experiments on these datasets, which measure how well our models can generate function representations for unseen API descriptions, which mimic user queries.

2 Related Work

Natural language querying of APIs has long been a goal in software engineering, related to the general problem of software reuse (Krueger, 1992). To date, a number of industrial scale products are available in this area.[2] To our knowledge, most implementations use shallow term matching and/or information-extraction techniques (Lv et al., 2015), differing from our methods that use more conventional NLP components and techniques. As we show in this paper and in RK, term matching and related techniques can sometimes serve as a competitive baseline, but are almost always outperformed by our translation approach.

More recently, there has been increased interest in machine learning on learning code representations from APIs, especially using resources such as GitHub or StackOverflow. However, this work tends to look at learning from many API collections (Gu et al., 2016), making such systems hard to evaluate and to apply to querying specific APIs. Other work looks at learning to generate longer code from source code annotations for natural language programming (Allamanis et al., 2015), often focusing narrowly on a specific programming language (e.g., Java) or set of APIs. To our knowledge, none of these approaches include companion software that facilitate building custom pipelines for specific APIs and querying.

Technically, our approach is related to work on semantic parsing, which looks at generating formal representations from text input for natural language understanding applications, notably question-answering. Many existing methods take direct inspiration from work on MT (Wong and Mooney, 2006) and parsing (Zettlemoyer and Collins, 2009). Please see RK for more discussion and pointers to related work.

3 Technical Approach

In this paper, we focus on learning to generate function representations from textual descriptions inside of source code collections, or APIs. We will refer to these target function representations as *API components*. Each component specifies a function name, a list of arguments, and other optional information such as a namespace.

Given a set of example text-component pairs from an example API, $D = \{(x_i, z_i)\}_{i=1}^{n}$, the goal

---

is to learn how to generate correct, well-formed components $z \in \mathcal{C}$ for each text x. When viewed as a semantic parsing problem, we can view each z as analogous to a target logical form. In this paper, we focus narrowly on Python source code projects, and thus Python functions z, however our methods are agnostic to the input natural language and output programming language as shown in RK.

When used for querying, our model takes a text input and attempts to generate the desired function representation. Technically, our approach follows our previous work and has two components: a simple and lightweight word-based translation model that generates candidate API components, and a discriminative model that reranks the translation model output using additional phrase and document-level features. All of these models are implemented natively in our tool, and we describe each part in turn.

3.1 Translation Model

Given an input text (or query) sequence $x = w_1, .., w_{|x|}$, the goal is to generate an output API component $z = u_i, .., u_{|z|}$, which involves learning a conditional distribution $p(z \mid x)$. We pursue a noisy-channel approach, where

$$p(z \mid x) \propto p(x \mid z)p(z)$$

By assuming a uniform prior $p(z)$ on output components, the model therefore involves computing $p(x \mid z)$, which under a word-based translation model can be expressed as:

$$p(x \mid z) = \sum_a p(x, a \mid z)$$

where the summation ranges over the set of all many-to-one (word) alignments a from $x \to z$.

While many different formulations of word-based models exist, we previously found that the simplest lexical translation model, or IBM Model 1 (Brown et al., 1993), outperforms even higher-order alignment models with location parameters. This model computes all alignments exactly using the following equation:

$$p(x \mid z) \approx \prod_{j=1}^{|x|} \sum_{i=0}^{|z|} p_t(w_j \mid u_i) \qquad (1)$$

where p_t defines a multinomial distribution over a given component term u_j for all words w_j.

While many parameter estimation strategies exist for training word-based models, we similarly found that the simplest EM procedure of Brown et al. (1993) works the best. In RK, we describe a linear-time decoding strategy (i.e., for generating components from input) over the number of components $\mathcal{C}$, which we use in this paper. Our tool also implements our types of conventional MT decoding strategies that are better suited for large APIs and more complex semantic languages.

3.2 Discriminative Reranking

Following most semantic parsing approaches (Zettlemoyer and Collins, 2009), we use a discriminative log-linear model to rerank the components generated from the underlying translation model. Such a model defines a conditional distribution: $p(z \mid x; \theta) \propto e^{\theta \cdot \phi(x,z)}$, for a parameter vector $\theta \in \mathbb{R}^b$, and a set of feature functions $\phi(x, z)$.

Our tool implements several different training and optimization methods. For the purpose of this paper, we train our models using an online, stochastic gradient ascent algorithm under a maximum conditional log-likelihood objective.

3.2.1 Features

For a given text input x and output component z, $\phi(x, z)$ defines a set of features between these two items. By default, our pipeline implementation uses three classes of features, identical to the feature set used in RK. The first class includes additional word-level features, such as word/component match, overlap, component syntax information, and so on. The second includes phrase and hierarchical phrase features between text and component candidates, which are extracted standardly from symmetric word-level alignment heuristics.

The other category of features includes document-level features. This includes information about the underlying API class hierarchy, and relations between words/phrases and abstract classes within this hierarchy. Also, we use additional textual description of parameters in the docstrings to indicate whether word-components candidate pairs overlap in these descriptions.

4 Implementation and Usage

All of the functionality above is implemented in the **Function Assistant** toolkit. The tool is part of the companion software release for our previous work called **Zubr**. For efficiency, the core

```
## pipeline parameters
params = [
 ("-baseline","baseline",False,"bool",
 "Use baseline model [default=False]","GPipeline")
]

## Zubr pipeline tasks
tasks = [
 "zubr.doc_extractor.DocExtractor",# extract docs
 "process_data", # custom function.
 "zubr.SymmetricAlignment",# learn trans. model.
 "zubr.Dataset", # build dataset obj.
 "zubr.FeatureExtractor",  ## build extractor obj.
 "zubr.Optimizer", ## train reranking model
 "zubr.QueryInterface", # build query interface
 "zubr.web.QueryServer", # launch HTTP server
]

def process_data(config):
    """Preprocess the extracted data using a custom
    function or outside library (e.g., nltk)

    :param config: The global configuration
    """
    preprocess_function(config,...)
```

Figure 2: An example pipeline script for building a translation model and query server.

functionality is written in Cython [3], which is a compiled superset of the Python language that facilitates native C/C++ integration.

The tool is designed to be used in two ways: first, as a black-box pipeline to build custom translation pipelines and API query engines. The tool can also be integrated with other components using our Cython and Python API. We focus on the first type of functionality.

4.1 Library Design and Pipelines

Our library uses dependency-injection OOP design principles. All of the core components are implemented as wholly independent classes, each of which has a number of associated configuration values. These components interact via a class called `Pipeline`, which glues together various user-specified components and dependencies, and builds a global configuration from these components. Subsequent instantiation and sharing of objects is dictated, or *injected*, by these global configurations settings, which can change dynamically throughout a pipeline run.

Pipelines are created by writing pipeline scripts, such as the one shown in Figure 2. This file is an ordinary Python file, with two mandatory variables. The first `params` variable specifies various high-level configuration parameters associated with the pipeline. In this case, there is a setting `--baseline`, which can be evoked to run

a baseline experiment, and will effect the subsequent processing pipeline.

The second, and most important, variable is called `tasks`, and this specifies an ordering of subprocesses that should be executed. The fields in this list are pointers to either core utilities in the underlying `Zubr` toolkit (each with the prefix `zubr.`), or user defined functions. This particular pipeline starts by building a dataset from a user specified source code repository, using `DocExtractor`, then builds a symmetric translation model `SymmetricAlignment`, a feature extractor `FeatureExtractor`, a discriminative reranker `Optimizer`, all via various intermediate steps. It finishes by building a query interface and query server, `QueryInterface` and `QueryServer`, which can then be used for querying the input API.

As noted already, each subprocesses has a number of associated configuration settings, which are joined into a global configuration object by the `Pipeline` instance. For the translation model, settings include, for example, the type of translation model to use, the number of iterations to use when training models, and so on. All of these settings can be specified on the terminal, or in a separate configuration file. As well, the user is free to define custom functions, such as `process_data`, or classes which can be used to modify the default processing pipeline or implement new ML features.

4.2 Web Server

The last step in this pipeline builds an HTTP web server that can be used to query the input API. Internally, the server makes calls to the trained translation model and discriminative reranker, which takes user queries and attempts to translate them into API function representations. These candidate translations are then returned to the user as potential answers to the query. Depending on the outcome, the user can either rephrase his/her question if the target function is not found, or look closer at the implementation by linking to the function's source code.

An example screen shot of the query server is shown in Figure 3. Here, the background API is the NLTK toolkit, and the query is *Train a sequence tagger model*. While not mentioned explicitly, the model returns training functions for the `HiddenMarkovModelTagger`. The right

[3] http://cython.org/

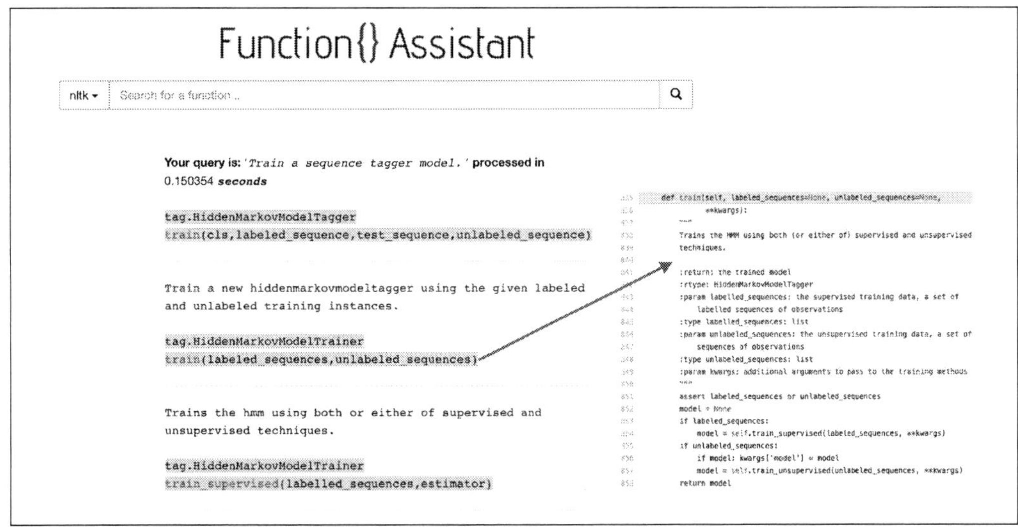

Figure 3: An example screen shot of the `Function Assistant` web server.

Project	# Pairs	# Symbols	# Words	Vocab.
scapy	757	1,029	7,839	1,576
zipline	753	1,122	8,184	1,517
biopython	2,496	2,224	20,532	2,586
renpy	912	889	10,183	1,540
pyglet	1,400	1,354	12,218	2,181
kivy	820	861	7,621	1,456
pip	1,292	1,359	13,011	2,201
twisted	5,137	3,129	49,457	4,830
vispy	1,094	1,026	9,744	1,740
orange	1,392	1,125	11,596	1,761
tensorflow	5,724	4,321	45,006	4,672
pandas	1,969	1,517	17,816	2,371
sqlalchemy	1,737	1,374	15,606	2,039
pyspark	1,851	1,276	18,775	2,200
nupic	1,663	1,533	16,750	2,135
astropy	2,325	2,054	24,567	3,007
sympy	5,523	3,201	52,236	4,777
ipython	1,034	1,115	9,114	1,771
orator	817	499	6,511	670
obspy	1,577	1,861	14,847	2,169
rdkit	1,006	1,380	9,758	1,739
django	2,790	2,026	31,531	3,484
ansible	2,124	1,884	20,677	2,593
statsmodels	2,357	2,352	21,716	2,733
theano	1,223	1,364	12,018	2,152
nltk	2,383	2,324	25,823	3,151
sklearn	1,532	1,519	13,897	2,115

Table 1: New English Github datasets.

side of the image shows the hyperlink path to the original source in Github for the `train` function.

5 Experiments

Our current `DocExtractor` implementation supports building parallel datasets from raw Python source code collections. Internally, the tool reads source code using the abstract syntax tree utility, `ast`, in the Python standard library, and extracts sets of function and description pairs. In addition, the tool also extracts class descriptions, parameter and return value descriptions, and information about the API's internal class hierarchy. This last type of information is then used to define document-level features.

To experiment with this feature, we built pipelines and ran experiments for 27 popular Python projects. The goal of these experiments is to test the robustness of our extractor, and see how well our models answer unseen queries for these resources using our previous experimental setup.

5.1 Datasets

The example projects are shown in Table 1. Each dataset is quantified in terms of **# Pairs**, or the number of parallel function-component representations, the **# Symbols** in the component output language, the # (NL) **Words** and **Vocab** size.

5.2 Experimental Setup

Each dataset is randomly split into train, test, and dev. sets using a 70%-30% (or 15%/15%) split. We can think of the held-out sets as mimicking queries that users might ask the model. Standardly, all models are trained on the training sets, and hyper-parameters are tuned to the dev. sets.

For a unseen text input during testing, the model generates a candidate list of component outputs. An output is considered correct if it matches *exactly* the gold function representation. As before, we measure the **Accuracy @1**, accuracy within top ten (**Accuracy @10**), and the **MRR**.

As in our previous work, three additional baselines are used. The first is a simple bag-of-words

Method	scapy	zipline	biopython	renpy	pyglet	kivy	pip	twisted	vispy
BoW	00.0 51.3 17.4	01.7 38.3 12.9	05.8 54.8 20.4	06.6 41.1 16.6	05.7 52.3 19.2	07.3 53.6 22.0	06.2 40.9 17.1	06.6 38.8 16.9	07.3 48.7 18.6
Term Match	**21.2** 43.3 28.7	28.5 50.8 36.2	23.5 48.1 31.7	25.7 59.5 38.7	20.4 50.9 31.2	30.0 62.6 41.3	19.1 50.2 30.7	17.6 44.1 26.2	29.2 64.0 41.1
Translation	20.3 61.9 34.7	27.6 62.5 40.7	29.6 75.6 45.8	30.8 61.7 42.0	26.1 69.5 41.3	33.3 67.4 45.3	18.6 56.4 32.3	27.7 61.4 39.4	28.6 70.1 42.3
Reranker	**21.2 67.2 37.2**	**30.3 70.5 45.3**	**32.3 79.1 48.6**	**38.9 73.5 48.9**	**29.0 77.1 45.5**	**35.7 75.6 49.1**	**25.9 65.8 39.9**	**28.8 65.8 42.2**	**33.5 80.4 50.3**

Method	orange	tensorflow	pandas	sqlalchemy	pyspark	nupic	astropy	sympy	ipython
BoW	13.4 60.5 29.1	09.4 47.4 21.2	03.7 40.6 15.6	07.3 45.0 18.4	07.5 50.9 20.8	06.4 55.0 22.8	07.7 52.0 21.1	06.4 44.4 18.5	01.9 41.2 13.9
Term Match	37.9 69.7 49.3	25.2 48.7 33.5	19.3 43.7 27.9	17.3 48.4 26.6	20.5 46.9 29.1	23.6 51.0 33.1	26.1 49.1 34.3	20.2 44.9 28.8	23.8 56.7 33.8
Translation	40.3 78.3 54.0	35.3 71.5 48.0	29.1 62.7 41.0	28.8 70.3 43.0	37.1 78.7 52.1	**30.9** 69.8 44.6	30.7 66.6 43.4	**32.8** 70.2 45.5	24.5 59.3 36.5
Reranker	**45.1 84.1 59.9**	**38.4 77.7 51.8**	**31.1 66.1 43.1**	**35.0 76.1 49.7**	**41.5 81.5 55.3**	29.3 **76.7 45.6**	**33.9 74.4 47.4**	32.1 **75.0 46.6**	**29.6 66.4 42.3**

Method	orator	obspy	rdkit	django	ansible	statsmodels	theano	nltk	sklearn
BoW	10.6 66.3 28.6	06.7 49.5 20.2	05.3 40.6 17.1	04.5 40.9 16.2	17.9 55.3 30.5	05.6 46.1 18.6	03.2 43.7 16.2	05.0 44.2 16.3	05.2 45.8 17.7
Term Match	31.9 64.7 43.7	19.9 46.6 30.0	13.3 46.6 23.9	19.3 48.0 29.1	24.8 54.0 35.8	16.7 39.9 25.1	16.3 37.1 24.0	19.8 45.6 28.4	24.4 50.6 32.5
Translation	**32.7** 79.5 47.5	33.8 75.8 48.3	**25.3** 60.6 37.2	22.9 57.8 34.6	35.5 71.6 47.5	25.4 64.8 37.8	26.2 58.4 37.8	28.2 68.0 41.5	27.9 67.6 41.3
Reranker	**32.7 82.7 49.7**	**37.7 80.0 52.3**	**25.3 63.3 39.6**	**25.8 64.5 39.4**	**40.5 77.0 53.1**	**28.8 69.1 41.7**	**27.3 66.1 39.9**	**31.6 72.5 45.7**	**29.2 75.5 44.5**

| Accuracy @1 | Accuracy @10 | Mean Reciprocal Rank (MRR) |

Table 2: Test results on our new Github datasets.

(**BoW**) model, which uses word-component pairs as features. The second is a **Term Match** baseline, which ranks candidates according to the number of matches between input words and component words. We also compare the results of the **Translation** (model) without the reranker.

6 Results and Discussion

Test results are shown in Table 2, and largely conform to our previous findings. The **BoW** and **Term Match** baselines are outperformed by all other models, which again shows that API querying is more complicated than simple word-component matching. The **Reranker** model leads to improvements on all datasets as compared with only using the **Translation** model, indicating that document-level and phrase features can help.

We note that these experiments are synthetic, in the sense that it's unclear whether the held-out examples bear any resemblance to actual user queries. Assuming, however, that each held-out set is a representative sample of the queries that real users would ask, we can then interpret the results as indicating how well our models answer queries. Whether or not these held-out examples reflect *real* queries, we believe that they still provide a good benchmark for model construction. All code and data will be released to facilitate further experimentation and application building. Future work will look at eliciting more naturalistic queries (e.g., through StackOverflow), and doing usage studies via a permanent web demo[4].

7 Conclusion

We introduce **Function Assistant**, a lightweight tool for querying API collections using uncon-strained natural language. Users can supply our tool with target source code projects and build custom translation or processing pipelines and query servers from scratch. In addition to the tool, we also created new resources for studying API querying, in the form of datasets built from 27 popular Github projects. While our approach uses simple components, we hope will that our tool and resources will serve as a benchmark for future work in this area, and ultimately help to solve everyday software search and reusability issues.

References

Miltiadis Allamanis, Daniel Tarlow, Andrew D Gordon, and Yi Wei. 2015. Bimodal modelling of source code and NL. In *Proceedings of ICML*.

Peter F Brown, Vincent J Della Pietra, Stephen A Della Pietra, and Robert L Mercer. 1993. The mathematics of SMT. *Computational linguistics*, 19(2).

Xiaodong Gu, Hongyu Zhang, Dongmei Zhang, and Sunghun Kim. 2016. Deep API Learning. *arXiv preprint arXiv:1605.08535*.

Charles W. Krueger. 1992. Software reuse. *ACM Computing Surveys (CSUR)*, 24(2).

Fei Lv, Hongyu Zhang, Jian-guang Lou, Shaowei Wang, Dongmei Zhang, and Jianjun Zhao. 2015. Codehow: Effective code search based on api understanding and extended boolean model (e). In *Proceedings of ASE*.

Kyle Richardson and Jonas Kuhn. 2017. Learning Semantic Correspondences in Technical Documentation. In *Proceedings of ACL*.

Yuk Wah Wong and Raymond J. Mooney. 2006. Learning for Semantic Parsing with Statistical Machine Translation. In *Proceedings of HLT-NAACL*.

Luke S. Zettlemoyer and Michael Collins. 2009. Learning context-dependent mappings from sentences to logical form. In *Proceedings of ACL*.

---

[4] see demo here: http://zubr.ims.uni-stuttgart.de/

MoodSwipe: A Soft Keyboard that Suggests Messages Based on User-Specified Emotions

Chieh-Yang Huang[1]   Tristan Labetoulle[2]   Ting-Hao (Kenneth) Huang[3]

Yi-Pei Chen[1]   Hung-Chen Chen[1]   Vallari Srivastava[4]   Lun-Wei Ku[1]

[1] Academia Sinica, Taiwan.

`{appleternity,ypc82,hankchen,lwku}@iis.sinica.edu.tw`

[2] IMT Atlantique, France. `contact@tristan-labetoulle.com`

[3] Carnegie Mellon University, USA. `tinghaoh@cs.cmu.edu`

[4] Institute of Engineering & Technology, DAVV, India. `vallari357@gmail.com`

Abstract

We present MoodSwipe, a soft keyboard that suggests text messages given the user-specified emotions utilizing the real dialog data. The aim of MoodSwipe is to create a convenient user interface to enjoy the technology of emotion classification and text suggestion, and at the same time to collect labeled data automatically for developing more advanced technologies. While users select the MoodSwipe keyboard, they can type as usual but sense the emotion conveyed by their text and receive suggestions for their message as a benefit. In MoodSwipe, the detected emotions serve as the medium for suggested texts, where viewing the latter is the incentive to correcting the former. We conduct several experiments to show the superiority of the emotion classification models trained on the dialog data, and further to verify good emotion cues are important context for text suggestion.

1 Introduction

Knowing how and when to express emotion is a key component of emotional intelligence (Salovey and Mayer, 1990). Effective leaders are good at expressing emotions (Bachman, 1988); expressing positive emotions in group activities improves group cooperation, fairness, and overall group performance (Barsade and Gibson, 1998); and expressing negative emotions can promote relationships (Graham et al., 2008). However, in the mobile device era where text-based communication is part of life, technologies are rarely utilized to assist users to *express* their emotions properly via text. For instance, business people in heated disputes with their clients may need assistance to rephrase their angry messages into neutral descriptions before sending them. Similarly, people may have trouble finding the perfect words to show how much they appreciate a friend's help. Or people may want to deliberately express anger to extract concessions in negotiations, or to make a joke, such as with the "Obama's Anger Translator" skit, in which the comedian "translates" the U.S. President's calm statements into emotional tirades. While emotion classification has been used in helping users to better understand other people's emotions (Wang et al., 2016; Huang et al., 2017), these technologies have rarely been used to support user needs in expressing emotions. Most prior work focuses on interface design, for instance using kinetic typography or dynamic text (Bodine and Pignol, 2003; Forlizzi et al., 2003; Lee et al., 2006) , affective buttons (Broekens and Brinkman, 2009), or text color and emoticons (Sánchez et al., 2006) to enable emotion expression in instant messengers. Other work explores the relations between user typing patterns and their emotions (Zimmermann et al., 2003; Alepis et al., 2006; Tech, 2016). However, the text itself is still the essential part of text-based communication; visual cues and typing patterns are only minor factors. Other work even describes attempts to incorporate body signals such as fluctuating skin conductivity levels (DiMicco et al., 2002), thermal feedback (Wilson et al., 2016), or facial expressions (El Kaliouby and Robinson, 2004) to enrich emotion expression, but these require additional equipment and are less scalable.

In this paper we introduce *MoodSwipe*[1], a soft keyboard that automatically suggests text according to user-specified emotions. As shown in Figure 1, MoodSwipe receives user input text from

---

[1]MoodSwipe is available at: `https://play.google.com/store/apps/details?id=sinica.moodswipe&hl=en`

Proceedings of the 2017 EMNLP System Demonstrations, pages 73–78
Copenhagen, Denmark, September 7–11, 2017. ©2017 Association for Computational Linguistics

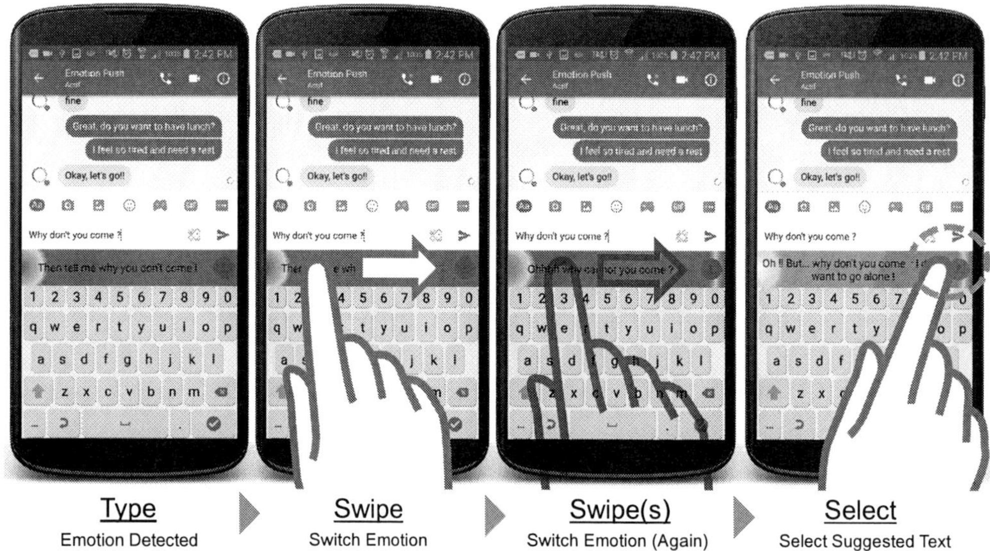

Figure 1: The user interface of MoodSwipe keyboard, which includes a standard soft keyboard, a color bar above the keyboard, and a circle button to the right of the color bar. Users swipe the color bar to specify their emotions and view the messages suggested for different emotions.

the keyboard, and immediately shows the detected emotion of the input message. Seven emotions (*Anger*, *Joy*, *Sadness*, *Fear*, *Anticipation*, *Tired* and *Neutral*) are detected and presented by their corresponding colors as defined by the research of psychologists and user studies (Wang et al., 2016). Users *swipe* the color bar to change the detected emotion according to their *mood* and view the messages suggested for different emotions. For example, if the user types "I disagree," MoodSwipe suggests a relevant message telling the user how one would say the same thing when he or she is happy, sad, or angry.

The contributions of this work are three-fold. First, we address the long-standing challenge of **collecting *self-reported* emotion labels for dialog messages**. Unlike posts on social media, where users often spontaneously tag their own emotions, self-reported emotion labels for dialog messages are expensive to collect. Users often feel disturbed when they are asked to annotate their own emotions on the fly. MoodSwipe provides a handy service which is entertaining and easy to use. It provides a natural incentive for users to label their own emotions on the spot. Second, MoodSwipe closes the loop of **bi-directional *interactive emotion sensing***. Most prior work powered by emotion detection focused on helping users when *receiving* messages (Wang et al., 2016) instead of when *sending* them. MoodSwipe enables auto-

Emotion	Color	Suggestion
Anger	Red (#F43131)	I'm in a pissy mood. I'm sorry.
Joy	Yellow (#E1D500)	I'm doing fine.
Sadness	Navy Blue (#518CCF)	I'm upset, but I'm fine.
Fear	Green (#17C617)	(no suggestion)
Anticipation	Orange (#E78300)	Oh, I'm fine, I'm widw awake. What's up?
Tired	Purple (#C350DF)	I'm working.
Neutral	White (#FFFFFF)	I'm fine.

Figure 2: Mapping between colors and emotions, and example suggestion texts for "I am fine."

mated support, helping users express their emotions in text, and therefore supplies the missing piece for an emotion-sensitive text-based communication environment. Finally, MoodSwipe introduces a **new interaction paradigm**, in which users explicitly provide feedback to systems about *why* they select this suggested response. Classic response suggestion tasks such as dialog generation (Li et al., 2016) or automated email reply (Kannan et al., 2016) assume that the in-the-moment context of each user (e.g., the current emotion) is unknown. MoodSwipe opens up possibilities for users to explicitly and actively provide context on the fly, which the automated models can use to provide better suggestions.

2 The MoodSwipe Keyboard

The user interface and workflow of MoodSwipe are shown in Figure 1. The MoodSwipe keyboard interface contains three major parts: *(i)* a standard soft keyboard, *(ii)* a color bar above the keyboard, and *(iii)* a circle button to the right of the color bar. When the user starts typing, MoodSwipe detects the emotion of the input text in real time, and the color bar background changes color on-the-fly to reflect the current emotion of the user input text. MoodSwipe's seven emotions and their colors are shown in Figure 2, which was developed based on psychological work and user studies (Wang et al., 2016). Based on the emotion MoodSwipe currently displays, the color bar also shows the user the suggested text. Those suggested messages for the input "I am fine" are also listed in Figure 2.

When the user *swipes* the color bar, one of MoodSwipe's seven emotion colors is brought up in descending order of the classification probability for the input message. The user swipes right to see the predicted emotion with a lower probability and its suggested text, or swipes left to see the previous one. In Figure 1, the user types "Why don't you come?" and MoodSwipe detects *Anger* (red) and suggests "Then tell me why you don't come!". The user swipes right to see the option "Ohhhh why cannot you come?" for emotion *Sadness* (blue). The user keeps swiping until he or she reaches a suitable message ("Oh!! But...why don't you come I don't want to go alone!") and then clicks the circle button at color bar's right side to replaces the user input with the suggested text. Then with this replacement, the user self-reports that the emotion label of the user's message "Why don't you come?" should be more *Fear* (green) than *Anger* (red) in the current dialog context.

MoodSwipe actively triggers emotion detection and updates color accordingly when the user presses the spacebar, which usually indicates the completion of a word, or has a 500ms pause after the last user input. To lighten server loads and reduce possible conflicts with the second condition, the minimum time interval between two triggers is set at 400ms. All users activities are recorded, including typed text, suggested texts, emotion labels selected/abandoned, and all the timestamps.

3 Use Cases

In this section we outline several possible use cases of MoodSwipe. First, MoodSwipe can help users to better **understand their own messages' emotions** perceived by other users. Our prior study (Huang et al., 2017) shows that not all users are clearly aware of what emotion their messages will convey. In this scenario, MoodSwipe is able to act as an early assistant or reminder when composing a message. Second, MoodSwipe can **assist users to better express themselves** when "words fail me." Sometimes users could experience strong emotions and have difficulty in finding good ways to express themselves via text, and they can type keywords into MoodSwipe to search for better messages from its dialog database. Third, users can **alternate the perceived emotions in their own texts** for various purposes. For instance, some people might need assistance to rephrase their angry messages into neutral descriptions, and some people may want to deliberately express anger to extract concessions in negotiations. Finally, MoodSwipe can be used as a tool to help new users quickly **adapt to the language style of a community.** MoodSwipe is powered by messages that were collected from young IM users. An elder new user who is not very familiar with the language styles of the young generation can use MoodSwipe to rephrase his/her sentence so that it can be better received by young users.

4 Back-end System, Experiments and Discussions

Two major functions of the MoodSwipe keyboard are to guess for the users the emotion of their current text message and to provide text suggestions based on that. In this section, we describe several models we developed and different settings used to evaluate their performance. Our advantage in conducting these experiments comes from our emotion-based chat app EmotionPush (Wang et al., 2016) and the social dialogs it has collected.

4.1 Experimental Materials

For the experiments, we adopted the Emotion-Push dataset (available soon). A total number of 162,031 message logs were collected for this dataset. To evaluate the performance of emotion classification, we had native speakers manually label the emotions of the randomly selected 8,818 messages. These manual emotion attribute were all chosen from the seven emotion labels defined for the keyboard. Among these 8,818 emotion labeled messages, 70% were for training, 10% for validation and 20% for testing. Two different emotion corpus, LJ40K (Yang and Liu, 2013) and the tweet data, are utilized for comparison. LJ40K contains 40 emotions and for each of the emotions, 1,000 blogs are collected. The 40 emotions are then mapped to the 7 emotions according to our previous work (Wang et al., 2016). On the other hand, the tweet data is built by Twitter streaming API[2] with a filter of using the 40 emotions as hashtag. A total number of 19,480 tweets are collected and further categorized into 7 emotions.

The text message suggestion function provided by MoodSwipe recommends responses given the input text message and its corresponding emotion label from users. For the experiments, we selected messages from the labeled 8,818 messages according to two rules: 1) to ensure a proper turn, the previous message must be sent from another user instead of the same message owner, and 2) the emotion label must not be neutral. We drop a small number of short messages containing hindi or pure punctuation (e.g., "!!!") for which text suggestions cannot be found, as in these cases we are unable to evaluate the performance of different settings. A total of 1,366 messages were collected for the sentence suggestion experiment (707 Joy, 223 Anger, 189 Sadness, 124 Anticipation, 72 Fear and 51 Tired). For the evaluation, text suggestions are generated for these messages using MoodSwipe.

4.2 Emotion Classification

Two models are developed for emotion classification: the general CNN (Kim, 2014) with 125 filters, including 25 filters for each filter length ranging from 1 to 5, and the LSTM (Hochreiter and Schmidhuber, 1997). These two models are trained on blog data, tweet data, and our dialog data, respectively, and then tested on the dialog data. In Table 1 we report the results of three major emotions with these two models, as the other emotions are minor and the training data insufficient to build a reliable model (anticipation 1.77%, tired 0.8%, fear 1.19%, total 3.77%). Only accuracies trained on the dialog data for three major emotions are all over 0.9 (see CNN[3] and LSTM[3]), which supports the use of dialogs in MoodSwipe. Considering time-consuming issue, we adopted CNN as the final model for MoodSwipe.

4.3 Text Suggestion & Results

The purpose of the experiments for test message suggestion is to determine whether the system generates better suggested texts given the user-specified emotion. We designed a retrieval-based model utilizing Lucene (McCandless et al., 2010)

Model	Joy	Anger	Sadness	Neutral
(Wang et al., 2016)	.779	.771	.853	.323
CNN[1]	.832	.960	.750	.513
CNN[2]	.645	.942	.503	.222
CNN[3]	.905	.962	.973	.820
LSTM[1]	.230	.967	.963	.222
LSTM[2]	.596	.959	.516	.222
LSTM[3]	.906	.965	.964	.816

Table 1: Accuracy of the emotion classification task tested on dialog data while trained on blog[1], tweet[2] and dialog[3] data.

and then applied it on the EmotionPush dataset which contains 162,031 social dialog messages. When searching for similar messages, Lucene first applies term matching on the dataset using query message. Messages containing at least one same word would be candidates which is then ranked by BM25 (Robertson et al., 2009). When the user received a message and is composing a response, the user manually specifies an emotion (*e.g.*, *Anger*) that he/she wants to convey in the message, and the following two settings for generating responses.

1. **[Baseline]:** Given the message that the user received, MoodSwipe first retrieves its most similar message (by Lucene) from the database, and then returns the response of that retrieved message as the suggestion.

2. **[+Emotion]:** The procedure is identical as [Baseline], just that the suggested text must convey the user-specified emotion. For instance, if the user specifies *Anger*, MoodSwipe takes the message that the user received and from database finds its most similar message whose response's emotion is labelled as *Anger* as the suggestion.

Note that the emotions in our database are annotated by automatic algorithms instead of humans.

To assess the quality of suggested messages in each setting, we used the 1,366 messages collected in sentence suggestion experiment to conduct human evaluations with crowd workers recruited via Amazon Mechanical Turk. For each message, we first show the crowd workers its 10 previous messages in the original chat log. We then show the following three messages, in a random order, as the *follow-up line candidates* of the displayed chat log: 1) the actual user input response, 2) the suggested texts in [Baseline], and 3) the suggested texts in [+Emotion]. Workers are asked to rank these three candidate messages based on their

Setting	Clarity	Comfort	Responsiveness
Rank of Messages and Suggested Texts			
Input	1.522	1.570	1.531
Baseline	2.245	2.220	2.244
+Emotion	2.233	2.210	2.225
Good Suggestion Rate (%)			
Baseline	26.12	28.38	26.44
+Emotion	26.09	28.65	26.70

Table 2: Human evaluation results. In Baseline the user-specified emotions are not available.

Good Suggestion Rate (%)		
Setting	Anger	Anticipation	Fear
Baseline	40.36	21.29	31.39
+Emotion	37.49	20.32	25.28
Setting	Joy	Sadness	Tired
Baseline	25.35	29.31	27.45
+Emotion	28.18	26.56	29.41

Table 3: Good suggestion rates of *comfort* for messages of different emotions.

clarity, *comfort*, and *responsiveness* of being the follow-up line of the given chat log (Liu et al., 2010) ($rank = 1, 2, or\ 3$. Lower is better.) For each message, we recruit 5 workers and average their results. Table 2 shows the average ranking and the "Good Suggestion Rate" of each setting, which is the proportion of the suggested messages that have a better (lower) ranking than the original user input response. While the original input responses still have a better (lower) average ranking, Table 2 shows that 26% to 28% of the suggested texts are considered good by crowd workers and thus could be useful to users. Results also show that the [+Emotion] setting on average generates slightly better suggestions than [Baseline] setting in all three aspects.

With the consideration that in the three evaluation aspects *comfort* is most relevant to emotions, we further analyze the *comfort* result of each emotion (Table 3.) Among all emotions, the Good Suggestion Rates for *Anger* messages are the highest (40.36% and 37.49%), which are even much higher than the average rates (about 28% as shown in Table 2). This result suggests that our method is particularly useful for expressing Anger emotions.

These results show the potential benefits of including emotion signals in a response suggestion application. While the simple retrieval-based model (where emotions act only as "filters") may be of limited use, MoodSwipe is still able to suggest responses that are better than the user responses around 25% of time. We believe that when MoodSwipe is deployed, more data can be collected and a more sophisticated models can be developed to boost the benefit of emotion context.

4.4 Collecting User-reported Labels

One merit of MoodSwipe is the capability to collect user-reported labels. MoodSwipe can obtain labels from two major user actions, select and swipe, respectively.

1. **[Select]** When the user first types a response, browses all suggestions, and finally selects one suggested text, MoodSwipe can record the user's original typed text and label its emotion as that of the selected text.

2. **[Swipe]** When the user first types a response, swipes directly to a specific emotion (*e.g.*, Joy) and stops there, even without selecting the suggested text, it often still indicates that the user wants to express this emotion (*e.g.*, Joy.) Therefore, MoodSwipe can record the user's current typed text and label it as the same emotion, even the user does not select the suggested text eventually.

5 Conclusion

We have developed the sender side MoodSwipe to cooperate with the receiver side applications and complete the emotion sensitive communication framework. MoodSwipe provided a convenient interface which facilitating users on using the modern emotion classification and text suggestion techniques. In MoodSwipe, data are labeled automatically according to frond-end cues in the background. We show that the user-specified emotion can benefit text suggestion, though the performance can still be improved by increasing the size of the dialog database. MoodSwipe is available at Google Play, and a demo video is provided at: `https://www.youtube.com/watch?v=SZ1biWoiq3Y`

Acknowledgments

Research of this paper was partially supported by Ministry of Science and Technology, Taiwan, under the contract 105-2221-E-001-007-MY3.

References

Efthymios Alepis, Maria Virvou, and Katerina Kabassi. 2006. Affective student modeling based on microphone and keyboard user actions. In *Advanced*

Learning Technologies, 2006. Sixth International Conference on, pages 139–141. IEEE.

Wallace Bachman. 1988. Nice guys finish first: A symlog analysis of us naval commands. *The SYMLOG practitioner: Applications of small group research*, pages 133–154.

Sigal G Barsade and Donald E Gibson. 1998. Group emotion: A view from top and bottom. *Research on managing groups and teams*, 1(4):81–102.

Kerry Bodine and Mathilde Pignol. 2003. Kinetic typography-based instant messaging. In *CHI'03 Extended Abstracts on Human Factors in Computing Systems*, pages 914–915. ACM.

Joost Broekens and Willem-Paul Brinkman. 2009. Affectbutton: Towards a standard for dynamic affective user feedback. In *Affective Computing and Intelligent Interaction and Workshops, 2009. ACII 2009. 3rd International Conference on*, pages 1–8. IEEE.

Joan Morris DiMicco, Vidya Lakshmipathy, and Andrew Tresolini Fiore. 2002. Conductive chat: Instant messaging with a skin conductivity channel. In *Proceedings of Conference on Computer Supported Cooperative Work*.

Rana El Kaliouby and Peter Robinson. 2004. Faim: integrating automated facial affect analysis in instant messaging. In *Proceedings of the 9th international conference on Intelligent user interfaces*, pages 244–246. ACM.

Jodi Forlizzi, Johnny Lee, and Scott Hudson. 2003. The kinedit system: affective messages using dynamic texts. In *Proceedings of the SIGCHI Conference on Human Factors in Computing Systems*, pages 377–384. ACM.

Steven M Graham, Julie Y Huang, Margaret S Clark, and Vicki S Helgeson. 2008. The positives of negative emotions: Willingness to express negative emotions promotes relationships. *Personality and Social Psychology Bulletin*, 34(3):394–406.

Sepp Hochreiter and Jürgen Schmidhuber. 1997. Long short-term memory. *Neural computation*, 9(8):1735–1780.

Chieh-Yang Huang, Lun-Wei Ku, et al. 2017. Challenges in providing automatic affective feedback in instant messaging applications. *arXiv preprint arXiv:1702.02736*.

Anjuli Kannan, Karol Kurach, Sujith Ravi, Tobias Kaufmann, Andrew Tomkins, Balint Miklos, Greg Corrado, László Lukács, Marina Ganea, Peter Young, et al. 2016. Smart reply: Automated response suggestion for email. *arXiv preprint arXiv:1606.04870*.

Yoon Kim. 2014. Convolutional neural networks for sentence classification. *arXiv preprint arXiv:1408.5882*.

Joonhwan Lee, Soojin Jun, Jodi Forlizzi, and Scott E Hudson. 2006. Using kinetic typography to convey emotion in text-based interpersonal communication. In *Proceedings of the 6th conference on Designing Interactive systems*, pages 41–49. ACM.

Jiwei Li, Will Monroe, Alan Ritter, Michel Galley, Jianfeng Gao, and Dan Jurafsky. 2016. Deep reinforcement learning for dialogue generation. *arXiv preprint arXiv:1606.01541*.

Leigh Anne Liu, Chei Hwee Chua, and Günter K Stahl. 2010. Quality of communication experience: definition, measurement, and implications for intercultural negotiations. *Journal of Applied Psychology*, 95(3):469.

Michael McCandless, Erik Hatcher, and Otis Gospodnetic. 2010. *Lucene in Action, Second Edition: Covers Apache Lucene 3.0*. Manning Publications Co., Greenwich, CT, USA.

Stephen Robertson, Hugo Zaragoza, et al. 2009. The probabilistic relevance framework: Bm25 and beyond. *Foundations and Trends® in Information Retrieval*, 3(4):333–389.

Peter Salovey and John D Mayer. 1990. Emotional intelligence. *Imagination, cognition and personality*, 9(3):185–211.

J Alfredo Sánchez, Norma P Hernández, Julio C Penagos, and Yulia Ostróvskaya. 2006. Conveying mood and emotion in instant messaging by using a two-dimensional model for affective states. In *Proceedings of VII Brazilian symposium on Human factors in computing systems*, pages 66–72. ACM.

Cornell Tech. 2016. This smartphone keyboard app can read your emotions.

Shih-Ming Wang, Chun-Hui Li, Yu-Chun Lo, Ting-Hao K Huang, and Lun-Wei Ku. 2016. Sensing emotions in text messages: An application and deployment study of emotionpush. *arXiv preprint arXiv:1610.04758*.

Graham Wilson, Dobromir Dobrev, and Stephen A Brewster. 2016. Hot under the collar: Mapping thermal feedback to dimensional models of emotion. In *Proceedings of the 2016 CHI Conference on Human Factors in Computing Systems*, pages 4838–4849. ACM.

Yi-Hsuan Yang and Jen-Yu Liu. 2013. Quantitative study of music listening behavior in a social and affective context. *Multimedia, IEEE Transactions on*, 15(6):1304–1315.

Philippe Zimmermann, Sissel Guttormsen, Brigitta Danuser, and Patrick Gomez. 2003. Affective computing—a rationale for measuring mood with mouse and keyboard. *International journal of occupational safety and ergonomics*, 9(4):539–551.

ParlAI: A Dialog Research Software Platform

Alexander H. Miller, Will Feng, Adam Fisch, Jiasen Lu,
Dhruv Batra, Antoine Bordes, Devi Parikh and Jason Weston
Facebook AI Research

Abstract

We introduce ParlAI (pronounced "par-lay"),
an open-source software platform for dialog
research implemented in Python, available at
`http://parl.ai`. Its goal is to provide a
unified framework for sharing, training and
testing dialog models; integration of Amazon
Mechanical Turk for data collection, human
evaluation, and online/reinforcement learning;
and a repository of machine learning models
for comparing with others' models, and improving upon existing architectures. Over 20
tasks are supported in the first release, including popular datasets such as SQuAD, bAbI
tasks, MCTest, WikiQA, QACNN, QADaily-
Mail, CBT, bAbI Dialog, Ubuntu, OpenSubtitles and VQA. Several models are integrated,
including neural models such as memory networks, seq2seq and attentive LSTMs.

1 Introduction

The purpose of language is to accomplish communication goals, which typically involve a dialog between
two or more communicators (Crystal, 2004). Hence,
trying to solve dialog is a fundamental goal for researchers in the NLP community. From a machine
learning perspective, building a learning agent capable of dialog is also fundamental for various reasons,
chiefly that the solution involves achieving most of the
subgoals of the field, and in many cases those subtasks
are directly impactful to the task.

On the one hand dialog can be seen as a single task
(learning how to talk) and on the other hand as thousands of related tasks that require different skills, all using the same input and output format. The task of book-
ing a restaurant, chatting about sports or the news, or
answering factual or perceptually-grounded questions
all fall under dialog. Hence, methods that perform task
transfer appear crucial for the end-goal. Memory, logical and commonsense reasoning, planning, learning
from interaction, learning compositionality and other
AI subgoals also have clear roles in dialog.

However, to pursue these research goals, we require
software tools that unify the different dialog sub-tasks

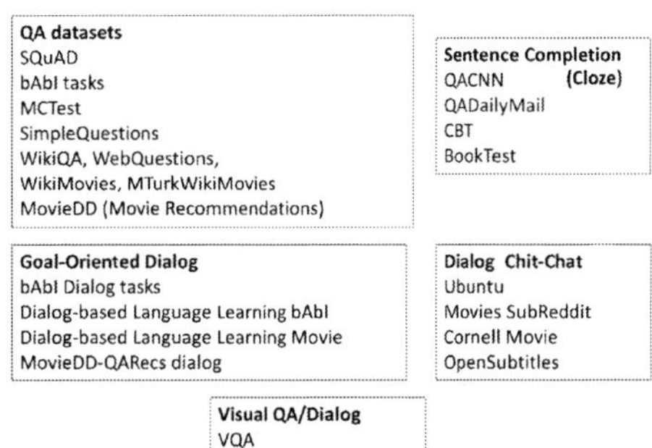

Figure 1: The tasks in the first release of ParlAI.

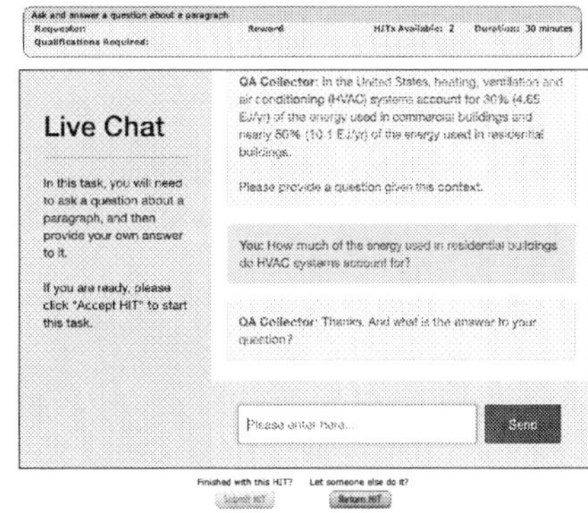

Figure 2: MTurk Live Chat for collecting QA datasets
in ParlAI.

and the agents that can learn from them. Working on
individual datasets can lead to siloed research, where
the overfitting to specific qualities of a dataset do not
generalize to solving other tasks. For example, methods that do not generalize beyond WebQuestions (Berant et al., 2013) because they specialize on knowledge
bases only, SQuAD (Rajpurkar et al., 2016) because
they predict start and end context indices (see Sec. 7),
or bAbI (Weston et al., 2015) because they use supporting facts or make use of its simulated nature.

In this paper we present a software platform, ParlAI (pronounced "par-lay"), that provides researchers
a unified framework for training and testing dialog
models, especially multitask training or evaluation over

79

many tasks at once, as well as seamless integration with Amazon Mechanical Turk. Over 20 tasks are supported in the first release, including many popular datasets, see Fig. 1. Included are examples of training neural models with PyTorch and Lua Torch[1]. Using Theano[2] or Tensorflow[3] instead is also straightforward.

The overarching goal of ParlAI is to build a community-based platform for easy access to both tasks and learning algorithms that perform well on them, in order to push the field forward. This paper describes our goals in detail, and gives a technical overview of the platform.

2 Goals

The goals of ParlAI are as follows:

A unified framework for development of dialog models. ParlAI aims to unify dialog dataset input formats fed to machine learning agents to a *single format*, and to standardize evaluation frameworks and metrics as much as possible. Researchers can submit their new tasks and their agent training code to the repository to share with others in order to aid reproducibility, and to better enable follow-on research.

General dialog involving many different skills. ParlAI contains a seamless combination of real and simulated language datasets, and encourages multitask model development & evaluation by making multitask models as easy to build as single task ones. This should reduce overfitting of model design to specific datasets and encourage models that perform task transfer, an important prerequisite for a general dialog agent.

Real dialog with people. ParlAI allows collecting, training and evaluating on live dialog with humans via Amazon Mechanical Turk by making it easy to connect Turkers with a dialog agent, see Fig. 2. This also enables comparison of Turk experiments across different research groups, which has been historically difficult.

Towards a common general dialog model. Our aim is to motivate the building of new tasks and agents that move the field towards a working dialog model. Hence, each new task that goes into the repository should build towards that common goal, rather than being seen solely as a piece of independent research.

3 General Properties of ParlAI

ParlAI consists of a number of tasks and agents that can be used to solve them. All the tasks in ParlAI have a single format (API) which makes applying any agent to any task, or multiple tasks at once, simple. The tasks include both fixed supervised/imitation learning datasets (i.e. conversation logs) and interactive (on-line or reinforcement learning) tasks, as well as both real language and simulated tasks, which can all be

---

[1] http://pytorch.org/ and http://torch.ch/
[2] http://deeplearning.net/software/theano/
[3] https://www.tensorflow.org/

```
teacher = SquadTeacher(opt)
agent = MyAgent(opt)
world = World(opt, [teacher, agent])
for i in range(num_exs):
  world.parley()
  print(world.display())
```

```
def parley(self):
  for agent in self.agents:
    act = agent.act()
    for other_agent in self.agents:
      if other_agent != agent:
        other_agent.observe(act)
```

Figure 3: ParlAI main for displaying data (top) and the code for the world.parley call (bottom).

seamlessly trained on. ParlAI also supports other media, e.g. images as well as text for visual question answering (Antol et al., 2015) or visually grounded dialog (Das et al., 2017). ParlAI automatically downloads tasks and datasets the first time they are used. One or more Mechanical Turkers can be embedded inside an environment (task) to collect data, train or evaluate learning agents.

Examples are included in the first release of training with PyTorch and Lua Torch. ParlAI uses ZeroMQ to talk to languages other than Python (such as Lua Torch). Both batch training and hogwild training of models are supported and built into the code. An example main for training an agent is given in Fig. 3.

4 Worlds, Agents and Teachers

The main concepts (classes) in ParlAI are worlds, agents and teachers:

- **world** – the environment. This can vary from being very simple, e.g. just two agents conversing, to much more complex, e.g. multiple agents in an interactive environment.
- **agent** – an agent that can act (especially, speak) in the world. An agent is either a learner (i.e. a machine learned system), a hard-coded bot such as one designed to interact with learners, or a human (e.g. a Turker).
- **teacher** – a type of agent that talks to the learner in order to teach it, e.g. implements one of the tasks in Fig. 1.

After defining a world and the agents in it, a main loop can be run for training, testing or displaying, which calls the function world.parley() to run one time step of the world. Example code to display data is given in Fig. 3, and the output of running it is in Fig. 4.

5 Actions and Observations

All agents (including teachers) speak to each other in a single common format – the observation/action object (a python dict), see Fig. 5. It is used to pass text, labels and rewards between agents. The same object type is used for both talking (acting) and listening (observing), but with different values in the fields. Hence,

```
python examples/display_data.py -t babi

[babi:Task1k:4]: The office is north of the kitchen.
The bathroom is north of the office.
What is north of the kitchen?
[cands: office|garden|hallway|bedroom|kitchen|bathroom]
   [RepeatLabelAgent]: office
- - - - - - - - - - - - - - - - - - - - -
--
[babi:Task1k:2]: Daniel went to the kitchen.
Daniel grabbed the football there.
Mary took the milk there.
Mary journeyed to the office.
Where is the milk?
[cands: office|garden|hallway|bedroom|kitchen|bathroom]
   [RepeatLabelAgent]: office
```

Figure 4: Example output to display data of a given task (see Fig. 3 for corresponding code).

Observation/action `dict`
Passed back and forth between agents & environment.

Contains:
  .text   *text of speaker(s)*
  .id   *id of speaker(s)*
  .reward   *for reinforcement learning*
  .episode_done *signals end of episode*

For supervised dialog datasets:
  .label
  .label_candidates *multiple choice options*
  .text_candidates *ranked candidate responses*
  .metrics   *evaluation metrics*

Other media:
  .image   *for VQA or Visual Dialog*

Figure 5: The observation/action dict is the central message passing object in ParlAI: agents send this message to speak, and receive a message of this form to observe other speakers and the environment.

the object is returned from agent.act() and passed in to agent.observe(), see Fig. 3.

The fields of the message are as follows:

- *text:* a speech act.
- *id:* the speaker's identity.
- *reward:* a real-valued reward assigned to the receiver of the message.
- *episode_done:* indicating the end of a dialog.

For supervised datasets, there are some additional fields that can be used:

- *label:* a set of answers the speaker is expecting to receive in reply, e.g. for QA datasets the right answers to a question.
- *label_candidates:* a set of possible ways to respond supplied by a teacher, e.g. for multiple choice datasets or ranking tasks.
- *text_candidates:* ranked candidate predictions from a learner. Used to evaluate ranking metrics, rather than just evaluate the single response in the *text* field.
- *metrics:* A teacher can communicate to a learning agent metrics on its performance.

Finally other media can also be supported with additional fields:

- *image:* an image, e.g. for Visual Question Answering or Visual Dialog datasets.

As the dict is extensible, we can add more fields over time, e.g. for audio and other sensory data, as well as actions other than speech acts.

Each of these fields are technically optional, depending on the dataset, though the *text* field will most likely be used in nearly all exchanges. A typical exchange from a ParlAI training set is shown in Fig. 6.

6 Code Structure

The ParlAI codebase has five main directories:

- **core**: the primary code for the platform.
- **agents**: contains agents which can interact with the worlds/tasks (e.g. learning models).
- **examples**: contains examples of different mains (display data, training and evaluation).
- **tasks**: contains code for the different tasks available from within ParlAI.
- **mturk**: contains code for setting up Mechanical Turk and sample MTurk tasks.

6.1 Core

The core library contains the following files:

- `agents.py`: defines the Agent base class for all agents, which implements the observe() and act() methods, the Teacher class which also reports metrics, and MultiTaskTeacher for multitask training.
- `dialog_teacher.py`: the base teacher class for doing dialog with fixed chat logs.
- `worlds.py`: defines the base World class, DialogPartnerWorld for two speakers, MultiAgentDialogWorld for more than two, and two containers that can wrap a chosen environment: BatchWorld for batch training, and HogwildWorld for training across multiple threads.
- `dict.py`: code for building language dictionaries.
- `metrics.py`: computes exact match, F1 and ranking metrics for evaluation.
- `params.py`: uses argparse to interpret command line arguments for ParlAI

6.2 Agents

The agents directory contains machine learning agents. Currently available within this directory:

- **drqa:** an attentive LSTM model DrQA (Chen et al., 2017) implemented in PyTorch that has competitive results on SQuAD (Rajpurkar et al., 2016) amongst other datasets.
- **memnn:** code for an end-to-end memory network (Sukhbaatar et al., 2015) in Lua Torch.

```
Teacher: {
    'text': 'Sam went to the kitchen.\n Pat gave Sam the
milk.\nWhere is the milk?',\\
    'labels': ['kitchen'],
    'label_candidates': ['hallway', 'kitchen', 'bathroom'],
    'episode_done': False
}

Student: {
    'text': 'hallway'
}

Teacher: {
    'text': 'Sam went to the hallway\nPat went to the
bathroom\nWhere is the milk?',
    'labels': ['hallway'],
    'label_candidates': ['hallway', 'kitchen', 'bathroom'],
    'done': True
}

Student: {
    'text': 'hallway'
}
...
```

Figure 6: A typical exchange from a ParlAI training set involves messages passed using the observation/action dict (the test set would not include labels). Shown here is the bAbI dataset.

- **remote_agent:** basic class for any agent connecting over ZeroMQ.
- **seq2seq:** basic GRU sequence to sequence model (Sutskever et al., 2014)
- **ir_baseline:** information retrieval (IR) baseline that scores responses with TFIDF-weighted matching (Ritter et al., 2011).
- **repeat_label:** basic class for merely repeating all data sent to it (e.g. for debugging).

6.3 Examples

This directory contains examples of different mains:.

- `display_data`: display data from a particular task provided on the command-line.
- `display_model`: show the predictions of a provided model.
- `eval_model`: compute evaluation metrics for a given model on a given task.
- `train_model`: execute a standard training procedure with a given task and model, including logging and possibly alternating between training and validation.

For example, one can display 10 random examples from the bAbI tasks (Weston et al., 2015):

```
python display_data.py -t babi -n 10
```

Display multitasking bAbI and SQuAD (Rajpurkar et al., 2016) at the same time:

```
python display_data.py -t babi,squad
```

Evaluate an IR baseline model on the Movies Subreddit:

```
python eval_model.py -m ir_baseline -t
'#moviedd-reddit' -dt valid
```

Train an attentive LSTM model on the SQuAD dataset with a batch size of 32 examples:

```
python train_model.py -m drqa -t squad
-b 32
```

6.4 Tasks

Over 20 tasks are supported in the first release, including popular datasets such as SQuAD (Rajpurkar et al., 2016), bAbI tasks (Weston et al., 2015), QACNN and QADailyMail (Hermann et al., 2015), CBT (Hill et al., 2015), bAbI Dialog tasks (Bordes and Weston, 2016), Ubuntu (Lowe et al., 2015) and VQA (Antol et al., 2015). All the datasets in the first release are shown in Fig. 1[4].

The tasks are separated into five categories:

- Question answering (QA): one of the simplest forms of dialog, with only 1 turn per speaker. Any intelligent dialog agent should be capable of answering questions, and there are many kinds of questions (and hence datasets) that one can build, providing a set of very important tests. Question answering is particularly useful in that the evaluation is simpler than other forms of dialog if the dataset is labeled with QA pairs and the questions are mostly unambiguous.
- Sentence Completion (Cloze Tests): the agent has to fill in a missing word in the next utterance in a dialog. Again, this is specialized dialog task, but it has the advantage that the datasets are cheap to make and evaluation is simple, which is why the community has built several such datasets.
- Goal-Oriented Dialog: a more realistic class of tasks is where there is a goal to be achieved by the end of the dialog. For example, a customer and a travel agent discussing a flight, one speaker recommending another a movie to watch, and so on.
- Chit-Chat: dialog tasks where there may not be an explicit goal, but more of a discussion — for example two speakers discussing sports, movies or a mutual interest.
- Visual Dialog: dialog is often grounded in physical objects in the world, so we also include dialog tasks with images as well as text.

Choosing a task in ParlAI is as easy as specifying it on the command line, as shown in the dataset display utility, Fig. 4. If the dataset has not been used before, ParlAI will automatically download it. As all datasets are treated in the same way in ParlAI (with a single dialog API, see Sec. 5), a dialog agent can switch training and testing between any of them. Importantly, one can specify many tasks at once (multitasking) by simply providing a comma-separated list, e.g. the command line arguments `-t babi,squad`, to use those two datasets, or even all the QA datasets at once (`-t #qa`) or indeed every task in ParlAI at once (`-t #all`). The aim is to make it easy to build and evaluate very rich dialog models.

Each task is contained in a folder with the following standardized files:

---

[4]All dataset descriptions and references are at `http://parl.ai` in the `README.md` and `task_list.py`.

- `build.py`: file for setting up data for the task, including downloading the data the first time it is requested.
- `agents.py`: contains teacher class(es), agents that live in the world of the task.
- `worlds.py`: optionally added for tasks that need to define new/complex environments.

To add a new task, one must implement build.py to download any required data, and agents.py for the teacher. If the data consist of fixed logs/dialog scripts such as in many supervised datasets (SQuAD, Ubuntu, etc.) there is very little code to write. For more complex setups where an environment with interaction has to be defined, new worlds and/or teachers can be implemented.

6.5 Mechanical Turk

An important part of ParlAI is seamless integration with Mechanical Turk for data collection, training or evaluation. Human Turkers are also viewed as agents in ParlAI and hence human-human, human-bot, or multiple humans and bots in group chat can all converse within the standard framework, switching out the roles as desired with no code changes to the agents. This is because Turkers also receive and send via the same interface: using the fields of the observation/action dict. We provide two examples in the first release:

(i) **qa_collector:** an agent that talks to Turkers to collect question-answer pairs given a context paragraph to build a QA dataset, see Fig. 2.
(ii) **model_evaluator:** an agent which collects ratings from Turkers on the performance of a bot on a given task.

Running a new MTurk task involves implementing and running a main file (like run.py) and defining several task specific parameters for the world and agent(s) you wish humans to talk to. For data collection tasks the agent should pose the problem and ask the Turker for e.g. the answers to questions, see Fig. 2. Other parameters include the task description, the role of the Turker in the task, keywords to describe the task, the number of hits and the rewards for the Turkers. One can run in a sandbox mode before launching the real task where Turkers are paid.

For online training or evaluation, the Turker can talk to your machine learning agent, e.g. LSTM, memory network or other implemented technique. New tasks can be checked into the repository so researchers can share data collection and data evaluation procedures and reproduce experiments.

7 Demonstrative Experiment

To demonstrate ParlAI in action, we give results in Table 1 of DrQA, an attentive LSTM architecture with single task and multitask training on the SQuAD and bAbI tasks, a combination not shown before with any method, to our knowledge.

This experiment simultaneously shows the power of ParlAI — how easy it is to set up this experiment — and the limitations of current methods. Almost all methods working well on SQuAD have been designed to predict a phrase from the given context (they are given labeled start and end indices in training). Hence, those models cannot be applied to all dialog datasets, e.g. some of the bAbI tasks include yes/no questions, where yes and no do not appear in the context. This highlights that researchers should not focus models on a single dataset. ParlAI does not provide start and end label indices as its API is dialog only, see Fig. 5. This is a deliberate choice that discourages such dataset overfitting/ specialization. However, this also results in a slight drop in performance because less information is given[5] (66.4 EM vs. 69.5 EM, see (Chen et al., 2017), which is still in the range of many existing well-performing methods, see `https://stanford-qa.com`).

Overall, while DrQA can solve *some* of the bAbI tasks and performs well on SQuAD, it does not match the best performing methods on bAbI (Seo et al., 2016; Henaff et al., 2016), and multitasking does not help. Hence, ParlAI lays out the challenge to the community to find learning algorithms that are generally applicable and that benefit from training over many dialog datasets.

8 Related Software

There are many existing independent dialog datasets, and training code for individual models that work on some of them. Many are framed in slightly different ways (different formats, with different types of supervision), and ParlAI attempts to unify this fragmented landscape.

There are some existing software platforms that are related in their scope, but not in their specialization. OpenAI's Gym and Universe[6] are toolkits for developing and comparing reinforcement learning (RL) algorithms. Gym is for games like Pong or Go, and Universe is for online games and websites. Neither focuses on dialog or covers the case of supervised datasets as we do.

CommAI[7] is a framework that uses textual communication for the goal of developing artificial general intelligence through incremental tasks that test increasingly more complex skills, as described in (Mikolov et al., 2015). CommAI is in a RL setting, and contains only synthetic datasets, rather than real natural language datasets as we do here. In that regard it has a different focus to ParlAI, which emphasizes the more immediate task of real dialog, rather than directly on evaluation of machine intelligence.

---

[5] As we now do not know the location of the true answer, we randomly pick the start and end indices of any context phrase matching the given training set answer, in some cases this is unique.

[6] `https://gym.openai.com/` and `https://universe.openai.com/`

[7] `https://github.com/facebookresearch/CommAI-env`

	Task	Single	Multitask
bAbI 10k	1: Single Supporting Fact	100	100
	2: Two Supporting Facts	98.1	54.3
	3: Three Supporting Facts	45.4	58.1
	4: Two Arg. Relations	100	100
	5: Three Arg. Relations	98.9	98.2
	11: Basic Coreference	100	100
	12: Conjunction	100	100
	13: Compound Coref.	100	100
	14: Time Reasoning	99.8	99.9
	16: Basic Induction	47.7	48.2
SQuAD	(Dev. Set)	66.4	63.4

Table 1: Test Accuracy of DrQA on bAbI 10k and SQuAD (Exact Match metric) using ParlAI. The subset of bAbI tasks for which the answer is exactly contained in the text is used.

9 Conclusion and Outlook

ParlAI is a framework allowing the research community to share existing and new tasks for dialog as well as agents that learn on them, and to collect and evaluate conversations between agents and humans via Mechanical Turk. We hope this tool enables systematic development and evaluation of dialog agents, helps push the state of the art in dialog further, and benefits the field as a whole.

Acknowledgments

We thank Mike Lewis, Denis Yarats, Douwe Kiela, Michael Auli, Y-Lan Boureau, Arthur Szlam, Marc'Aurelio Ranzato, Yuandong Tian, Maximilian Nickel, Martin Raison, Myle Ott, Marco Baroni, Leon Bottou and other members of the FAIR team for discussions helpful to building ParlAI.

References

Stanislaw Antol, Aishwarya Agrawal, Jiasen Lu, Margaret Mitchell, Dhruv Batra, C Lawrence Zitnick, and Devi Parikh. 2015. VQA: Visual Question Answering. In *Proceedings of the IEEE International Conference on Computer Vision*, pages 2425–2433.

Jonathan Berant, Andrew Chou, Roy Frostig, and Percy Liang. 2013. Semantic parsing on freebase from question-answer pairs. In *EMNLP*, volume 2, page 6.

Antoine Bordes and Jason Weston. 2016. Learning end-to-end goal-oriented dialog. *arXiv preprint arXiv:1605.07683*.

Danqi Chen, Adam Fisch, Jason Weston, and Antoine Bordes. 2017. Reading wikipedia to answer open-domain questions. *arXiv:1704.00051*.

David Crystal. 2004. *The Cambridge encyclopedia of the English language*. Ernst Klett Sprachen.

Abhishek Das, Satwik Kottur, José MF Moura, Stefan Lee, and Dhruv Batra. 2017. Learning cooperative visual dialog agents with deep reinforcement learning. *arXiv preprint arXiv:1703.06585*.

Mikael Henaff, Jason Weston, Arthur Szlam, Antoine Bordes, and Yann LeCun. 2016. Tracking the world state with recurrent entity networks. *arXiv preprint arXiv:1612.03969*.

Karl Moritz Hermann, Tomas Kocisky, Edward Grefenstette, Lasse Espeholt, Will Kay, Mustafa Suleyman, and Phil Blunsom. 2015. Teaching machines to read and comprehend. In *Advances in Neural Information Processing Systems*, pages 1693–1701.

Felix Hill, Antoine Bordes, Sumit Chopra, and Jason Weston. 2015. The goldilocks principle: Reading children's books with explicit memory representations. *arXiv preprint arXiv:1511.02301*.

Ryan Lowe, Nissan Pow, Iulian Serban, and Joelle Pineau. 2015. The ubuntu dialogue corpus: A large dataset for research in unstructured multi-turn dialogue systems. *arXiv preprint arXiv:1506.08909*.

Tomas Mikolov, Armand Joulin, and Marco Baroni. 2015. A roadmap towards machine intelligence. *arXiv preprint arXiv:1511.08130*.

Pranav Rajpurkar, Jian Zhang, Konstantin Lopyrev, and Percy Liang. 2016. Squad: 100,000+ questions for machine comprehension of text. *arXiv:1606.05250*.

Alan Ritter, Colin Cherry, and William B Dolan. 2011. Data-driven response generation in social media. In *EMNLP*, pages 583–593. Association for Computational Linguistics.

Minjoon Seo, Sewon Min, Ali Farhadi, and Hannaneh Hajishirzi. 2016. Query-reduction networks for question answering. *arXiv preprint arXiv:1606.04582*.

Sainbayar Sukhbaatar, Jason Weston, Rob Fergus, et al. 2015. End-to-end memory networks. In *Advances in neural information processing systems*, pages 2440–2448.

Ilya Sutskever, Oriol Vinyals, and Quoc V Le. 2014. Sequence to sequence learning with neural networks. In *Advances in neural information processing systems*, pages 3104–3112.

Jason Weston, Antoine Bordes, Sumit Chopra, Alexander M Rush, Bart van Merriënboer, Armand Joulin, and Tomas Mikolov. 2015. Towards ai-complete question answering: A set of prerequisite toy tasks. *arXiv:1502.05698*.

HeidelPlace: An Extensible Framework for Geoparsing

Ludwig Richter and **Johanna Geiß** and **Andreas Spitz** and **Michael Gertz**
Institute of Computer Science, Heidelberg University
Im Neuenheimer Feld 205, 69120 Heidelberg
`ludwig.richter@posteo.de`
`{geiss,spitz,gertz}@informatik.uni-heidelberg.de`

Abstract

Geographic information extraction from textual data sources, called *geoparsing*, is a key task in text processing and central to subsequent spatial analysis approaches. Several geoparsers are available that support this task, each with its own (often limited or specialized) gazetteer and its own approaches to toponym detection and resolution. In this demonstration paper, we present HeidelPlace, an extensible framework in support of geoparsing. Key features of HeidelPlace include a generic gazetteer model that supports the integration of place information from different knowledge bases, and a pipeline approach that enables an effective combination of diverse modules tailored to specific geoparsing tasks. This makes HeidelPlace a valuable tool for testing and evaluating different gazetteer sources and geoparsing methods. In the demonstration, we show how to set up a geoparsing workflow with HeidelPlace and how it can be used to compare and consolidate the output of different geoparsing approaches.

1 Introduction

The ever-growing amount of available text data raises the need for automated Information Extraction (IE) to obtain structured information from text. A central step in such an extraction procedure is the semantic annotation of the contained information (Zhang and Rettinger, 2014). For tasks such as event detection or content analysis, temporal and spatial information play a crucial role. In particular, the linking of place mentions to geographic databases, so-called *geoparsing*, is an integral element of textual analyses (Andogah et al., 2012). Geoparsing describes the process of identifying place mentions in text (so called *toponyms*) and linking them to unambiguous spatial references. Consider the example text *"Heidelberg was founded in 1196 AD"*, which contains the place mention *"Heidelberg"*. Typically, geoparsing involves three components: *gazetteers*, *toponym recognition* and *toponym resolution*. A Gazetteer is a dictionary of geographic features that serves as a knowledge repository for places of interest. Toponym recognition deals with the detection of place names in documents. For instance, *"Heidelberg"* can be detected by matching candidate strings to a gazetteer of city names. With the help of toponym resolution (also called *toponym linking*), each identified toponym is then matched to an unambiguous spatial reference (e.g., latitude and longitude coordinates). In our example above, the spatial reference may be taken from the matched gazetteer entry. Due to ambiguous names of mentioned places, this task often requires *toponym disambiguation*. For instance, *"Heidelberg"* refers to several places world-wide. If the gazetteer contains founding dates, we can infer that the text refers to Heidelberg in Germany.

Linguistic peculiarities, as well as the relevance of different places and place features, greatly vary with the application domain. Hence, geoparsing is a non-trivial process that requires fine tuning according to the respective use-case. As a result, a variety of geoparsing approaches have been proposed (Hoffart, 2015; Leidner, 2007; Lieberman and Samet, 2011, 2012), many of which are domain-specific. There exist several specialized gazetteers, such as GeoNames[1], a large gazetteer for a broad spectrum of place types, OpenStreetMap[2], a community-built geo-

---

[1] `http://geonames.org`
[2] `http://openstreetmap.org`

85

Proceedings of the 2017 EMNLP System Demonstrations, pages 85–90
Copenhagen, Denmark, September 7–11, 2017. ©2017 Association for Computational Linguistics

graphic knowledge-base, and Pleiades[3], a historic gazetteer. However, reusing and comparing existing geoparsers is often difficult, since they generally come with their own gazetteer and processing pipeline. Configurability and extensibility are rarely considered. As a result, it is often problematic to adjust a geoparser to other application domains or to include other algorithms. Especially the adjustment to a different gazetteer source tends to be troublesome. Each gazetteer uses its own data model and most geoparsers use the data model of their primary gazetteer resource. If the underlying gazetteer data model is not designed to be flexible, or if the geoparser is too tightly coupled with a specific gazetteer source, a reuse may not be possible.

CLAVIN[4], an open-source geoparsing framework, strives to overcome these issues by providing an extensible toolbox of geoparsing methods. However, the framework strongly relies on GeoNames as gazetteer, which is often not an ideal choice. Switching to another data source would entail a significant rewrite of the code base.

Thus, a generalized gazetteer data model is required that is compatible with different gazetteer sources. Only then can significant software modifications due to gazetteer specific data modeling be avoided, and the adaptation work be reduced to the transformation of data sources to the generic data model. While CLAVIN's modular design allows to add new modules, its processing pipeline is too restrictive to enable complex geoparsing approaches that rely on information exchange between different modules.

Contributions. In this work, we present HeidelPlace, a geoparsing framework that includes a generic gazetteer model and an implementation of the entire geoparsing process. The generic gazetteer model supports the integration and management of heterogeneous, large-scale gazetteer sources, and is flexible enough to integrate concepts from different gazetteers. A variety of concepts proposed in gazetteer research are included (Hill, 2000; Keler et al., 2009; Moura and Davis, 2014), which allow the description of places in a comprehensive and yet flexible manner.

The extensibility of HeidelPlace is realized in two ways. First, modularization is a central design aspect, with different geoparsing approaches being represented as modules. They can be used and combined in a plug-in like manner, allowing the integration of newly developed modules. Second, interactions between the different components are handled transparently by the framework, using an annotation-based processing pipeline. Therefore, the user can focus on obtaining appropriate configurations through experimentation. To further increase the efficiency of developing new geoparsing methods, we include user-friendly GUIs that make the geoparsing process transparent. The open-source project HeidelPlace and the data used for this demonstration are available for download from the EventAE project website[5].

2   Framework and System Overview

HeidelPlace includes a geoparsing framework for developing new geoparsers as well as GUIs to make the geoparsing process transparent to the user. The architecture of our proposed geoparsing framework is visualized in Figure 1, which highlights the three major components that we describe in the following. The GUIs are introduced towards the end of this section and in Section 3.

Annotation Pipeline: In order to execute the geoparsing process (either entirely or partially) on input documents, we utilize the annotation pipeline of the Stanford CoreNLP toolkit (Manning et al., 2014), which is built atop three key interdependent concepts, namely `Annotation objects`, `Annotators`, and `AnnotationPipelines`. An `Annotation object` stores key-value information about a document with arbitrary structure. As depicted in Figure 1, this may be the original text of a processed document, identified tokens, or mentions of named entities. An `Annotator` is a configurable module that performs some processing task on a given document. It can read and write analysis information from and to the `Annotation objects`, allowing to pass information among different `Annotators`. The annotator does not implement the processing task itself, but delegates between different modules that implement the same functionality. For instance, `Tokenizer` modules scan the original text of a document with specific strategies and return a set of identified tokens. A `TokenizerAnnotator` is configured by the user to utilize a particular `Tokenizer`

[3]http://pleiades.stoa.org
[4]https://clavin.bericotechnologies.com
[5]http://event.ifi.uni-heidelberg.de/?page_id=517

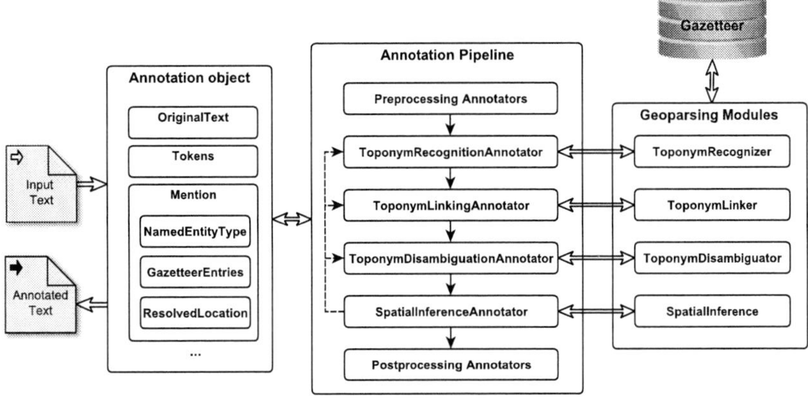

Figure 1: The geoparsing framework architecture, including the three major components: annotation pipeline, geoparsing modules, and gazetteer.

module. It passes all required information to the module and adds annotations for retrieved output tokens. This additional layer of abstraction allows to separate pipeline maintenance tasks from the implementation of the actual data processing methods. The `AnnotationPipeline` consists of a set of `Annotators`, which are run sequentially over the input document.

Geoparsing Modules: The main objective of our framework is the unification of the geoparsing process, with a focus on extensibility and usability. Therefore, we use a modular design and an easy-to-use processing pipeline as described above. The geoparsing process is divided into four steps, which are represented by modules:

- `ToponymRecognizer`: Extracts toponyms from a given input text document.
- `ToponymLinker`: Links each toponym to places in the gazetteer. Due to ambiguity, multiple matches per toponym are possible.
- `ToponymDisambiguator`: Resolves ambiguous matches.
- `SpatialInference`: Infers the location of unlinked toponyms.

For each step, an `Annotator` feeds the correct input to the respective module and then adds its output to the `Annotation object`.

The processing steps need to be executed in sequence, but may be re-run multiple times. For example, running a disambiguation process before the entity recognition step does not make sense. However, re-running a recognition module after a first complete geoparsing pass may improve the results in the second run.

Gazetteer: We developed a generic gazetteer model that allows to incorporate a wide spectrum of place related information. Its central concept is a *geographic place*, which may have multiple names, footprints, types, properties, and relationships, depending on the available data. This allows us to incorporate data from multiple heterogeneous sources.

To enable multilingual and context sensitive geoparsing, we allow each place name to have a language entry and a set of flags (e.g., *is historic* or *is official*). By supporting multiple footprints per place, different spatial representations like points, lines, or polygons are possible. This enables the use of different geographic resolutions and allows us to capture irregularities such as historic changes or political border conflicts. Since a place may fulfil different functions, multiple types can be assigned to each geographic place. In addition, each place may have an arbitrary number of properties with an assigned type and value (e.g., its *population* or a *Wikipedia link*). To link places within the gazetteer, typed place relationships can be defined (e.g., *sister city* or *topographic neighbor*) and used to implement administrative hierarchies. Optionally, relationships may have a value assigned, e.g., a place co-occurrence score (Overell and Rüger, 2008; Spitz et al., 2016). With a flexible type scheme, complex ontologies for place types, property types, and relationship types can be created by using *parent-child* and *similar-to* relationships among types. This allows the integration of type systems of existing gazetteers, while maintaining expressiveness by linking related types. Figure 2

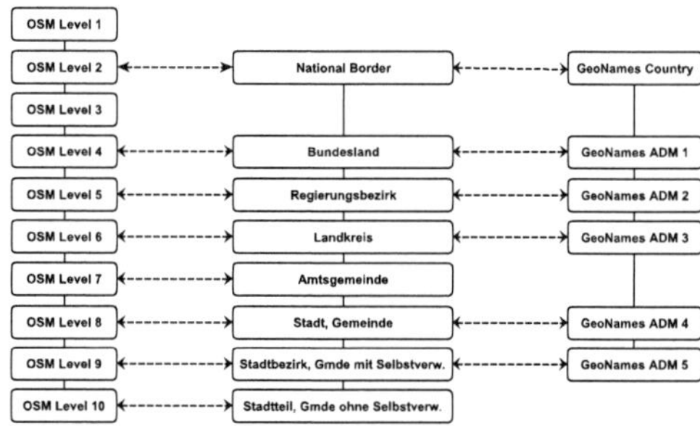

Figure 2: Mapping of GeoNames and OSM administrative levels to a German administrative hierarchy in the HeidelPlace gazetteer model.

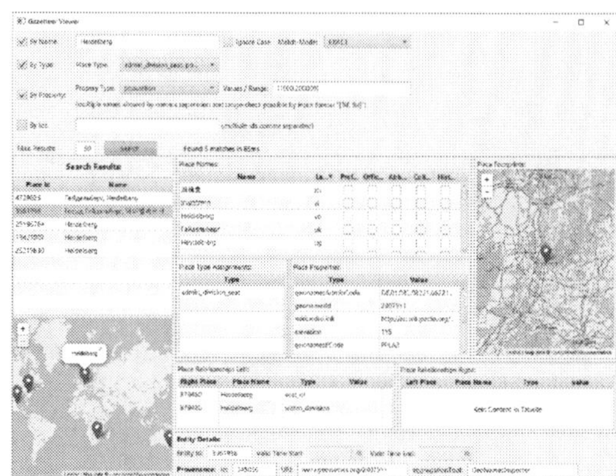

Figure 3: The gazetteer browsing GUI. The search filters can be specified at the top. On the left side the places are listed and shown on a map. The data for a selected place is displayed on the right side.

shows an exemplary mapping of GeoNames and OSM administrative levels to administrative hierarchies in the `PlaceType` entity class of the HeidelPlace gazetteer model. Furthermore, *provenance* and *validity times* can be recorded for each place and its descriptors. This allows to document data origin and temporal validity such as the change in population, which is especially important for historic text corpora.

To support easy access to the gazetteer database, we provide an API written in Java using JPA. This includes a mapping of the database schema to Java classes as well as a flexible query interface. It serves as an abstraction layer for complex database-level access to the underlying data model. A set of predefined filters for each place descriptor can be used to narrow the place search. Users may implement more filters through the JPA Criteria API. For advanced use cases, plain SQL queries support low-level access if desired.

Gazetteer Creation and Integration: Before we can perform actual geoparsing, we first need to fill our gazetteer with data. To demonstrate the applicability of the proposed gazetteer model, we implemented the model in a relational database schema using PostgreSQL 9.4 with PostGIS 2.2. We developed an importer for GeoNames to illustrate how the transformation and integration of data into our model works. A subset of the GeoNames dump from September 7th, 2016 was imported into the gazetteer database. It consists of 4.6 million places, with high coverage of higher-level administrative divisions and many populated places. We obtain basic POI coverage by adding hotels, airports, and castles. More than 6.3 million place names were extracted, 3.8 million of which are distinct (1.66 places per toponym, 1.38

toponyms per place). We use this data for the demonstration scenario. Due to the complexity of merging gazetteers, we refrain from elaborating on the conflation of gazetteers in this demonstration.

3 Demonstration Scenario

In the following, we describe the demonstration of four key usage scenarios of the framework.

Gazetteer Browsing: To make the geoparsing process transparent to the user, visual feedback is important. For the gazetteer component, we provide a user-friendly GUI called "Gazetteer Viewer", which was developed using JavaFX (see Figure 3). The GUI allows users to conveniently browse the gazetteer data and aids them in understanding the underlying data model. The user can narrow search results by specifying a set of filters in the filter mask in the top area. By clicking "Search", the gazetteer is scanned for places that match the specified criteria. A list of identified places and an overview map with their locations are displayed on the left side. If a place is selected in the list or map, its details are shown on the right side. To follow links between places, double clicking on an entry in the relationship table opens a separate view with details of the related place.

With this tool, data exploration can be greatly improved. Neither manual database queries nor knowledge about the database layout are required. Furthermore, the data is clearly structured and visualized to quickly convey relevant information. To display the geoparsing process, we developed a second GUI as described in the following.

Figure 4: The geoparsing GUI. The input filed for text and the modules selection is located at the top. The annotations are shown below in an interactive area where the user can gain more information. For each geoparsing method a separate result view is shown.

Performing Geoparsing: The usage of the geoparsing framework is demonstrated with a set of exemplary geoparsing modules. Here, the focus lies on showcasing the interplay between the modules and not on methodical sophistication. For toponym recognition, we include three modules. The first module applies the location name finder of OpenNLP, while the second uses Stanford NER to detect location entities. The third module is based on gazetteer look-ups for proper nouns as well as basic linguistic considerations. A single toponym linking module is also provided, which links toponyms to gazetteer entries via an exact name matching filter. For toponym disambiguation, two basic modules are implemented. The first module gives precedence to places with higher population, whereas the second module gives precedence to pairs of candidate places that are geographically closer. Since spatial inference is a non-trivial task, we implement no exemplary inference module in this demonstration.

To exemplify how a geoparser can be implemented based on our geoparsing framework, we provide a JavaFX-based GUI called "Geoparser Viewer". The viewer is depicted in Figure 4. It supports a set of pre-configured modules and visualizes the geoparsing process. In the viewer, the user first provides an input text document and selects a module per geoparsing step. The geopars-

ing process can then be run by clicking "Geoparse". Alternatively, geoparsing can be executed step-by-step by clicking the respective buttons. Resulting annotations are visualized in the bottom part of the window (in Figure 4, results for multiple geoparsing methods are shown, as described in the last use-case). This visualization helps the user to analyze the geoparsing results, as we discuss in the next scenario. The simple replacement of modules highlights the benefit of a modular design and clearly structured processing pipeline.

Analyzing Geoparsing Results: If a geoparsing method produces unexpected output or if its behavior is not clear, detailed analysis of the process is required. The result view of the "Geoparser Viewer" allows to conveniently analyze the geoparsing results. On the left side, identified named entities are highlighted in the original text. Since geoparsers may use general NER tools like StanfordNER, our recognition module can also add annotations for named entities other than locations. Knowing the type of other entities may be of use for later processing steps (e.g., disambiguation). Therefore, each color represents a named entity type (among others, yellow for persons, red for locations, blue for organizations). Additionally, a list with all identified named entities is shown. Selections in the text are reflected in the list and vice versa. If a location entity is selected, a list of linked places from the gazetteer is shown. A map displays the location for a selected linked place to quickly surmise the geographic context.

The results of the geoparsing process highly depend on the gazetteer data. For example, the type, administrative level, population, or mention frequency of a place may influence the recognition and disambiguation step. Hence, it may be of interest to see what information is stored for a linked place to draw conclusions about the geoparser decisions. By double-clicking on a linked place entry, a separate view is shown that is similar to the "Gazetteer Viewer". With such a visual analysis, experimentation and debugging of geoparsing methods is greatly simplified.

Comparing Geoparsing Methods: Another valuable feature is the comparison of different geoparsing modules. In the "Geoparser Viewer", multiple geoparsing methods can be compared qualitatively. If multiple modules per geoparsing step are selected, each combination from the cross product of all module combinations is considered a *geoparsing method*. After clicking "Geoparse" or any of the step-by-step buttons, a result view for each method is shown (see Figure 4).

The clearly structured and interactive visualization allows the user to quickly surmise the differences between several geoparsing methods. Of course, this does not replace quantitative performance analyses that allow for a more representative performance evaluation. Instead, it provides the means to easily test special cases and helps to better understand the geoparsing process and the employed modules.

4   Conclusion and Ongoing Work

In this paper, we presented HeidelPlace, a flexible and extensible geoparsing framework built on two paradigms. On the one hand, it introduces a generic gazetteer model that supports the integration of heterogeneous gazetteer sources. A comfortable query API and a user-friendly GUI aid users in maintaining and exploring the gazetteer. On the other hand, HeidelPlace utilizes a modularized pipeline for the entire geoparsing process. Since each geoparsing step is represented as a module within a flexible annotation-based processing pipeline, new approaches can easily be integrated and tested.

Our ongoing work includes the implementation of an evaluation component that enables a standardized quantitative comparison of different geoparsing approaches, the development of an UIMA component to simplify integration into existing IE pipelines, a web-service that supports remote queries to the gazetteer and geoparser, and the implementation of state-of-the-art modules as a starting point for a production-ready toolbox that can be improved and expanded by the community.

References

Geoffrey Andogah, Gosse Bouma, and John Nerbonne. 2012. Every Document Has a Geographical Scope. *Data Knowl. Eng.*, 81-82:1–20.

Linda L Hill. 2000. Core Elements of Digital Gazetteers: Placenames, Categories, and Footprints. *ECDL*, LNCS 1923:280–290.

Johannes Hoffart. 2015. *Discovering and Disambiguating Named Entities in Text*. Dissertation, Saarland University.

Carsten Keler, Krzyzstof Janowicz, and Mohamed Bishr. 2009. An Agenda for the Next Generation Gazetteer: Geographic Information Contribution and Retrieval. In *GIS '09*, pages 91–100.

Jochen L. Leidner. 2007. *Toponym Resolution in Text: Annotation, Evaluation and Applications of Spatial Grounding of Place Names*. Dissertation, University of Edinburgh.

Michael D. Lieberman and Hanan Samet. 2011. Multifaceted Toponym Recognition for Streaming News. In *SIGIR '11*, pages 843–852.

Michael D. Lieberman and Hanan Samet. 2012. Adaptive Context Features for Toponym Resolution in Streaming News. In *SIGIR '12*, pages 731–740.

Christopher D Manning, John Bauer, Jenny Finkel, Steven J Bethard, Mihai Surdeanu, and David McClosky. 2014. The Stanford CoreNLP Natural Language Processing Toolkit. In *ACL '14*, pages 55–60.

Tiago H. V. M. Moura and Clodoveu A. Davis. 2014. Integration of Linked Data Sources for Gazetteer Expansion. In *GIR '14*, pages 5:1–5:8.

Simon E. Overell and Stefan M. Rüger. 2008. Using Co-Occurrence Models for Placename Disambiguation. *Int. Journal of Geographical Inf. Science*, 22(3):265–287.

Andreas Spitz, Johanna Geiß, and Michael Gertz. 2016. So Far Away and Yet So Close: Augmenting Toponym Disambiguation and Similarity with Text-based Networks. In *SIGMOD GeoRich '16*, pages 2:1–2:6.

Lei Zhang and Achim Rettinger. 2014. X-LiSA: Cross-lingual Semantic Annotation. *Proceedings of the VLDB Endowment*, 7(13):1693–1696.

Unsupervised, Knowledge-Free, and Interpretable Word Sense Disambiguation

**Alexander Panchenko[‡], Fide Marten[‡], Eugen Ruppert[‡], Stefano Faralli[†],
Dmitry Ustalov[*], Simone Paolo Ponzetto[†], and Chris Biemann[‡]**

[‡]Language Technology Group, Department of Informatics, Universität Hamburg, Germany
[†]Web and Data Science Group, Department of Informatics, Universität Mannheim, Germany
[*]Institute of Natural Sciences and Mathematics, Ural Federal University, Russia
{panchenko,marten,ruppert,biemann}@informatik.uni-hamburg.de
{simone,stefano}@informatik.uni-mannheim.de
dmitry.ustalov@urfu.ru

Abstract

Interpretability of a predictive model is a powerful feature that gains the trust of users in the correctness of the predictions. In word sense disambiguation (WSD), *knowledge-based* systems tend to be much more interpretable than *knowledge-free* counterparts as they rely on the wealth of manually-encoded elements representing word senses, such as hypernyms, usage examples, and images. We present a WSD system that bridges the gap between these two so far disconnected groups of methods. Namely, our system, providing access to several state-of-the-art WSD models, aims to be *interpretable* as a knowledge-based system while it remains completely *unsupervised* and *knowledge-free*. The presented tool features a Web interface for all-word disambiguation of texts that makes the sense predictions human readable by providing interpretable word sense inventories, sense representations, and disambiguation results. We provide a public API, enabling seamless integration.

1 Introduction

The notion of word sense is central to computational lexical semantics. Word senses can be either *encoded manually* in lexical resources or *induced automatically* from text. The former knowledge-based sense representations, such as those found in the BabelNet lexical semantic network (Navigli and Ponzetto, 2012), are easily interpretable by humans due to the presence of definitions, usage examples, taxonomic relations, related words, and images. The cost of such interpretability is that every element mentioned above is encoded manually in one of the underlying resources, such as Wikipedia. Unsupervised knowledge-free approaches, e.g. (Di Marco and Navigli, 2013; Bartunov et al., 2016), require no manual labor, but the resulting sense representations lack the above-mentioned features enabling interpretability. For instance, systems based on sense embeddings are based on dense uninterpretable vectors. Therefore, the meaning of a sense can be interpreted only on the basis of a list of related senses.

We present a system that brings interpretability of the knowledge-based sense representations into the world of unsupervised knowledge-free WSD models. The contribution of this paper is the first *system* for word sense induction and disambiguation, which is unsupervised, knowledge-free, and interpretable at the same time. The system is based on the WSD approach of Panchenko et al. (2017) and is designed to reach interpretability level of knowledge-based systems, such as Babelfy (Moro et al., 2014), within an unsupervised knowledge-free framework. Implementation of the system is open source.[1] A live demo featuring several disambiguation models is available online.[2]

2 Related Work

In this section, we list prominent WSD systems with openly available implementations.

Knowledge-Based and/or Supervised Systems
IMS (Zhong and Ng, 2010) is a supervised all-words WSD system that allows users to integrate additional features and different classifiers. By default, the system relies on the linear support vector machines with multiple features. The AutoExtend (Rothe and Schütze, 2015) approach can be used to learn embeddings for lexemes and synsets

---

[1]https://github.com/uhh-lt/wsd
[2]http://jobimtext.org/wsd

Proceedings of the 2017 EMNLP System Demonstrations, pages 91–96
Copenhagen, Denmark, September 7–11, 2017. ©2017 Association for Computational Linguistics

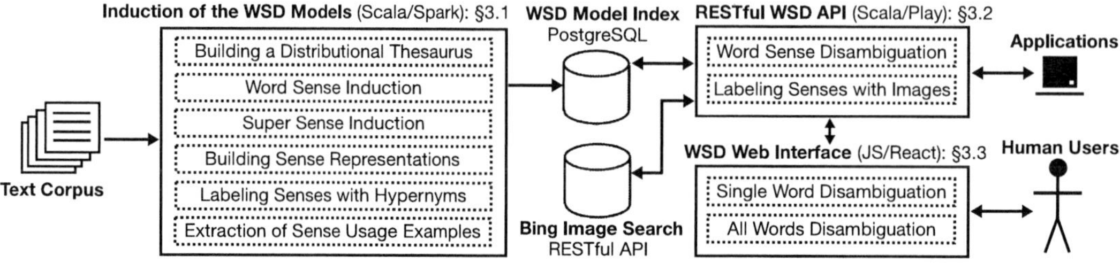

Figure 1: Software and functional architecture of the WSD system.

of a lexical resource. These representations were successfully used to perform WSD using the IMS.

DKPro WSD (Miller et al., 2013) is a modular, extensible Java framework for word sense disambiguation. It implements multiple WSD methods and also provides an interface to evaluation datasets. PyWSD[3] project also provides implementations of popular WSD methods, but these are implemented in the Python language.

Babelfy (Moro et al., 2014) is a system based on the BabelNet that implements a multilingual graph-based approach to entity linking and WSD based on the identification of candidate meanings using the densest subgraph heuristic.

Knowledge-Free and Unsupervised Systems
Neelakantan et al. (2014) proposed a multi-sense extension of the Skip-gram model that features an open implementation. AdaGram (Bartunov et al., 2016) is a system that learns sense embeddings using a Bayesian extension of the Skip-gram model and provides WSD functionality based on the induced sense inventory. SenseGram (Pelevina et al., 2016) is a system that transforms word embeddings to sense embeddings via graph clustering and uses them for WSD. Other methods to learn sense embeddings were proposed, but these do not feature open implementations for WSD.

Among all listed systems, only Babelfy implements a user interface supporting interpretable visualization of the disambiguation results.

3 Unsupervised Knowledge-Free Interpretable WSD

This section describes (1) how WSD models are learned in an unsupervised way from text and (2) how the system uses these models to enable human interpretable disambiguation in context.

3.1 Induction of the WSD Models

Figure 1 presents architecture of the WSD system. As one may observe, no human labor is used to learn interpretable sense representations and the corresponding disambiguation models. Instead, these are induced from the input text corpus using the JoBimText approach (Biemann and Riedl, 2013) implemented using the Apache Spark framework[4], enabling seamless processing of large text collections. Induction of a WSD model consists of several steps. First, a graph of semantically related words, i.e. a distributional thesaurus, is extracted. Second, word senses are induced by clustering of an ego-network of related words (Biemann, 2006). Each discovered word sense is represented as a cluster of words. Next, the induced sense inventory is used as a pivot to generate sense representations by aggregation of the context clues of cluster words. To improve interpretability of the sense clusters they are labeled with hypernyms, which are in turn extracted from the input corpus using Hearst (1992) patterns. Finally, the obtained WSD model is used to retrieve a list of sentences that characterize each sense. Sentences that mention a given word are disambiguated and then ranked by prediction confidence. Top sentences are used as sense usage examples. For more details about the model induction process refer to (Panchenko et al., 2017). Currently, the following WSD models induced from a text corpus are available:

Word senses based on cluster word features. This model uses the cluster words from the induced word sense inventory as sparse features that represent the sense.

Word senses based on context word features. This representation is based on a sum of word vectors of all cluster words in the induced sense inventory weighted by distributional similarity scores.

Super senses based on cluster word features.
To build this model, induced word senses are
first globally clustered using the Chinese Whispers
graph clustering algorithm (Biemann, 2006). The
edges in this sense graph are established by disambiguation of the related words (Faralli et al., 2016;
Ustalov et al., 2017). The resulting clusters represent semantic classes grouping words sharing a
common hypernym, e.g. "animal". This set of semantic classes is used as an automatically learned
inventory of super senses: There is only one global
sense inventory shared among all words in contrast
to the two previous traditional "per word" models.
Each semantic class is labeled with hypernyms.
This model uses words belonging to the semantic
class as features.

Super senses based on context word features.
This model relies on the same semantic classes
as the previous one but, instead, sense representations are obtained by averaging vectors of words
sharing the same class.

3.2 WSD API

To enable fast access to the sense inventories and
effective parallel predictions, the WSD models obtained at the previous step were indexed in a relational database.[5] In particular, each word sense
is represented by its hypernyms, related words,
and usage examples. Besides, for each sense, the
database stores an aggregated context word representation in the form of a serialized object containing a sparse vector in the Breeze format.[6] During the disambiguation phrase, the input context is
represented in the same sparse feature space and
the classification is reduced to the computation of
the cosine similarity between the context vector
and the vectors of the candidate senses retrieved
from the database. This back-end is implemented
as a RESTful API using the Play framework.[7]

3.3 User Interface for Interpretable WSD

The graphical user interface of our system is implemented as a single page Web application using
the React framework.[8] The application performs
disambiguation of a text entered by a user. In particular, the Web application features two modes:

Single word disambiguation mode is illustrated in Figure 2. In this mode, a user specifies

an ambiguous word and its context. The output of
the system is a ranked list of all word senses of the
ambiguous word ordered by relevance to the input
context. By default, only the best matching sense
is displayed. The user can quickly understand the
meaning of each induced sense by looking at the
hypernym and the image representing the sense.
Faralli and Navigli (2012) showed that Web search
engines can be used to acquire information about
word senses. We assign an image to each word in
the cluster by querying an image search API[9] using a query composed of the ambiguous word and
its hypernym, e.g. "jaguar animal". The first hit
of this query is selected to represent the induced
word sense. Interpretability of each sense is further ensured by providing to the user the list of
related senses, the list of the most salient context
clues, and the sense usage examples (cf. Figure 2).
Note that all these elements are obtained without
manual intervention.

Finally, the system provides the reasons behind
the sense predictions by displaying context words
triggered the prediction. Each common feature is
clickable, so a user is able to trace back sense cluster words containing this context feature.

All words disambiguation mode is illustrated
in Figure 3. In this mode, the system performs disambiguation of all nouns and entities in the input
text. First, the text is processed with a part-of-
speech and a named entity taggers.[10] Next, each
detected noun or entity is disambiguated in the
same way as in the single word disambiguation
mode described above, yet the disambiguation results are represented as annotations of a running
text. The best matching sense is represented by a
hypernym and an image as depicted in Figure 3.
This mode performs "semantification" of a text,
which can, for instance, assist language learners
with the understanding of a text in a foreign language: Meaning of unknown to the learner words
can be deduced from hypernyms and images.

4 Evaluation

In our prior work (Panchenko et al., 2017), we performed a thorough evaluation of the method implemented in our system on two datasets showing
the state-of-the-art performance of the approach as
compared to other unsupervised knowledge-free

---

[5]https://www.postgresql.org
[6]https://github.com/scalanlp/breeze
[7]https://www.playframework.com
[8]https://facebook.github.io/react

[9]https://azure.microsoft.com/en-us/
services/cognitive-services/search
[10]http://www.scalanlp.org

Figure 2: Single word disambiguation mode: results of disambiguation of the word "Jaguar" (B) in the sentence "*Jaguar* is a large spotted predator of tropical America similar to the leopard." (A) using the WSD disambiguation model based on cluster word features (C). The predicted sense is summarized with a hypernym and an image (D) and further represented with usage examples, semantically related words, and typical context clues. Each of these elements is extracted automatically. The reasons of the predictions are provided in terms of common sparse features of the input sentence and a sense representation (E). The induced senses are linked to BabelNet using the method of Faralli et al. (2016) (F).

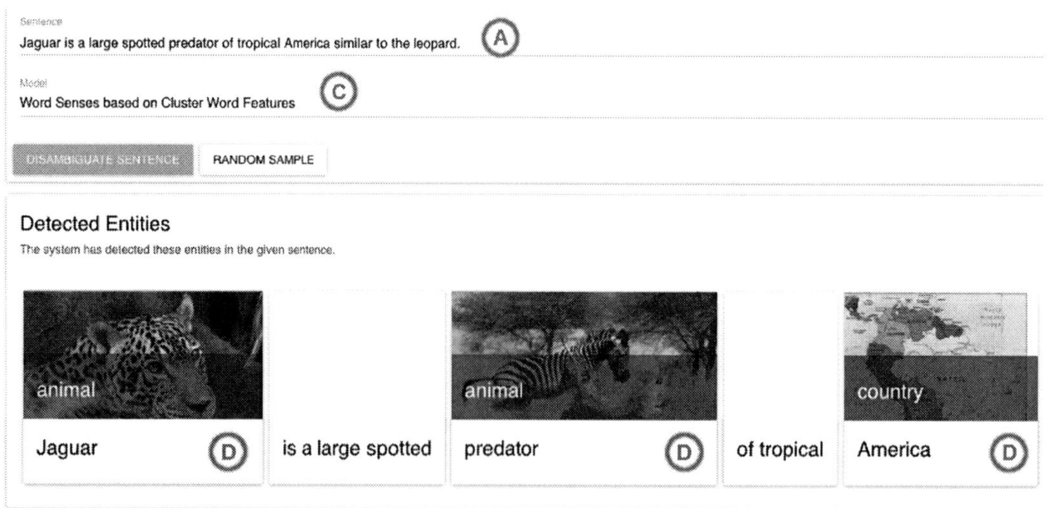

Figure 3: All words disambiguation mode: results of disambiguation of all nouns in a sentence.

# Words	# Senses	Avg. Polysemy	# Contexts
863	2,708	3.13	11,712

Table 1: Evaluation dataset based on BabelNet.

methods for WSD, including participants of the SemEval 2013 Task 13 (Jurgens and Klapaftis, 2013) and two unsupervised knowledge-free WSD systems based on word sense embeddings (Bartunov et al., 2016; Pelevina et al., 2016). These evaluations were based on the "lexical sample" setting, where the system is expected to predict a sense identifier of the ambiguous word.

In this section, we perform an extra evaluation that assesses how well hypernyms of ambiguous words are assigned in context by our system. Namely, the task is to assign a correct hypernym of an ambiguous word, e.g. "animal" for the word "*Jaguar*" in the context "*Jaguar* is a large spotted predator of tropical America". This task does not depend on a fixed sense inventory and evaluates at the same time WSD performance and the quality of the hypernymy labels of the induced senses.

4.1 Dataset

In this experiment, we gathered a dataset consisting of definitions of BabelNet 3.7 senses of 1,219 frequent nouns.[11] In total, we collected 56,003 sense definitions each labeled with gold hypernyms coming from the IsA relations of BabelNet.

The average polysemy of words in the gathered dataset was 15.50 senses per word as compared to 2.34 in the induced sense inventory. This huge discrepancy in granularities lead to the fact that some test sentences cannot be correctly predicted by definition: some (mostly rare) BabelNet senses simply have no corresponding sense in the induced inventory. To eliminate the influence of this idiosyncrasy, we kept only sentences that contain at least one common hypernym with all hypernyms of all induced senses. The statistics of the resulting dataset are presented in Table 1, it is available in the project repository.

4.2 Evaluation Metrics

WSD performance is measured using the accuracy with respect to the sentences labeled with the direct hypernyms (*Hypers*) or an extended set of hypernym including hypernyms of hypernyms (*Hy-*

---

[11]Most of the nouns come from the TWSI (Biemann, 2012) dataset, while the remaining nouns were manually selected.

WSD Model		Accuracy	
Inventory	Features	Hypers	HyperHypers
Word Senses	Random	0.257	0.610
Word Senses	MFS	0.292	0.682
Word Senses	Cluster Words	0.291	0.650
Word Senses	Context Words	**0.308**	**0.686**
Super Senses	Random	0.001	0.001
Super Senses	MFS	0.001	0.001
Super Senses	Cluster Words	**0.174**	**0.365**
Super Senses	Context Words	0.086	0.188

Table 2: Performance of the hypernymy labeling in context on the BabelNet dataset.

perHypers). A correct match occurs when the predicted sense has at least one common hypernym with the gold hypernyms of the target word in a test sentence.

4.3 Discussion of Results

Word Senses. All evaluated models outperform both random and most frequent sense baselines, see Table 2. The latter picks the sense that corresponds to the largest sense cluster (Panchenko et al., 2017). In the case of the traditional "per word" inventories, the model based on the context features outperform the models based on cluster words. While sense representations based on the clusters of semantically related words contain highly accurate features, such representations are sparse as one sense contains at most 200 features. As the result, often the model based on the cluster words contain no common features with the features extracted from the input context. The sense representations based on the aggregated context clues are much less sparse, which explains their superior performance.

Super Senses. In the case of the super sense inventory, the model based solely on the cluster words yielded better results that the context-based model. Note here that (1) the clusters that represent super senses are substantially larger than word sense clusters and thus less sparse, (2) words in the super sense clusters are unweighted in contrast to word sense cluster, thus averaging of word vectors is more noise-prone. Besides, the performance scores of the models based on the super sense inventories are substantially lower compared to their counterparts based on the traditional "per word" inventories. Super sense models are able to perform classification for any unknown word missing in the training corpus, but their disambiguation task is more complex (the models need to choose one of 712 classes as compared to an average of 2–3 classes for the "per word" inventories). This is illustrated by the near-zero scores of the random and the MFS baselines for this model.

5 Conclusion

We present the first openly available word sense disambiguation system that is unsupervised, knowledge-free, and interpretable at the same time. The system performs extraction of word and super sense inventories from a text corpus. The disambiguation models are learned in an unsupervised way for all words in the corpus on the basis on the induced inventories. The user interface of the system provides efficient access to the produced WSD models via a RESTful API or via an interactive Web-based graphical user interface. The system is available online and can be directly used from external applications. The code and the WSD models are open source. Besides, in-house deployments of the system are made easy due to the use of the Docker containers.[12] A prominent direction for future work is supporting more languages and establishing cross-lingual sense links.

Acknowledgments

We acknowledge the support of the DFG under the "JOIN-T" project, the RFBR under project no. 16-37-00354 mol_a, Amazon via the "AWS Research Grants" and Microsoft via the "Azure for Research" programs. Finally, we also thank four anonymous reviewers for their helpful comments.

References

S. Bartunov, D. Kondrashkin, A. Osokin, and D. Vetrov. 2016. Breaking Sticks and Ambiguities with Adaptive Skip-gram. In *Proc. AISTATS*. Cadiz, Spain, pp. 130–138.

C. Biemann. 2006. Chinese Whispers: An Efficient Graph Clustering Algorithm and Its Application to Natural Language Processing Problems. In *Proc. TextGraphs*. New York, NY, USA, pp. 73–80.

C. Biemann. 2012. Turk Bootstrap Word Sense Inventory 2.0: A Large-Scale Resource for Lexical Substitution. In *Proc. LREC*. Istanbul, Turkey, pp. 4038–4042.

C. Biemann and M. Riedl. 2013. Text: now in 2D! A framework for lexical expansion with contextual similarity. *Journal of Language Modelling* 1(1):55–95.

A. Di Marco and R. Navigli. 2013. Clustering and Diversifying Web Search Results with Graph-Based Word Sense Induction. *Computational Linguistics* 39(3):709–754.

S. Faralli and R. Navigli. 2012. A New Minimally-Supervised Framework for Domain Word Sense Disambiguation. In *Proc. EMNLP-CoNLL*. Jeju Island, Korea, pp. 1411–1422.

S. Faralli, A. Panchenko, C. Biemann, and S. P. Ponzetto. 2016. Linked Disambiguated Distributional Semantic Networks. In *Proc. ISWC, Part II*. Kobe, Japan, pp. 56–64.

M. A. Hearst. 1992. Automatic Acquisition of Hyponyms from Large Text Corpora. In *Proc. COLING*. Nantes, France, pp. 539–545.

D. Jurgens and I. Klapaftis. 2013. SemEval-2013 Task 13: Word Sense Induction for Graded and Non-Graded Senses. In *Proc. SemEval*. Atlanta, GA, USA, pp. 290–299.

T. Miller et al. 2013. DKPro WSD: A Generalized UIMA-based Framework for Word Sense Disambiguation. In *Proc. ACL*. Sofia, Bulgaria, pp. 37–42.

A. Moro, A. Raganato, and R. Navigli. 2014. Entity Linking meets Word Sense Disambiguation: A Unified Approach. *Transactions of the Association for Computational Linguistics* 2:231–244.

R. Navigli and S. P. Ponzetto. 2012. BabelNet: The automatic construction, evaluation and application of a wide-coverage multilingual semantic network. *Artificial Intelligence* 193:217–250.

A. Neelakantan, J. Shankar, A. Passos, and A. McCallum. 2014. Efficient Non-parametric Estimation of Multiple Embeddings per Word in Vector Space. In *Proc. EMNLP*. Doha, Qatar, pp. 1059–1069.

A. Panchenko, E. Ruppert, S. Faralli, S. P. Ponzetto, and C. Biemann. 2017. Unsupervised Does Not Mean Uninterpretable: The Case for Word Sense Induction and Disambiguation. In *Proc. EACL*. Valencia, Spain, pp. 86–98.

M. Pelevina, N. Arefiev, C. Biemann, and A. Panchenko. 2016. Making Sense of Word Embeddings. In *Proc. RepL4NLP*. Berlin, Germany, pp. 174–183.

S. Rothe and H. Schütze. 2015. AutoExtend: Extending Word Embeddings to Embeddings for Synsets and Lexemes. In *Proc. ACL-IJCNLP*. Beijing, China, pp. 1793–1803.

D. Ustalov, A. Panchenko, and C. Biemann. 2017. Watset: Automatic Induction of Synsets from a Graph of Synonyms. In *Proc. ACL*. Vancouver, Canada.

Z. Zhong and H. T. Ng. 2010. It Makes Sense: A Wide-Coverage Word Sense Disambiguation System for Free Text. In *Proc. ACL Demos*. Uppsala, Sweden, pp. 78–83.

---

[12]`https://www.docker.com`

NeuroNER: an easy-to-use program for
named-entity recognition based on neural networks

Franck Dernoncourt[*]
MIT
`francky@mit.edu`

Ji Young Lee[*]
MIT
`jjylee@mit.edu`

Peter Szolovits
MIT
`psz@mit.edu`

Abstract

Named-entity recognition (NER) aims at identifying entities of interest in a text. Artificial neural networks (ANNs) have recently been shown to outperform existing NER systems. However, ANNs remain challenging to use for non-expert users. In this paper, we present NeuroNER, an easy-to-use named-entity recognition tool based on ANNs. Users can annotate entities using a graphical web-based user interface (BRAT): the annotations are then used to train an ANN, which in turn predict entities' locations and categories in new texts. NeuroNER makes this annotation-training-prediction flow smooth and accessible to anyone.

1 Introduction

Named-entity recognition (NER) aims at identifying entities of interest in the text, such as location, organization and temporal expression. Identified entities can be used in various downstream applications such as patient note de-identification and information extraction systems. They can also be used as features for machine learning systems for other natural language processing tasks.

Early systems for NER relied on rules defined by humans. Rule-based systems are time-consuming to develop, and cannot be easily transferred to new types of texts or entities. To address these issues, researchers have developed machine-learning-based algorithms for NER, using a variety of learning approaches, such as fully supervised learning, semi-supervised learning, unsupervised learning, and active learning. NeuroNER is based on a fully supervised learning algorithm, which is the most studied approach (Nadeau and Sekine, 2007).

Fully supervised approaches to NER include support vector machines (SVM) (Asahara and Matsumoto, 2003), maximum entropy models (Borthwick et al., 1998), decision trees (Sekine et al., 1998) as well as sequential tagging methods such as hidden Markov models (Bikel et al., 1997), Markov maximum entropy models (Kumar and Bhattacharyya, 2006), and conditional random fields (CRFs) (McCallum and Li, 2003; Tsai et al., 2006; Benajiba and Rosso, 2008; Filannino et al., 2013). Similar to rule-based systems, these approaches rely on handcrafted features, which are challenging and time-consuming to develop and may not generalize well to new datasets.

More recently, artificial neural networks (ANNs) have been shown to outperform other supervised algorithms for NER (Collobert et al., 2011; Lample et al., 2016; Lee et al., 2016; Labeau et al., 2015; Dernoncourt et al., 2016). The effectiveness of ANNs can be attributed to their ability to learn effective features jointly with model parameters directly from the training dataset, instead of relying on handcrafted features developed from a specific dataset. However, ANNs remain challenging to use for non-expert users.

Contributions NeuroNER makes state-of-the-art named-entity recognition based on ANN available to anyone, by focusing on usability. To enable users to create or modify annotations for a new or existing corpus, NeuroNER interfaces with the web-based annotation program BRAT (Stenetorp et al., 2012). NeuroNER makes the annotation-training-prediction flow smooth and accessible to anyone, while leveraging the state-of-the-art prediction capabilities of ANNs. NeuroNER is open source and freely available online[1].

---

[*] These authors contributed equally to this work.

[1]NeuroNER is available at: `https://github.com/Franck-Dernoncourt/NeuroNER`

Proceedings of the 2017 EMNLP System Demonstrations, pages 97–102
Copenhagen, Denmark, September 7–11, 2017. ©2017 Association for Computational Linguistics

2   Related Work

Existing publicly available NER systems geared toward non-experts do not use ANNs. For example, Stanford NER (Finkel et al., 2005), ABNER (Settles, 2005), the MITRE Identification Scrubber Toolkit (MIST) (Aberdeen et al., 2010), (Boag et al., 2015), BANNER (Leaman et al., 2008) and NERsuite (Cho et al., 2010) rely on CRFs. GAPSCORE uses SVMs (Chang et al., 2004). Apache cTAKES (Savova et al., 2010) and Gate's ANNIE (Cunningham et al., 1996; Maynard and Cunningham, 2003) use mostly rules. NeuroNER, the first ANN-based NER system for non-experts, is more generalizable to new corpus due to the ANNs' capability to learn effective features jointly with model parameters.

Furthermore, in many cases, the NER systems assume that the user already has an annotated corpus formatted in a specific data format. As a result, users often have to connect their annotation tool with the NER systems by reformatting annotated data, which can be time-consuming and error-prone. Moreover, if users want to manually improve the annotations predicted by the NER system (e.g., if they use the NER system to accelerate the human annotations), they have to perform additional data conversion. NeuroNER streamlines this process by incorporating BRAT, a widely-used and easy-to-use annotation tool.

3   System Description

NeuroNER comprises two main components: an NER engine and an interface with BRAT. NeuroNER also comes with real-time monitoring tools for training, and pre-trained models that can be loaded to the NER engine in case the user does not have access to labelled training data. Figure 1 presents an overview of the system.

3.1   NER engine

The NER engine takes as input three sets of data with gold labels: the training set, the validation set, and the test set. Additionally, it can also take as input the deployment set, which refers to any new text without gold labels that the user wishes to label. The files that comprise each set of data should be in the same format as used for the annotation tool BRAT or the CoNLL-2003 NER shared task dataset (Tjong Kim Sang and De Meulder, 2003), and organized in the corresponding folder.

The NER engine's ANN contains three layers:

- Character-enhanced token-embedding layer,
- Label prediction layer,
- Label sequence optimization layer.

The character-enhanced token-embedding layer maps each token to a vector representation. The sequence of vector representations corresponding to a sequence of tokens is then input to label prediction layer, which outputs the sequence of vectors containing the probability of each label for each corresponding token. Lastly, the label sequence optimization layer outputs the most likely sequence of predicted labels based on the sequence of probability vectors from the previous layer. All layers are learned jointly. The model architecture is detailed in (Dernoncourt et al., 2016).

The ANN as well as the training process have several hyperparameters such as character embedding dimension, character-based token-embedding LSTM dimension, token embedding dimension, and dropout probability. All hyperparameters may be specified in a configuration file that is human-readable, so that the user does not have to dive into any code. Listing 1 presents an excerpt of the configuration file.

```
[dataset]
dataset_folder                = dat/conll

[character_lstm]
using_character_lstm          = True
char_embedding_dimension      = 25
char_lstm_dimension           = 50

[token_lstm]
token_emb_pretrained_file     = glove.txt
token_embedding_dimension     = 200
token_lstm_dimension          = 300

[crf]
using_crf                     = True
random_initial_transitions    = True

[training]
dropout                       = 0.5
patience                      = 10
maximum_number_of_epochs      = 100
maximum_training_time         = 10
number_of_cpu_threads         = 8
```

Listing 1: Excerpt of the configuration file used to define the ANN as well as the training process. Only the `dataset_folder` parameter needs to be changed by the user: the other parameters have reasonable default values, which the user may optionally tune.

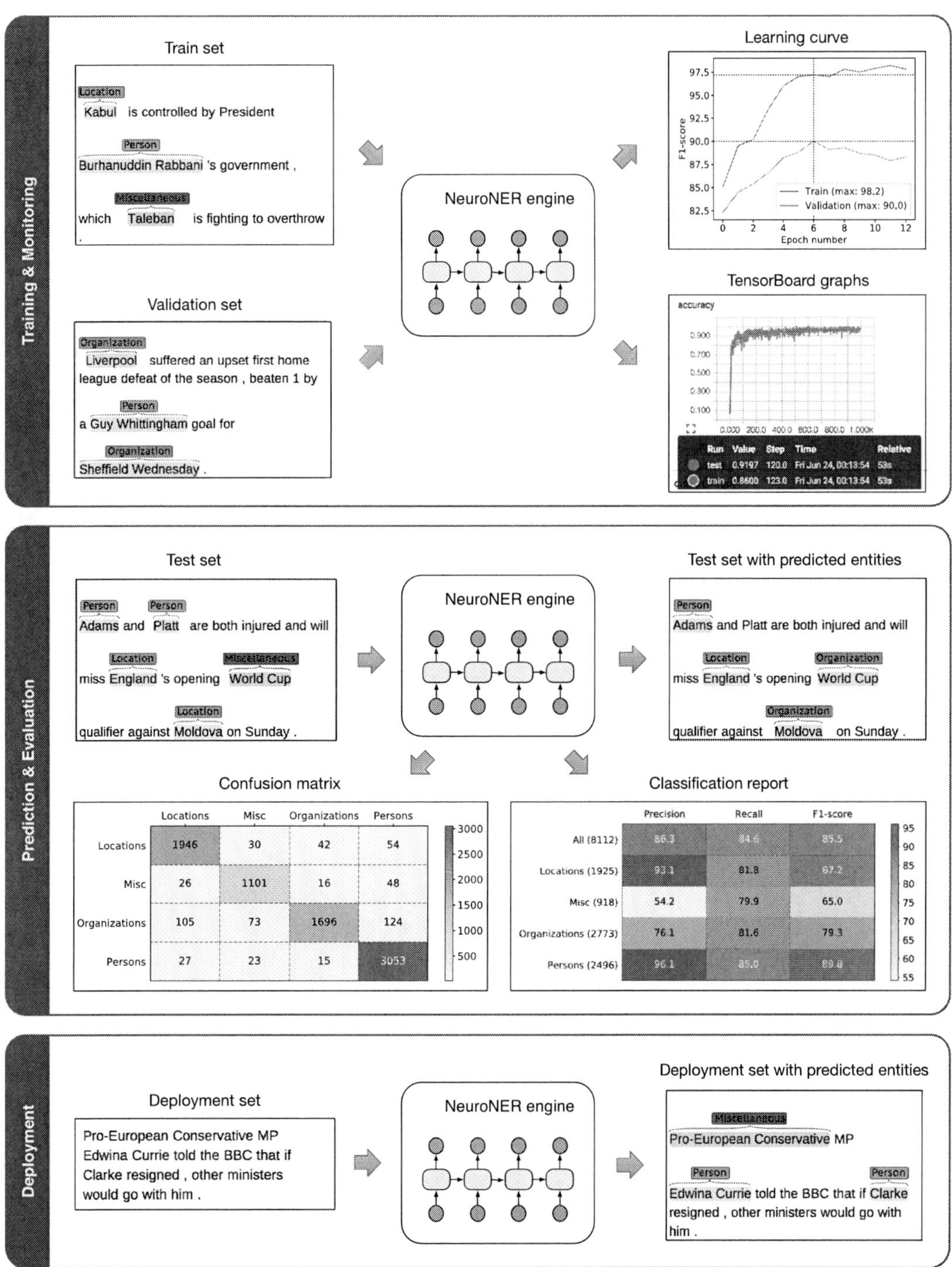

Figure 1: NeuroNER system overview. In the NeuroNER engine, the training set is used to train the parameters of the ANN, and the validation set is used to determine when to stop training. The user can monitor the training process in real time via the learning curve and TensorBoard. To evaluate the trained ANN, the labels are predicted for the test set: the performance metrics can be calculated and plotted by comparing the predicted labels with the gold labels. The evaluation can be done at the same time as the training if the test set is provided along with the training and validation sets, or separately after the training or using a pre-trained model. Lastly, the NeuroNER engine can label the deployment set, i.e. any new text without gold labels.

3.2 Real-time monitoring for training

As training an ANN may take many hours, or even a few days on very large datasets, NeuroNER provides the user with real-time feedback during the training for monitoring purpose. Feedback is given through two different means: plots generated by NeuroNER, and TensorBoard.

Plots NeuroNER generates several plots showing the training progress and outcome at each epoch. Plots include the evolution of the overall F1-score over time, confusion matrices visualizing the number of correct versus incorrect predictions for each class, and classification reports showing the F1-score, precision and recall for each class.

TensorBoard As NeuroNER is based on TensorFlow , it leverages the functionalities of TensorBoard. TensorBoard is a suite of web applications for inspecting and understanding TensorFlow runs and graphs. It allows to view in real time the performances achieved by the ANN being trained. Moreover, since it is web-based, these performances can be conveniently shared with anyone remotely. Lastly, since graphs generated by TensorBoard are interactive, the user may gain further insights on the ANN performances.

3.3 Pre-trained models

Some users may prefer not to train any ANN model, either due to time constraints or unavailable gold labels. For example, if the user wants to tag protected health information, they might not be able to have access to a labeled identifiable dataset. To address this need, NeuroNER provides a set of pre-trained models. Users are encouraged to contribute by uploading their own trained models. NeuroNER also comes with several pre-trained token embeddings, either with word2vec (Mikolov et al., 2013a,b) or GloVe (Pennington et al., 2014), which the NeuroNER engine can load easily once specified in the configuration file.

3.4 Annotations

NeuroNER is designed to smoothly integrate with the freely available web-based annotation tool BRAT, so that non-expert users may create or improve annotations. Specifically, NeuroNER addresses two main use cases:

- creating new annotations from scratch, e.g. if the goal is to annotate a dataset for which no gold label is available,

- improving the annotations of an already labeled dataset: the annotations may have been done by another human or by a previous run of NeuroNER.

In the latter case, the user may use NeuroNER interactively, by iterating between manually improving the annotations and running the NeuroNER engine with the new annotations to obtain more accurate annotations.

NeuroNER can take as input datasets in the BRAT format, and outputs BRAT-formatted predictions, which makes it easy to start training directly from the annotations as well as visualize and analyze the predictions. We chose BRAT for two main reasons: it is easy to use, and it can be deployed as a web application, which allows crowdsourcing. As a result, the user may quickly gather a vast amount of annotations by using crowdsourcing marketplaces such as Amazon Mechanical Turk (Buhrmester et al., 2011) and CrowdFlower (Finin et al., 2010).

One limitation of NeuroNER is that it does not allow overlapping annotations in the BRAT format. However, NeuroNER is not restricted to named-entity recognition: it may be used for any sequence labeling, such as part-of-speech tagging and chunking.

3.5 System requirements

NeuroNER runs on Linux, Mac OS X, and Microsoft Windows. It requires Python 3.5, TensorFlow 1.0 (Abadi et al., 2016), scikit-learn (Pedregosa et al., 2011), and BRAT. A setup script is provided to make the installation straightforward. It can use the GPU if available, and the number of CPU threads and GPUs to use can be specified in the configuration file.

3.6 Performances

To assess the quality of NeuroNER's predictions, we use two publicly and freely available datasets for named-entity recognition: CoNLL 2003 and

Model	CoNLL 2003	i2b2 2014
Best published	90.9	97.9
NeuroNER	90.5	97.7

Table 1: F1-scores (%) on the test set comparing NeuroNER with the best published methods in the literature, viz. (Passos et al., 2014) for CoNLL 2003, (Dernoncourt et al., 2016) for i2b2 2014.

i2b2 2014. CoNLL 2003 (Tjong Kim Sang and De Meulder, 2003) is a widely studied dataset with 4 usual types of entity: persons, organizations, locations and miscellaneous names. We use the English version.

The i2b2 2014 dataset (Stubbs et al., 2015) was released as part of the 2014 i2b2/UTHealth shared task Track 1. It is the largest publicly available dataset for de-identification, which is a form of named-entity recognition where the entities are protected health information such as patients' names and patients' phone numbers. 22 systems were submitted for this shared task.

Table 1 compares NeuroNER with state-of-the-art systems on CoNLL 2003 and i2b2 2014. Although the hyperparameters of NeuroNER were not optimized for these datasets (the default hyperparameters were used), the performances of NeuroNER are on par with the state-of-the-art systems.

4   Conclusions

In this article we have presented NeuroNER, an ANN-based NER tool that is accessible to non-expert users and yields state-of-the-art results. Addressing the need of many users who want to create or improve annotations, NeuroNER smoothly integrates with the web-based annotation tool BRAT.

References

Martín Abadi, Ashish Agarwal, Paul Barham, Eugene Brevdo, Zhifeng Chen, Craig Citro, Greg S Corrado, Andy Davis, Jeffrey Dean, Matthieu Devin, et al. 2016. Tensorflow: Large-scale machine learning on heterogeneous distributed systems. *arXiv preprint arXiv:1603.04467*.

John Aberdeen, Samuel Bayer, Reyyan Yeniterzi, Ben Wellner, Cheryl Clark, David Hanauer, Bradley Malin, and Lynette Hirschman. 2010. The mitre identification scrubber toolkit: design, training, and assessment. *International journal of medical informatics*, 79(12):849–859.

Masayuki Asahara and Yuji Matsumoto. 2003. Japanese named entity extraction with redundant morphological analysis. In *Proceedings of the 2003 Conference of the North American Chapter of the Association for Computational Linguistics on Human Language Technology-Volume 1*, pages 8–15. Association for Computational Linguistics.

Yassine Benajiba and Paolo Rosso. 2008. Arabic named entity recognition using conditional random fields. In *Proc. of Workshop on HLT & NLP within the Arabic World, LREC*, volume 8, pages 143–153. Citeseer.

Daniel M Bikel, Scott Miller, Richard Schwartz, and Ralph Weischedel. 1997. Nymble: a high-performance learning name-finder. In *Proceedings of the fifth conference on Applied natural language processing*, pages 194–201. Association for Computational Linguistics.

William Boag, Kevin Wacome, Tristan Naumann, and Anna Rumshisky. 2015. Cliner: A lightweight tool for clinical named entity recognition. *AMIA Joint Summits on Clinical Research Informatics (poster)*.

Andrew Borthwick, John Sterling, Eugene Agichtein, and Ralph Grishman. 1998. Nyu: Description of the mene named entity system as used in muc-7. In *In Proceedings of the Seventh Message Understanding Conference (MUC-7)*. Citeseer.

Michael Buhrmester, Tracy Kwang, and Samuel D Gosling. 2011. Amazon's mechanical turk a new source of inexpensive, yet high-quality, data? *Perspectives on psychological science*, 6(1):3–5.

Jeffrey T Chang, Hinrich Schütze, and Russ B Altman. 2004. Gapscore: finding gene and protein names one word at a time. *Bioinformatics*, 20(2):216–225.

HC Cho, N Okazaki, M Miwa, and J Tsujii. 2010. Nersuite: a named entity recognition toolkit. *Tsujii Laboratory, Department of Information Science, University of Tokyo, Tokyo, Japan*.

Ronan Collobert, Jason Weston, Léon Bottou, Michael Karlen, Koray Kavukcuoglu, and Pavel Kuksa. 2011. Natural language processing (almost) from scratch. *The Journal of Machine Learning Research*, 12:2493–2537.

Hamish Cunningham, Yorick Wilks, and Robert J Gaizauskas. 1996. Gate: a general architecture for text engineering. In *Proceedings of the 16th conference on Computational linguistics-Volume 2*, pages 1057–1060. Association for Computational Linguistics.

Franck Dernoncourt, Ji Young Lee, Ozlem Uzuner, and Peter Szolovits. 2016. De-identification of patient notes with recurrent neural networks. *Journal of the American Medical Informatics Association (JAMIA)*.

Michele Filannino, Gavin Brown, and Goran Nenadic. 2013. Mantime: Temporal expression identification and normalization in the tempeval-3 challenge. *arXiv preprint arXiv:1304.7942*.

Tim Finin, Will Murnane, Anand Karandikar, Nicholas Keller, Justin Martineau, and Mark Dredze. 2010. Annotating named entities in twitter data with crowdsourcing. In *Proceedings of the NAACL HLT 2010 Workshop on Creating Speech and Language Data with Amazon's Mechanical Turk*, pages 80–88. Association for Computational Linguistics.

Jenny Rose Finkel, Trond Grenager, and Christopher Manning. 2005. Incorporating non-local information into information extraction systems by gibbs sampling. In *Proceedings of the 43rd annual meeting on association for computational linguistics*, pages 363–370. Association for Computational Linguistics.

N Kumar and Pushpak Bhattacharyya. 2006. Named entity recognition in Hindi using MEMM. *Techbical Report, IIT Mumbai*.

Matthieu Labeau, Kevin Löser, and Alexandre Allauzen. 2015. Non-lexical neural architecture for fine-grained POS tagging. In *Proceedings of the 2015 Conference on Empirical Methods in Natural Language Processing*, pages 232–237, Lisbon, Portugal. Association for Computational Linguistics.

Guillaume Lample, Miguel Ballesteros, Sandeep Subramanian, Kazuya Kawakami, and Chris Dyer. 2016. Neural architectures for named entity recognition. *arXiv preprint arXiv:1603.01360*.

Robert Leaman, Graciela Gonzalez, et al. 2008. Banner: an executable survey of advances in biomedical named entity recognition. In *Pacific symposium on biocomputing*, volume 13, pages 652–663.

Ji Young Lee, Franck Dernoncourt, Ozlem Uzuner, and Peter Szolovits. 2016. Feature-augmented neural networks for patient note de-identification. *COLING Clinical NLP*.

Diana Maynard and Hamish Cunningham. 2003. Multilingual adaptations of annie, a reusable information extraction tool. In *Proceedings of the tenth conference on European chapter of the Association for Computational Linguistics-Volume 2*, pages 219–222. Association for Computational Linguistics.

Andrew McCallum and Wei Li. 2003. Early results for named entity recognition with conditional random fields, feature induction and web-enhanced lexicons. In *Proceedings of the seventh conference on Natural language learning at HLT-NAACL 2003-Volume 4*, pages 188–191. Association for Computational Linguistics.

Tomas Mikolov, Kai Chen, Greg Corrado, and Jeffrey Dean. 2013a. Efficient estimation of word representations in vector space. *arXiv preprint arXiv:1301.3781*.

Tomas Mikolov, Ilya Sutskever, Kai Chen, Greg S Corrado, and Jeff Dean. 2013b. Distributed representations of words and phrases and their compositionality. In *Advances in neural information processing systems*, pages 3111–3119.

David Nadeau and Satoshi Sekine. 2007. A survey of named entity recognition and classification. *Lingvisticae Investigationes*, 30(1):3–26.

Alexandre Passos, Vineet Kumar, and Andrew McCallum. 2014. Lexicon infused phrase embeddings for named entity resolution. In *Proceedings of the Eighteenth Conference on Computational Natural Language Learning*, pages 78–86, Ann Arbor, Michigan. Association for Computational Linguistics.

Fabian Pedregosa, Gaël Varoquaux, Alexandre Gramfort, Vincent Michel, Bertrand Thirion, Olivier Grisel, Mathieu Blondel, Peter Prettenhofer, Ron Weiss, Vincent Dubourg, et al. 2011. Scikit-learn: Machine learning in python. *Journal of Machine Learning Research*, 12(Oct):2825–2830.

Jeffrey Pennington, Richard Socher, and Christopher D Manning. 2014. GloVe: global vectors for word representation. *Proceedings of the Empiricial Methods in Natural Language Processing (EMNLP 2014)*, 12:1532–1543.

Guergana K Savova, James J Masanz, Philip V Ogren, Jiaping Zheng, Sunghwan Sohn, Karin C Kipper-Schuler, and Christopher G Chute. 2010. Mayo clinical text analysis and knowledge extraction system (ctakes): architecture, component evaluation and applications. *Journal of the American Medical Informatics Association*, 17(5):507–513.

Satoshi Sekine et al. 1998. Nyu: Description of the japanese ne system used for met-2. In *Proc. Message Understanding Conference*.

Burr Settles. 2005. ABNER: An open source tool for automatically tagging genes, proteins, and other entity names in text. *Bioinformatics*, 21(14):3191–3192.

Pontus Stenetorp, Sampo Pyysalo, Goran Topić, Tomoko Ohta, Sophia Ananiadou, and Jun'ichi Tsujii. 2012. Brat: a web-based tool for nlp-assisted text annotation. In *Proceedings of the Demonstrations at the 13th Conference of the European Chapter of the Association for Computational Linguistics*, pages 102–107. Association for Computational Linguistics.

Amber Stubbs, Christopher Kotfila, and Özlem Uzuner. 2015. Automated systems for the de-identification of longitudinal clinical narratives: Overview of 2014 i2b2/uthealth shared task track 1. *Journal of biomedical informatics*, 58:S11–S19.

Erik F Tjong Kim Sang and Fien De Meulder. 2003. Introduction to the conll-2003 shared task: Language-independent named entity recognition. In *Proceedings of the seventh conference on Natural language learning at HLT-NAACL 2003-Volume 4*, pages 142–147. Association for Computational Linguistics.

Richard Tzong-Han Tsai, Cheng-Lung Sung, Hong-Jie Dai, Hsieh-Chuan Hung, Ting-Yi Sung, and Wen-Lian Hsu. 2006. Nerbio: using selected word conjunctions, term normalization, and global patterns to improve biomedical named entity recognition. *BMC bioinformatics*, 7(5):S11.

SUPWSD: A Flexible Toolkit for
Supervised Word Sense Disambiguation

Simone Papandrea, Alessandro Raganato and **Claudio Delli Bovi**
Department of Computer Science
Sapienza University of Rome
`papandrea.simone@gmail.com`
`{raganato,dellibovi}@di.uniroma1.it`

Abstract

In this demonstration we present SUP-WSD, a Java API for supervised Word Sense Disambiguation (WSD). This toolkit includes the implementation of a state-of-the-art supervised WSD system, together with a Natural Language Processing pipeline for preprocessing and feature extraction. Our aim is to provide an easy-to-use tool for the research community, designed to be modular, fast and scalable for training and testing on large datasets. The source code of SUPWSD is available at `http://github.com/SI3P/SupWSD`.

1 Introduction

Word Sense Disambiguation (Navigli, 2009, WSD), is one of the long-standing challenges of Natural Language Understanding. Given a word in context and a pre-specified sense inventory, the task of WSD is to determine the intended meaning of that word depending on the context. Several WSD approaches have been proposed over the years and extensively studied by the research community, ranging from knowledge-based systems to semi-supervised and fully supervised models (Agirre et al., 2014; Moro et al., 2014; Taghipour and Ng, 2015b; Iacobacci et al., 2016). Nowadays a new line of research is emerging, and WSD is gradually shifting from a purely monolingual (i.e. English) setup to a wider multilingual setting (Navigli and Moro, 2014; Moro and Navigli, 2015). Since scaling up to multiple languages is considerably easier for knowledge-based systems, as they do not require sense-annotated training data, various efforts have been made towards the automatic construction of high-quality sense-annotated corpora for multiple lan-

guages (Otegi et al., 2016; Delli Bovi et al., 2017), aimed at overcoming the so-called *knowledge acquisition bottleneck* of supervised models (Pilehvar and Navigli, 2014). These efforts include the use of Wikipedia, which can be considered a full-fledged, manually sense-annotated resource for numerous languages, and hence exploited as training data (Dandala et al., 2013).

Beside the automatic harvesting of sense-annotated data for different languages, a variety of multilingual preprocessing pipelines has also been developed across the years (Padr and Stanilovsky, 2012; Agerri et al., 2014; Manning et al., 2014). To date, however, very few attempts have been made to integrate these data and tools with a supervised WSD framework; as a result, multilingual WSD has been almost exclusively tackled with knowledge-based systems, despite the fact that supervised models have been proved to consistently outperform knowledge-based ones in all standard benchmarks (Raganato et al., 2017). As regards supervised WSD, It Makes Sense (Zhong and Ng, 2010, IMS) is indeed the de-facto state-of-the-art system used for comparison in WSD, but it is available only for English, with the last major update dating back to 2010.

The publicly available implementation of IMS also suffers from two crucial drawbacks: (i) the design of the software makes the current code difficult to extend (e.g. with classes taking as input more than 15 parameters); (ii) the implementation is not optimized for larger datasets, being rather time- and resource-consuming. These difficulties hamper the work of contributors willing to update it, as well as the effort of researchers that would like to use it with languages other than English.

In this paper we present SUPWSD, whose objective is to overcome the aforementioned drawbacks, and facilitate the use of a supervised WSD software for both end users and researchers. SUP-

103

Proceedings of the 2017 EMNLP System Demonstrations, pages 103–108
Copenhagen, Denmark, September 7–11, 2017. ©2017 Association for Computational Linguistics

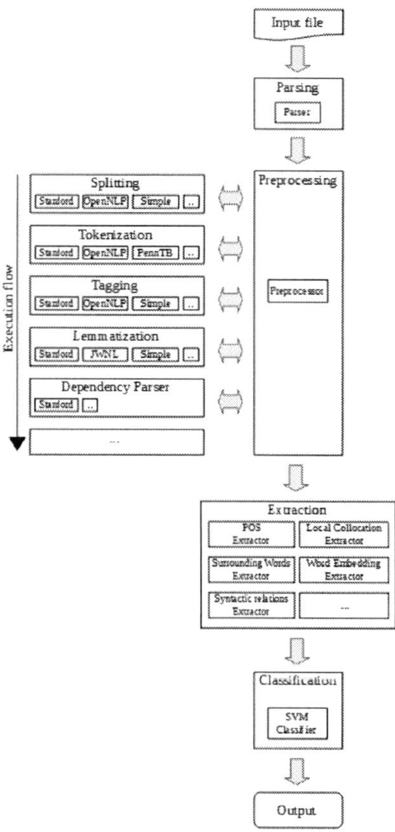

Figure 1: Architecture design of SUPWSD.

WSD is designed to be modular and highly flexible, enabling contributors to extend it with ease. Its usage is simple and immediate: it is based on a jar file with only 2 commands and 3 parameters, along with an XML configuration file for specifying customized settings. SUPWSD supports the most widely used preprocessing tools in the research community: Stanford coreNLP (Manning et al., 2014), openNLP[1], and TreeTagger (Schmid, 2013); as such, SUPWSD can directly handle all the languages supported by these tools. Finally, its architecture design relies on commonly used design patterns in Java (such as Factory and Observer among others), which make it flexible for a programmatic use and easily expandable.

2 SUPWSD: Architecture

In this section we describe the workflow of SUPWSD. Figure 1 shows the architecture design of our framework: it is composed of four main modules, common for both the training and testing phase: (i) input parsing, (ii) text preprocessing, (iii) features extraction and (iv) classification.

Input parsing. Given either a plain text or an XML file as input, SUPWSD first parses the file and extracts groups of sentences to provide them as input for the subsequent text preprocessing module. Sentence grouping is used to parallelize the preprocessing module's execution and to make it less memory-intensive. Input files are loaded in memory using a lazy procedure (i.e. the parser does not load the file entirely at once, but processes it according to the segments of interest) which enables a smoother handling of large datasets. The parser specification depends on the format of the input file via a Factory patterns, in such a way that new additional parsers can easily be implemented and seamlessly integrated in the workflow (c.f. Section 3). SUPWSD currently features 6 different parsers, targeted to the various formats of the Senseval/SemEval WSD competition (both all-words and lexical sample), along with a parser for plain text.

Text preprocessing. The text preprocessing module runs the pre-specified preprocessing pipeline on the input text, all the way from sentence splitting to dependency parsing, and retrieves the data used by the feature extraction module to construct the features. This module consists of a five-step pipeline: sentence splitting, tokenization, part-of-speech tagging, lemmatization and dependency parsing. SUPWSD currently supports two preprocessing options: *Stanford* and *Hybrid*. Both can be switched on and off using the configuration file. The former (default choice) provides a wrapper for the Stanford NLP pipeline, and selects the default Stanford model for each component. The latter, instead, enables the user to customize their model choice for each and every preprocessing step. For instance, one possible customization is to use the openNLP models for tokenization and sentence splitting, and the Stanford models for part-of-speech tagging and lemmatization. In addition, the framework enables the user to provide an input text where preprocessing information is already included.

The communication between the input parsing and the text preprocessing modules (Figure 1) is handled by the `Analyzer`, a component that handles a fixed thread pool and outputs the feature information collected from the input text.

```xml
<?xml version="1.0" encoding="UTF-8"?>
<supWSD xmlns:xsi="http://www.w3.org/2001/XMLSchema-instance"
    xsi:noNamespaceSchemaLocation="supWSD.xsd">
    <working_directory>path</working_directory>
    <parser mns="file">lexical|senseval|semeval7|semeval13|semeval15|plain</parser>
    <preprocessing>
        <splitter model="">stanford|open_nlp|simple|none</splitter>
        <tokenizer model="">stanford|open_nlp|penn_tree_bank|simple|none</tokenizer>
        <tagger model="">stanford|open_nlp|tree_tagger|simple|none</tagger>
        <lemmatizer model="">stanford|jwnl|tree_tagger|simple|none</lemmatizer>
        <dependency_parser model="">stanford|none</dependency_parser>
    </preprocessing>
    <extraction>
        <features>
            <pos_tags cutoff="0">true|false</pos_tags>
            <local_collocations cutoff="0">true|false</local_collocations>
            <surrounding_words cutoff="0" window="1">true|false</surrounding_words>
            <word_embeddings strategy="EXP|FRA|AVG" window="10" vectors="file" vocab="file"
                                   cache="[0...1]">true|false</word_embeddings>
            <syntactic_relations>true|false</syntactic_relations>
        </features>
    </extraction>
    <classifier>liblinear|libsvm</classifier>
    <writer>all|single|plain</writer>
    <sense_inventory dict="file">wordnet|babelnet|none</sense_inventory>
</supWSD>
```

Figure 2: The XML configuration file used by SUPWSD.

Features extraction. The feature extraction
module takes as input the data extracted at preprocessing time, and constructs a set of features
that will be used in the subsequent stage to train
the actual SUPWSD model. As in the previous
stage, the user can rely on the configuration file
(Figure 2) to select which features to enable or
disable. SUPWSD currently supports five standard features: (i) *part-of-speech tag* of the target
word and part-of-speech tags surrounding the target word (with a left and a right window of length
3); (ii) *surrounding words*, i.e. the set of word
tokens (excluding stopwords from a pre-specified
list) appearing in the context of the target word;
(iii) *local collocations*, i.e. ordered sequences of
tokens around the target word; (iv) pre-trained
word embedding, integrated according to three different strategies, as in Iacobacci et al. (2016);[2] (v)
syntactic relations, i.e. a set of features based on
the dependency tree of the sentence, as in Lee and
Ng (2002). SUPWSD allows the user to select appropriate cutoff parameters for features (i) to (iii),
in order to filter them out according to a minimum
frequency threshold.

Classification. The classification module con-
stitutes the last stage of the SUPWSD pipeline.
On the basis of the feature set constructed in the
previous stage, this module leverages an off-the-
shelf machine learning library to run a classification algorithm and generate a model for each
sense-annotated word type in the input text. The
current version of SUPWSD relies on two widely
used machine learning frameworks: LIBLIN-
EAR[3] and LIBSVM[4]. The classification module
of SUPWSD operates on top of these two libraries.

Using the configuration file (Figure 2) the user
can select which library to use and, at the same
time, choose the underlying sense inventory. The
current version of SUPWSD supports two sense
inventories: WordNet (Miller et al., 1990)[5] and
BabelNet (Navigli and Ponzetto, 2012)[6]. Specifying a sense inventory enables SUPWSD to exploit
the Most Frequent Sense (MFS) back-off strategy
at test time for those target words for which no
training data are available.[7] If no sense inventory
is specified, the model will not provide an answer
for those target words.

3 SUPWSD: Adding New Modules

In this section we illustrate how to implement new
modules for SUPWSD and integrate them into the
framework at various stages of the pipeline.

Adding a new input parser. In order to
integrate a new XML parser, it is enough
to extend the `XMLHandler` class and implement the methods `startElement`,
`endElement` and `characters` (see the
example in Figure 3). With the global variable
`mAnnotationListener`, the programmatic
user can directly specify when to transmit the
parsed text to the text preprocessing module.
Instead, in order to integrate a general parser for
custom text, it is enough to extend the `Parser`

---

[2] We implemented a cache mechanism in order to deal efficiently with large word embedding files.

[3] http://liblinear.bwaldvogel.de
[4] https://www.csie.ntu.edu.tw/~cjlin/
libsvm
[5] https://wordnet.princeton.edu
[6] http://babelnet.org
[7] The MFS is based on the lexicographic order provided
by the sense inventory (either WordNet or BabelNet).

```java
public class NewXMLHandler extends XMLHandler {

    @Override
    public void startElement(String uri, String localName,
            String name, Attributes attributes) throws SAXException {

        NewLexicalTags tag=NewLexicalTags.valueOf(name.toUpperCase());

        switch (tag) {
            ...
        }
        this.push(tag);

    }

    @Override
    public void endElement(String uri, String localName, String name)
            throws SAXException {

        NewLexicalTags tag=NewLexicalTags.valueOf(name.toUpperCase());

        switch (tag) {
            ...
            case TEXT:
                this.mAnnotationListener.notifyAnnotations(...);
        }
        this.pop();

    }

    @Override
    public void characters(char ch[], int start, int length)
            throws SAXException {

        String sentence = new String(ch, start, length);
        switch ((NewLexicalTags)this.get()) {
            ...
        }

    }
}
```

Figure 3: An example of XML parser.

class and implement the `parse` method. An example is provided by the `PlainParser` class that implements a parser for a plain textual file.

Adding a new preprocessing module. To add a new preprocessing module into the pipeline, it is enough to implement the interfaces in the package `modules.preprocessing.units`. It is also possible to add a brand new step to the pipeline (e.g. a Named Entity Recognition module) by extending the class `Unit` and implementing the methods to load the models asynchronously.

```java
public abstract class FeatureExtractor {

    private final int mCutOff;

    public FeatureExtractor(int cutoff){

        this.mCutOff=cutoff;
    }

    public final int getCutOff(){

        return this.mCutOff;
    }

    public abstract void load() throws Exception
    public abstract void unload();
    public abstract Class<? extends Feature> getFeatureClass();
    public abstract Collection<Feature> extract(Lexel lexel,
            Annotation annotation);

}
```

Figure 4: The abstract class modeling a feature extractor.

Adding a new feature. A new feature for SUP-WSD can be implemented with a two-step procedure. The first step consists in creating a class

```java
public abstract class Classifier<T,V> {

    public abstract Object train(AmbiguityTrain ambiguity);
    protected abstract double[] predict(T model, V[] featuresNodes);
    protected abstract V[] getFeatureNodes(SortedSet<Feature> features);

    public final Collection<Result> evaluate(AmbiguityTest ambiguity,
            Object model,String cls) {[]
```

Figure 5: The abstract class modeling a classifier.

that extends the abstract class `Feature`. The builder of this class requires a unique key and a name. It is also possible to set a default value for the feature by implementing the method `getDefaultValue`. The second step consists in implementing an extractor for the new feature via the abstract class `FeatureExtractor` (Figure 4). Each `FeatureExtractor` has a cut-off value and declares the name of the class through the method `getFeatureClass`.

Adding a new classifier. A new classifier for SUPWSD can be implemented by extending the generic abstract class `Classifier` (Figure 5), which declares the methods to train and test the models. Feature conversion is carried out with the generic method `getFeatureNodes`.

```
$ supWSD.jar train config.xml corpus keys
$ supWSD.jar test  config.xml corpus keys
```
Figure 6: Command line usage for SUPWSD.

4 SUPWSD: Usage

SUPWSD can be used effectively via the command line with just 4 parameters (Figure 6): the first parameter toggles between the train and test mode; the second parameter contains the path to the configuration file; the third and fourth parameters contain the paths to the dataset and the associated key file (i.e. the file containing the annotated senses for each target word) respectively.

Figure 2 shows an example configuration file for SUPWSD. As illustrated throughout Section 2, the SUPWSD pipeline is entirely customizable by changing these configuration parameters, and allows the user to employ specific settings at each stage of the pipeline (from preprocessing to actual classification). The `working directory` tag encodes the path in the file system where the trained models are to be saved. Finally, the `writer` tag enables the user to choose the preferred way of printing the test results (e.g. with or without confidence scores for each sense).

SUPWSD can also be used programmatically through its Java API, either using the toolkit (the

Tr. Corpus	System	Senseval-2	Senseval-3	SemEval-07	SemEval-13	SemEval-15
SemCor	IMS	70.9	69.3	61.3	65.3	69.5
	SupWSD	71.3	68.8	60.2	65.8	70.0
	IMS+emb	71.0	69.3	60.9	**67.3**	71.3
	SupWSD+emb	**72.7**	**70.6**	63.1	66.8	71.8
	IMS$_{-s}$+emb	72.2	70.4	62.6	65.9	71.5
	SupWSD$_{-s}$+emb	72.2	70.3	**63.3**	66.1	71.6
	Context2Vec	71.8	69.1	61.3	65.6	**71.9**
	MFS	65.6	66.0	54.5	63.8	67.1
SemCor + OMSTI	IMS	72.8	69.2	60.0	65.0	69.3
	SupWSD	72.6	68.9	59.6	64.9	69.5
	IMS+emb	70.8	68.9	58.5	66.3	69.7
	SupWSD+emb	**73.8**	**70.8**	**64.2**	**67.2**	71.5
	IMS$_{-s}$+emb	73.3	69.6	61.1	66.7	70.4
	SupWSD$_{-s}$+emb	73.1	70.5	62.2	66.4	70.9
	Context2Vec	72.3	68.2	61.5	**67.2**	**71.7**
	MFS	66.5	60.4	52.3	62.6	64.2

Table 1: F-scores (%) of different models in five all-words WSD datasets.

main class `SupWSD`, provided with the two static methods `train` and `test`, shares the same usage of the command line interface) or using an HTTP RESTful service.

5 Evaluation

We evaluated SupWSD on the evaluation framework of Raganato et al. (2017)[8], which includes five test sets from the Senseval/Semeval series and two training corpus of different size, i.e. Sem-Cor (Miller et al., 1993) and OMSTI (Taghipour and Ng, 2015a). As sense inventory, we used WordNet 3.0 (Miller et al., 1990) for all open-class parts of speech. We compared SupWSD with the original implementation of IMS, including the best configurations reported in Iacobacci et al. (2016) which exploit word embedding as features. As shown in Table 1, the performance of SupWSD consistently matches up to the original implementation of IMS in terms of F-Measure, sometimes even outperforming its competitor by a considerable margin; this suggests that a neat and flexible implementation not only brings benefits in terms of usability of the software, but also impacts on the accuracy of the model.

5.1 Speed Comparisons

We additionally carried out an experimental evaluation on the performance of SupWSD in terms of execution time. As in the previous experiment, we compared SupWSD with IMS and,

	IMS	SupWSD
train Semcor/sec.	~ 360	~ 120
train Semcor+OMSTI/sec.	~ 3000	~ 510
test/sec.	~ 110	~ 22

Table 2: Speed comparison for both the training and testing phases.

given that both implementations are written in Java, we tested their programmatic usage within a Java program. We relied on a testing corpus with 1M words and more than 250K target instances to disambiguate, and we used both frameworks on SemCor and OMSTI as training sets. All experiments were performed using an Intel i7-4930K CPU 3.40GHz twelve-core machine. Figures in Table 2 show a considerable gain in execution time achieved by SupWSD, which is around 3 times faster than IMS on Semcor, and almost 6 times faster than IMS on OMSTI.

6 Conclusion and Release

In this demonstration we presented SupWSD, a flexible toolkit for supervised Word Sense Disambiguation which is designed to be modular, highly customizable and easy to both use and extend for end users and researchers. Furthermore, beside the Java API, SupWSD provides an HTTP RESTful service for programmatic access to the SupWSD framework and the pre-trained models.

Our experimental evaluation showed that, in addition to its flexibility, SupWSD can replicate or outperform the state-of-the-art results reported by

---

[8]http://lcl.uniroma1.it/wsdeval

the best supervised models on standard benchmarks, while at the same time being optimized in terms of execution time.

The SUPWSD framework (including the source code, the pre-trained models, and an online demo) is available at `http://github.com/SI3P/SupWSD`. We release the toolkit here described under the GNU General Public License v3.0, whereas the RESTful service is licensed under a Creative Commons Attribution-Non Commercial-Share Alike 3.0 License.

Acknowledgments

The authors gratefully acknowledge the support of the Sapienza Research Grant 'Avvio alla Ricerca 2016'. 

References

Rodrigo Agerri, Josu Bermudez, and German Rigau. 2014. Ixa pipeline: Efficient and ready to use multilingual nlp tools. In *LREC*, pages 3823–3828.

Eneko Agirre, Oier Lopez de Lacalle, and Aitor Soroa. 2014. Random Walks for Knowledge-Based Word Sense Disambiguation. *Computational Linguistics*, 40(1):57–84.

Bharath Dandala, Rada Mihalcea, and Razvan Bunescu. 2013. Multilingual word sense disambiguation using wikipedia. In *Proceedings of the Sixth International Joint Conference on Natural Language Processing*, pages 498–506.

Claudio Delli Bovi, José Camacho-Collados, Alessandro Raganato, and Roberto Navigli. 2017. Eurosense: Automatic harvesting of multilingual sense annotations from parallel text. In *Proc. of ACL*.

Ignacio Iacobacci, Mohammad Taher Pilehvar, and Roberto Navigli. 2016. Embeddings for Word Sense Disambiguation: An Evaluation Study. In *Proc. of ACL*, pages 897–907.

Yoong Keok Lee and Hwee Tou Ng. 2002. An empirical evaluation of knowledge sources and learning algorithms for word sense disambiguation. In *Proc. of EMNLP*.

Christopher D. Manning, Mihai Surdeanu, John Bauer, Jenny Finkel, Steven J. Bethard, and David McClosky. 2014. The Stanford CoreNLP natural language processing toolkit. In *Association for Computational Linguistics (ACL) System Demonstrations*, pages 55–60.

George A. Miller, R.T. Beckwith, Christiane D. Fellbaum, D. Gross, and K. Miller. 1990. WordNet: an online lexical database. *International Journal of Lexicography*, 3(4):235–244.

George A. Miller, Claudia Leacock, Randee Tengi, and Ross T. Bunker. 1993. A semantic concordance. In *Proc. of HLT*, pages 303–308.

Andrea Moro and Roberto Navigli. 2015. SemEval-2015 Task 13: Multilingual All-Words Sense Disambiguation and Entity Linking. In *Proc. of SemEval*, pages 288–297.

Andrea Moro, Alessandro Raganato, and Roberto Navigli. 2014. Entity Linking meets Word Sense Disambiguation: a Unified Approach. *TACL*, 2:231–244.

Roberto Navigli. 2009. Word sense disambiguation: A survey. *ACM Computing Surveys*, 41(2):10.

Roberto Navigli and Andrea Moro. 2014. Multilingual word sense disambiguation and entity linking. In *COLING (Tutorials)*, pages 5–7.

Roberto Navigli and Simone Paolo Ponzetto. 2012. BabelNet: The Automatic Construction, Evaluation and Application of a Wide-Coverage Multilingual Semantic Network. *Artificial Intelligence*, 193:217–250.

Arantxa Otegi, Nora Aranberri, Antonio Branco, Jan Hajic, Steven Neale, Petya Osenova, Rita Pereira, Martin Popel, Joao Silva, Kiril Simov, and Eneko Agirre. 2016. QTLeap WSD/NED Corpora: Semantic Annotation of Parallel Corpora in Six Languages. In *Proceedings of LREC*, pages 3023–3030.

Llus Padr and Evgeny Stanilovsky. 2012. Freeling 3.0: Towards wider multilinguality. In *Proceedings of the Language Resources and Evaluation Conference (LREC 2012)*, Istanbul, Turkey. ELRA.

Mohammad Taher Pilehvar and Roberto Navigli. 2014. A large-scale pseudoword-based evaluation framework for state-of-the-art word sense disambiguation. *Computational Linguistics*, 40(4).

Alessandro Raganato, Jose Camacho-Collados, and Roberto Navigli. 2017. Word Sense Disambiguation: A Unified Evaluation Framework and Empirical Comparison. In *Proc. of EACL*.

Helmut Schmid. 2013. Probabilistic part-of-speech tagging using decision trees. In *New methods in language processing*, page 154. Routledge.

Kaveh Taghipour and Hwee Tou Ng. 2015a. One Million Sense-Tagged Instances for Word Sense Disambiguation and Induction. In *Proceedings of CoNLL*, pages 338–344.

Kaveh Taghipour and Hwee Tou Ng. 2015b. Semisupervised word sense disambiguation using word embeddings in general and specific domains. In *HLT-NAACL*, pages 314–323.

Zhi Zhong and Hwee Tou Ng. 2010. It makes sense: A wide-coverage word sense disambiguation system for free text. In *Proc. of ACL System Demonstrations*.

Interactive Abstractive Summarization for Event News Tweets

Ori Shapira[1], Hadar Ronen[2], Meni Adler[1], Yael Amsterdamer[1],
Judit Bar-Ilan[2] and Ido Dagan[1]

[1]Department of Computer Science, Bar-Ilan University, Ramat-Gan, Israel
[2]Department of Information Science, Bar-Ilan University, Ramat-Gan, Israel
{obspp18,hadarg,meni.adler}@gmail.com
yael.amsterdamer@biu.ac.il, judit.bar-ilan@biu.ac.il, dagan@cs.biu.ac.il

Abstract

We present a novel interactive summarization system that is based on *abstractive* summarization, derived from a recent consolidated knowledge representation for multiple texts. We incorporate a couple of interaction mechanisms, providing a bullet-style summary while allowing to attain the most important information first and interactively drill down to more specific details. A usability study of our implementation, for event news tweets, suggests the utility of our approach for text exploration.

1 Introduction

Multi-document summarization (MDS) techniques aim to assist readers in obtaining the most important information when reading multiple texts on a topic. The dominant MDS approach focuses on constructing a short summary of some targeted length, capturing the most important information, mimicking a manually-crafted "static" summary. As an alternative, few papers considered *interactive summarization*, where the presented information can be interactively explored by the user according to needs and interest (Christensen et al., 2014; Leuski et al., 2003; Yan et al., 2011).

In this paper we propose further contribution to this approach, focusing on interactive *abstractive* summarization. We suggest that an abstractive summarization approach, based on extracted "atomic" facts, is particularly suitable in the interactive setting as it allows more flexible information presentation. Intuitively, it makes more sense for a user to explore information at the level of individual facts, rather than the coarser level of full original sentences, as in prior work on interactive *extractive* summarization (see Section 6).

We build on the abstractive approach in supporting two useful modes of interaction. First, we present information in a *bullet-style summary*, where the most important information is initially displayed in bullet sentences, while further details may be obtained by *unfolding* additional bullets. Specifically, we implemented this approach for summarizing news tweets on a certain event along a time line (see Figure 2). Our second mode of interaction is *concept expansion*, which allows viewing complementary information about a concept via its alternative term mentions, while tracking the concept occurrences throughout the summary (see Figure 3). This information is hidden in static summaries that use original sentences (extractive) or a single term per concept (abstractive).

To facilitate the modular construction of interactive summaries, we utilize as input a consolidated representation of texts, in particular the recent Open Knowledge Representation (OKR) of Wities et al. (2017). Briefly, this representation captures the propositions of the texts, where co-referring concepts or propositions are collapsed together while keeping links to the original mentions (see Section 2). We leverage OKR structures to extract information at the level of atomic facts, to expand information from collapsed mentions and to retrieve the sources from which summary sentences were derived.

The novelties of our interactive scheme call for verifying its effectiveness and usefulness for users. For that, we have implemented our approach in a prototype system (Sections 3-4). This system automatically produces an interactive summary from input OKR data, which we assume to be parsed from original texts by an external black-box tool. We have examined our system through a set of standard usability tests (Brooke, 1996;

109

Proceedings of the 2017 EMNLP System Demonstrations, pages 109–114
Copenhagen, Denmark, September 7–11, 2017. ©2017 Association for Computational Linguistics

Lund, 2001) on gold standard OKR datasets that enabled us to study its contribution in isolation (Section 5). Our results show that the proposed system is highly valuable for readers, providing an appealing alternative to standard static summarization.

2 Preliminaries

As mentioned above, our interactive summarization system is based on a consolidated representation for the information in multiple texts. We next review some background on such representations and then describe the particular Open Knowledge Representation that we use.

2.1 Consolidated Representation

Motivated by summarization and text exploration, recent work considered the consolidation of textual information in various structures. As prominent examples, the studies of Liu et al. (2015) and Li et al. (2016) construct graph-based representations whose nodes are predicates or arguments thereof, extracted from the original text, and the predicate-argument relations are captured by edges. Identical or coreferring concepts are collapsed in a single node.

Rospocher et al. (2016) present a more supervised approach where concepts in the graph are linked to DBPedia[1] entries. This along with other metadata is used to detect coreferences and disambiguate concepts.

None of these works considers interactive summaries, and in particular none incorporates sufficient data for our modes of user interaction. We next briefly review the Open Knowledge Representation recently introduced by Wities et al. (2017), which is used by our system.

2.2 Open Knowledge Representation

We illustrate the components of the OKR formalism that are central to our summarization method via the example OKR structure in Figure 1 (see Wities et al. (2017) for full details). On the top, there are four original tweets. On the bottom, there are two consolidated propositions (marked P1 and P2) and four entities (marked E1-E4) derived from these tweets. The figure depicts three types of links captured in OKR, as follows.

Mention links connect each proposition or entity with its set of mention terms, namely, ev-

[1]http://wiki.dbpedia.org/

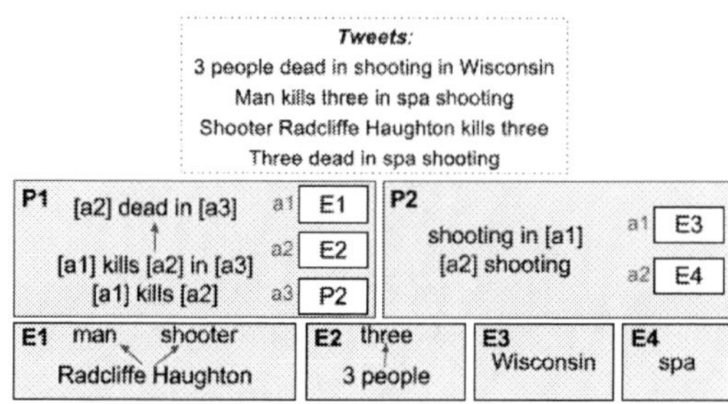

Figure 1: Four tweets on an event and their OKR structure.

ery form of reference to the entity/proposition throughout the texts. E.g., E1 from Figure 1 is mentioned in the tweets as *"man"*, *"shooter"* or *"Radcliffe Haughton"*. Mentions of propositions are stored as *templates* with argument placeholders, e.g., *"[a2] dead in [a3]"*. Through their mentions, entities and propositions are further linked with their occurrences in the original texts (omitted from the figure).

Argument links connect propositions with their arguments, which may be entities or (nested) propositions. Since a proposition may have several templates with different arguments, argument IDs (marked a1-a3 in P1) are used to capture coreferring arguments within the same proposition. For example, a2 and a3 appear as arguments in the two templates of P1, and refer to entity E2 and proposition P2 respectively.

Entailment links, marked by directed edges in Figure 1, track semantic entailment (in context) between different types of OKR components. For example, in E1, *"Radcliffe Haughton"* entails *"man"* or *"shooter"*, namely, the former is more specific/informative in the *given context*.

3 Comprehensive Summary Information

The architecture of our system consists of two main steps: (1) a preprocessing step in which we generate comprehensive summary information and (2) interactive display of selected information. In this section we describe the first step, which is based on an input OKR structure. Our UI for exploring the summary information interactively is described in the following section.

The general scheme for generating summary information in our system is as follows.

1. Partition the OKR propositions into *groups*.

2. Generate representative *summary sentences* for each group of propositions. These yield the bullet-style summary sentences.

3. Generate metadata for each representative sentence: a *knowledge score*, *concept expansions* and *timestamp*.

For the current system, we implemented a baseline method for each of these steps, which nonetheless achieved high satisfaction scores in the usability study (see Section 5).

We partition propositions, as captured in the OKR structure, into distinct groups such that the propositions of each group are (transitively) connected by argument links (ignoring link direction). E.g., in Figure 1, P2 is nested in P1 and thus the two are grouped together.

Next, for the "root" (i.e., not nested) proposition in a group, we generate alternative candidate sentences. This is done by filling, in its templates, all the possible combinations of relevant argument mentions, and recursively so for nested propositions. For example, for P1 we would generate *"[3 people] dead in [shooting in [Wisconsin]]"*, *"[3 people] dead in [[spa] shooting]"*, *"[Three] dead in [[spa] shooting]"*, and so on (22 candidate sentences in total).

From each set of candidates we choose one representative sentence. Importantly, this means that unlike bounded-length summary paragraphs our comprehensive summary information effectively covers *all* the propositions in the original texts. Instead of filtering upfront less salient information, it is only hidden initially in the UI and can be unfolded by the user (see Section 4). For a representative sentence, we choose a candidate with high *language model score*,[2] high *knowledge score* (defined below) and small length. This is done by optimizing a weighted sum of these factors.

The knowledge score of each sentence intuitively reflects how *common* its mentions are in the original texts as well as how *informative* (specific) they are, based on the OKR entailment links. Reconsidering Figure 1 for example, in the tweet *"Three dead in spa shooting"*, the concepts *"three"*, *"dead"* and *"spa shooting"* should be rewarded for appearing each in two tweets, but *"three"* should be rewarded less than *"3 people"*, which is more informative.

We use the following heuristically formulated equation to calculate the score of each generated

----

²For the language model, we trained an LSTM model (https://github.com/yandex/faster-rnnlm) on a collection of 100M tweets.

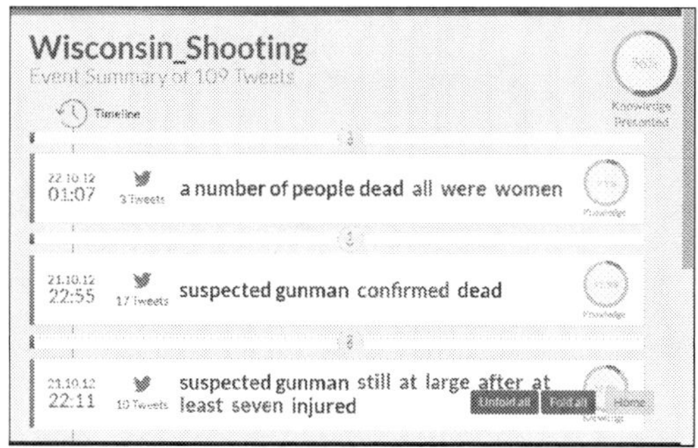

Figure 2: The initial view of a summary about a shooting in a Wisconsin spa covering 109 tweets. Ten generated sentences cover the most salient information throughout these tweets, and are ordered along the event timeline.

sentence s:

$$\text{score}(s) = \sum_{m \in \text{mentions}(s)} \alpha + \beta \cdot \text{depth}(m)$$

where $\text{mentions}(s)$ are the mentions of *predicates* and *entities* in the sentence. $\text{depth}(m)$ assigns a given mention m its depth in the relevant lexical entailment graph within the OKR. We have empirically set $\alpha = 1$, $\beta = 0.1$.

Each concept (entity or proposition) in the summary sentences is linked to its mentions and original texts using the OKR. The set of mentions is cleaned from duplicates (strings with small edit distance), yielding the *concept expansion* for sets with > 1 different mentions. This gives extra information about concepts that otherwise might have been missed. In Figure 3, for example, the *"suspected gunman"* is also identified as *"Jamaican"*. For the tweet summarization scenario, we also compute the *timestamp* of each representative sentence as the time of the first tweet mentioning its root proposition.

4   Interactive User Interface

We now describe the *web application*[3] we implemented, designed for the interactive exploration of multiple tweets on a specific event. Our backend is implemented in Python 2.7 and runs on a CentOS server. The frontend is implemented with the AngularJS library. JSON is used for data interchange.

Figure 2 shows the initial screen summarizing a set of 109 tweets about the shooting in a Wisconsin spa from our running example. Bullet-style sentences (generated as explained in Section 3) are

----

³http://u.cs.biu.ac.il/~shapirol/okr/

111

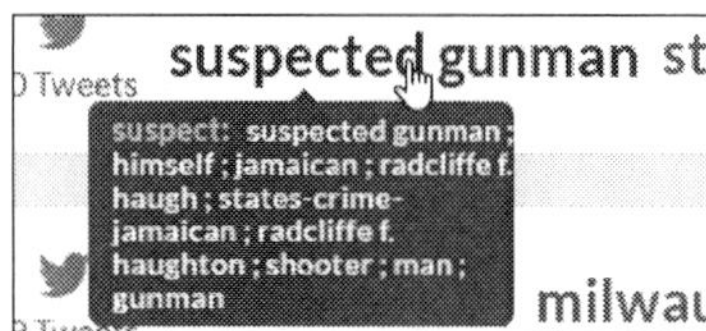

Figure 3: The *concept expansion* pop-up consisting of mentions referring to the same person as "suspected gunman", revealing further information (e.g. "Jamaican").

Figure 4: The tweets pop-up shows a scrollable pane with the source tweets for a generated sentence.

displayed along the event timeline, in descending order of their timestamps. As an indication of salience, to the right of each sentence, a pie chart shows the "percentage" of knowledge it covers according to its normalized knowledge score. The pie chart on the top shows the total knowledge "covered" by the currently visible sentences.

Initially, only sentences exceeding a certain information score threshold are displayed, as a concise bullet-style summary of the event. Other sentences are *folded* (e.g., between timestamps 01:07 and 22:55 in Figure 2). The user can then decide whether and which sentences to unfold, according to (a) time intervals of interest on the timeline; (b) the number of folded sentences, as indicated in the middle of the line; and (c) the amount of additional knowledge to be unfolded, which is highlighted on the top pie chart when hovering over folded sentences. By repeatedly unfolding sentences, the user can gradually discover the full timeline of the event with *all* consolidated data from the tweets.

Another mode of discovering information is via *concept expansion*: hovering over a highlighted concept (e.g., *"suspected gunman"*) opens a pop-up with different mentions of the same concept in the summary (Figure 3); clicking it further highlights all of its coreferences in the summary. Finally, the user can also click the Twitter icon to inspect the source tweets (Figure 4).

5   System Usability Tests

To assess and improve the value of our system, we have conducted two usability studies employing standard usability tests. The tests were performed on a dataset of human annotated OKR structures (of the form of Figure 1) released by Wities et al. (2017). We took their 6 largest clusters of event tweets, of about 100 tweets each. This gold-standard dataset enabled us to *study in isolation* the merits of our novel system. Given the positive results that we report below, we plan, in future work, to integrate and study our system in a fully automated pipeline.

5.1   Preliminary Usability Study

A first usability study was conducted with two goals: to examine the usefulness of our ideas and to understand user needs.

Methodology. The evaluation phase of a prototype requires only a few evaluators, according to the "discount" usability testing principle (Nielsen, 1993). Thus, six students not familiar with our project were recruited as evaluators. We asked them to perform a series of predefined tasks on one of the six selected events. During the system usage we observed the users' activity and employed a "think aloud" technique to obtain user remarks. Each on-screen activity was captured using "Debut Video Capturing Software"[4]. After performing all tasks, users were asked to fill the SU Scale (SUS) questionnaire (Brooke, 1996) for subjective usability evaluation.

Results. Table 1 lists the average scores obtained for each of the ten SUS questions, on a scale of 1 to 5. Overall, users found the prototype easy to use and showed willingness to use it frequently.

The SUS questionnaire yields an important single number in $[0, 100]$ representing a composite measure of the overall usability of the system. This number is calculated based on the ten question scores. As seen in Table 2, except for one dissatisfied user[5], the system received high scores ranging from 70 to 95. The observation and verbal reports during the test yielded a list of requirements that helped improve our prototype.

---

[4]http://www.nchsoftware.com/capture/

[5]This user had software quality assurance background and seemed to inspect for very minor software and user experience bugs, which we have later addressed.

SUS Question	Avg. Score
I think that I would like to use this system frequently.	3.83
I found the system unnecessarily complex.	2.33
I thought the system was easy to use.	3.33
I think that I would need the support of a technical person to be able to use this system.	2.17
I found the various functions in this system were well integrated.	3.83
I thought there was too much inconsistency in this system.	1.67
I would imagine that most people would learn to use this system very quickly.	3.5
I found the system very cumbersome to use.	1.33
I felt very confident using the system.	3.67
I needed to learn a lot of things before I could get going with this system.	2.17

Table 1: The ten SUS questions asked after the usability study and the average answer score on a scale of 1 to 5.

User	1	2	3	4	5	6
SUS Score	70	80	95	72.5	82.5	27.5

Table 2: SUS scores for each user, calculated based on the ten SUS question scores.

5.2 Comparative Usability Test

After updating our system to incorporate improvements obtained from the preliminary study, we conducted another comparative study to examine the relative effectiveness of our system.

Methlogy. We have compared our system, here denoted by IAS (for Interactive Abstractive Summary), with two baseline approaches:

- Tweet: a list of all the original tweets in the event dataset.
- Static: the full ordered list of sentences generated by our system (Section 3), with no interactive features nor metadata (such as concept expansion, knowledge scores, etc.).

As mentioned earlier, we have used the gold-standard OKR structures for 6 of the events released by Wities et al. (2017). Six users were each presented with two events in each interface (IAS, Tweet, Static), where the assignment of event to interface and order of interfaces were different for each user. The users explored the information that describes each event in the assigned interface, and at the end were asked to complete the USE Questionnaire (Lund, 2001).

Dimension	Tweet	Static	IAS
Usefulness	2.1	1.8	**2.3**
Knowledge Exploration	2.0	1.8	**2.6**
Satisfaction	2.0	1.7	**2.3**
Ease of Use	**2.5**	2.3	2.1
Ease of Learning	**2.7**	2.5	2.3

Table 3: USE questionnaire dimensions score comparison of the three system interfaces on a scale of 1 to 3.

This questionnaire required users to rank each of the three interfaces on a scale from 1 to 3 according to 33 statements. The original 30 USE statements represent four dimensions: Usefulness, Satisfaction, Ease of Use, and Ease of Learning. We added three statements to rank user's experience of knowledge exploration.[6]

Results. Table 3 shows the average rank of each interface in each of the examined dimensions. While our system was naturally somewhat more complex to use than the baselines, which only require reading, it consistently received the highest ranks in the dimensions of Usefulness, Satisfaction and Knowledge Exploration. This indicates that interactivity indeed provides substantial value to the user, regardless of the summary sentences (as evident by the comparison to baseline Static).

The ranked USE statements also serve as an indication for the *quality* of our summary when compared to the other baselines. Standard summarization metrics are designed for static summaries[7] and are thus not expressly adequate for our interactive system due to its content being dynamic and user-manipulated. Having demonstrated here that interactive summaries are useful, designing and conducting dedicated quality tests for interactive summaries is a priority in our future work.

6 Related Work

A vast body of work has been dedicated to the problem of multi-text summarization. We focus here on the rather few studies that enhance summarization with user interaction.

The iNeATS system (Leuski et al., 2003) was an early attempt for interactive summarization, allowing explicit control over parameters such as

---

[6] The three additional statements are: The system motivated me to actively explore more information; The system made me feel that I know the highlights of the event; The system helped me notice the important details of the event.

[7] The ROUGE and Pyramid methods are the common metrics to evaluate summaries.

length, participating elements, etc. Yan et al. (2011) have studied a more *implicit* approach, attempting to discover user preferences such as topics and contexts via user clicks. Both approaches involve repeatedly updating a summary paragraph based on user feedback.

The more recent SUMMA system (Christensen et al., 2014) resembles ours in supporting *hierarchical summarization*. Salient summary sentences are high in the hierarchy and further details can be discovered by drilling down into lower levels.

All of the aforementioned methods compute *extractive* summaries, which are composed of sentences from the original texts. In comparison, our *abstractive* approach has a few appealing advantages. Most importantly, this approach facilitates the construction of flexible bullet-style summaries since we are not confined to existing sentences, which may combine several atomic facts of varying saliency or require textual context. This, in turn, allows users to browse data at the level of atomic facts and avoids the need to regenerate the summary in order to incorporate user feedback.

7 Conclusion and Future Work

In this paper we presented a novel system for the interactive exploration of abstractive summary information. Our system builds on the Open Knowledge Representation (Wities et al., 2017) for consolidating the information of multiple texts, and produces a summary that fully captures this information. The interactive UI allows focusing on the most salient facts as well as gradually obtaining further details via different interaction modes. Our usability studies provide supportive evidence for the usefulness of our approach.

Our results shed light on a few important directions for future research. In general, our interactive abstractive method should be ported to other domains and types of corpora. E.g., while in the case of news tweets, sentence ordering was done along a timeline, the ordering of consolidated summary sentences may in general be a nontrivial task. Further, our approach for summary sentence generation can be enhanced, e.g., by using machine learning techniques to select the best representative sentences. For evaluation, we will design tests adequate for assessing the quality of an interactive summary, and use them in a more extensive user study that will incorporate a fully automated pipeline (i.e., an OKR parser).

Acknowledgments

This work was supported in part by grants from the MAGNET program of the Israeli Office of the Chief Scientist (OCS); the German Research Foundation through the German-Israeli Project Cooperation (DIP, grant DA 1600/1-1); by Contract HR0011-15-2-0025 with the US Defense Advanced Research Projects Agency (DARPA); by the BIU Center for Research in Applied Cryptography and Cyber Security in conjunction with the Israel National Cyber Bureau in the Prime Ministers Office; and by the Israel Science Foundation (grant No. 1157/16).

References

John Brooke. 1996. *SUS - "A quick and dirty" usability scale. Usability evaluation in industry*. CRC Press.

Janara Christensen, Stephen Soderland, Gagan Bansal, and Mausam. 2014. Hierarchical summarization: Scaling up multi-document summarization. In *ACL*.

Anton Leuski, Chin-Yew Lin, and Eduard H. Hovy. 2003. iNeATS: Interactive multi-document summarization. In *ACL*.

Wei Li, Lei He, and Hai Zhuge. 2016. Abstractive news summarization based on event semantic link network. In *COLING*.

Fei Liu, Jeffrey Flanigan, Sam Thomson, Norman M. Sadeh, and Noah A. Smith. 2015. Toward abstractive summarization using semantic representations. In *HLT-NAACL*.

Arnold M. Lund. 2001. Measuring usability with the USE questionnaire. *STC Usability SIG Newsletter*, 8(2).

Jakob Nielsen. 1993. *Usability engineering*. Academic Press.

Marco Rospocher, Marieke van Erp, Piek T. J. M. Vossen, Antske Fokkens, Itziar Aldabe, German Rigau, Aitor Soroa, Thomas Ploeger, and Tessel Bogaard. 2016. Building event-centric knowledge graphs from news. *J. Web Sem.*, 37-38.

Rachel Wities, Vered Shwartz, Gabriel Stanovsky, Meni Adler, Ori Shapira, Shyam Upadhyay, Dan Roth, Eugenio Martinez Camara, Iryna Gurevych, and Ido Dagan. 2017. A consolidated open knowledge representation for multiple texts. In *LSDSem, EACL*.

Rui Yan, Jian-Yun Nie, and Xiaoming Li. 2011. Summarize what you are interested in: An optimization framework for interactive personalized summarization. In *EMNLP*.

LANGPRO: Natural Language Theorem Prover

Lasha Abzianidze
CLCG, University of Groningen
The Netherlands
L.Abzianidze@rug.nl

Abstract

LangPro is an automated theorem prover for natural language.[1] Given a set of premises and a hypothesis, it is able to prove semantic relations between them. The prover is based on a version of analytic tableau method specially designed for natural logic. The proof procedure operates on logical forms that preserve linguistic expressions to a large extent. The nature of proofs is deductive and transparent. On the FraCaS and SICK textual entailment datasets, the prover achieves high results comparable to state-of-the-art.

1 Introduction

Nowadays many formal logics come with their own proof systems and with the automated theorem provers based on these systems. If we share Montagues's famous belief that there is "no important theoretical difference between natural languages and the artificial languages of logicians", then there plausibly exists a proof system for natural languages too. On the other hand, studies on Natural Logic seek a formal logic whose formulas are as close as possible to linguistic expressions. Inspired by these research ideas, Muskens (2010) proposed an analytic tableau system for natural logic, where higher-order logic based on a simple type theory is used as natural logic and a version of analytic tableau method is designed for it. Later, Abzianidze (2015b,a, 2016a) made the tableau system suitable for wide-coverage reasoning by extending it and implementing a theorem prover based on it.

This paper presents the Prolog implementation of the theorem prover, called LangPro, in detail and completes the previous publications in terms

---

[1] https://github.com/kovvalsky/LangPro

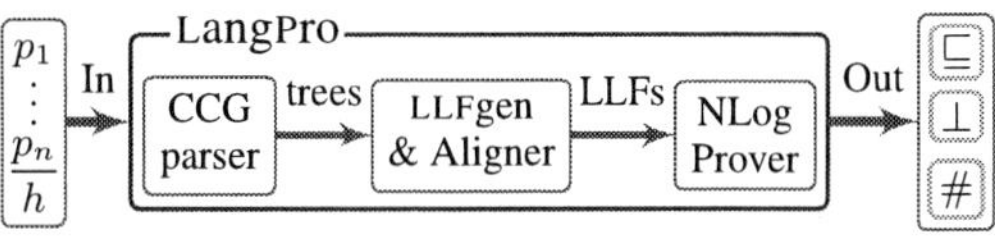

Figure 1: LangPro checks whether a set of premises $p_1, \ldots, p_n$ entails ($\sqsubseteq$), contradicts ($\bot$) or is neutral ($\#$) to a hypothesis h.

of the system description. The rest of the paper is organized as follows. First, we briefly introduce the tableau system and the employed natural logic. Then we characterize the architecture and functionality of LangPro (see Figure 1). Before concluding, we briefly compare the prover to the related textual entailment systems.

2 Natural Tableau

An *analytic tableau method* is a proof procedure which searches a model, i.e. a possible situation, satisfying a set of logic formulas. The search is performed by gradually applying inference rules, also called *tableau rules*, to the formulas. A tableau rule has antecedents and consequent and is easy to read, e.g., according to $\text{NO}_{\mathbb{T}}$ in Figure 3, if no A is B, then for any entity c, either it is not A or it is not B. A tableau proof, in short a *tableau*, is often depicted as an upside-down tree with initial formulas at its root (Figure 2). After each rule application, new inferred formulas are introduced in the tableau. Depending on the applied rules, the tableau can branch or grow in depth. A tableau branch models a situation that satisfies all the formulas in the branch. Closed branches, marked with ×, correspond to inconsistent situations. The search for a possible situation fails if all branches are closed—the tableau is closed.

The natural tableau is a tableau method for a

Proceedings of the 2017 EMNLP System Demonstrations, pages 115–120
Copenhagen, Denmark, September 7–11, 2017. ©2017 Association for Computational Linguistics

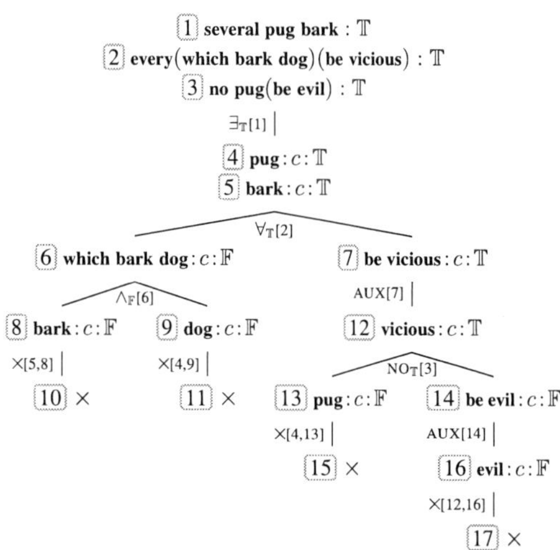

Figure 2: The tableau proves: *several pugs bark. every dog which barks is vicious. ⊥ no pug is evil.*

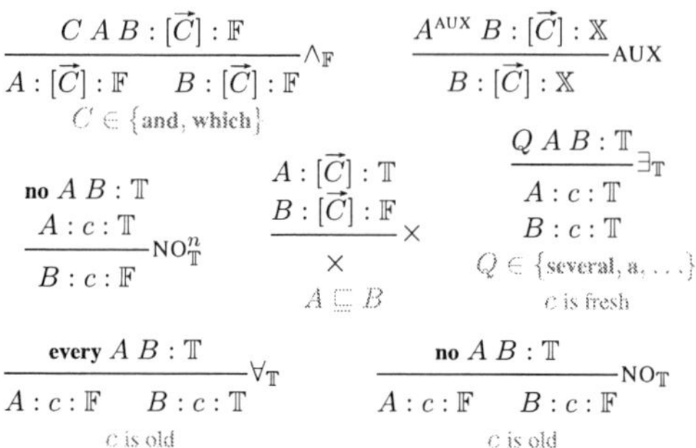

Figure 3: The inference rules employed in the tableau proof of Figure 2. An entity term is *old* (*fresh*) wrt a branch iff it is (not) in the branch.

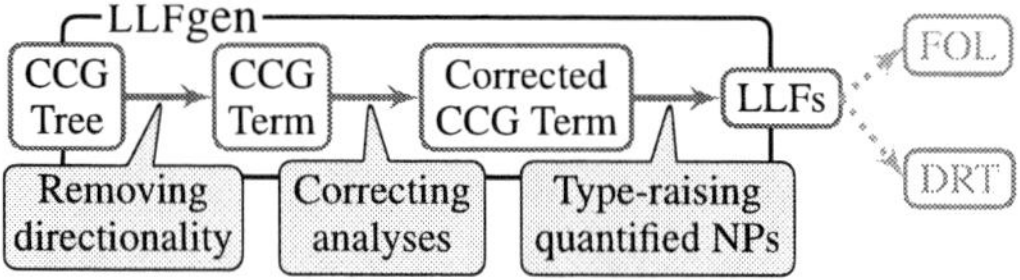

Figure 4: The LLF generator produces a list of LLFs from a single CCG derivation tree.

version of natural logic.[2] The terms of the natural logic, called *Lambda Logical Forms* (LLFs), are simply typed λ-terms built up from variables and constant lexical terms with the help of function application and λ-abstraction. The format of a tableau entry, i.e. node, is a tuple consisting of a modifier list, an LLF, an argument list and a truth sign. The parts are delimited with a colon. The empty lists are omitted for conciseness. For example, the entries (1) and (2) both mean that it is true that c barks loudly in Paris, where (α, β) is a functional type that expects an argument of type α and returns a value of type β.[3]

$$\mathbf{in}_{np,vp,vp}\mathbf{Paris}_{np} : \mathbf{loudly}_{vp,vp}\mathbf{bark}_{vp} : c_e : \mathbb{T} \quad (1)$$

$$\left(\mathbf{in}_{np,vp,vp}\mathbf{Paris}_{np}\right)\left(\mathbf{loudly}_{vp,vp}\mathbf{bark}_{vp} \, c_e\right) : \mathbb{T} \quad (2)$$

In order to prove a certain logical relation between premises and a hypothesis, the natural tableau searches a situation for the counterexample of the relation. The relation is proved if the situation is not found, otherwise it is refuted. An example of a closed natural tableau is shown in Figure 2. It proves the contradiction relation as it fails to find a situation for the counterexample— the premises and the hypothesis being true. In or-

der to facilitate reading tableau proofs, type information is omitted, the entries are enumerated and arcs are labeled with tableau rule applications. For example, [4] and [5] are obtained by applying $\exists_{\mathbb{T}}$ to [1]: if it is true that several pugs bark, then there is some entity c which is a pug and which barks.

3 LLF Generator

A Natural Tableau-based theorem prover for natural language requires automatic generation of LLFs from raw text. To do so, we implement a module, called LLFgen, that generates LLFs from syntactic derivations of Combinatory Categorial Grammar (CCG, Steedman 2000). Given a CCG derivation, LLFgen returns several LLFs that model different orders of quantifier scopes (see Figure 4).[4] Figure 5 displays a CCG derivation where VP_i abbreviates $S_i \backslash NP$.

LLFs are obtained from a CCG tree in three major steps (Figure 4): (i) removing directionality from CCG trees, (ii) correcting semantically inadequate analyses, and (iii) type-raising quantified NPs (QNPs). Below we briefly describe each of these steps and give corresponding examples.

Directionality information encoded in CCG categories and combinatory rules is redundant from a semantic perspective, therefore we discard it in

---

[2] It is an extended version of Muskens' original tableau system. The extension is three-fold and concerns the type system, the format of tableau entries and the inventory of tableau rules (Abzianidze, 2015b).

[3] LLFs are typed with syntactic and semantic types. Interaction between these types is established via the subtyping relation, e.g., entities being a subtype of NPs, $e <: np$, makes $\mathbf{bark}_{vp} \, c_e$ well-formed, where vp abbreviates (np, s).

[4] See Abzianidze (2016a, Ch. 3) for a detailed description.

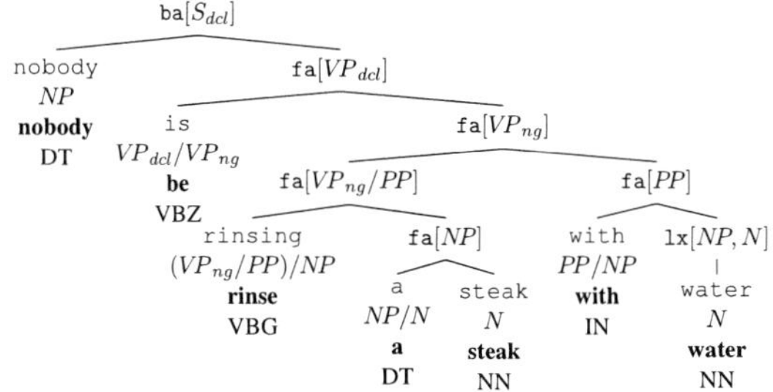

Figure 5: The CCG tree by C&C for *nobody is rinsing a steak with water* (SICK-1379).

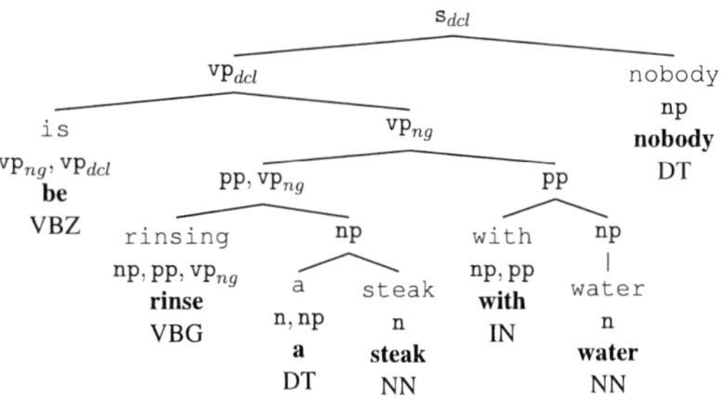

Figure 6: The CCG term obtained from the CCG tree of Figure 5. NB: the lexical rule remains.

the first step: CCG categories are converted into types ($Y\backslash X$ and $Y/X \rightsquigarrow$ (x, y)), and argument constituents are placed after function ones in binary combinatory rules. Resulted structures are called *CCG terms* (Figure 6).

Obtained CCG terms are often semantically inadequate. One of the reasons for this is *lexical* (i.e. *type-changing*) rules (e.g., $N \mapsto NP$ in Figure 5) of the CCG parsers which still remain in CCG terms (e.g., $[\mathbf{water_n}]_{np}$ in Figure 6). These rules are destructive from a compositional point of view. We designed 13 schematic rewriting rules of general type that *correct* CCG terms—make them semantically more adequate and transparent. The rules make use of types, part-of-speech (POS) and named entity (NE) tags to match semantically inadequate analyses:[5]

- Certain non-compositional multiword expressions are treated as constant terms: *a lot of, in front of, a few, because of, next to*, etc.

- Type-changing rules are *explained* by changing lexical types, decomposing terms or inserting new terms. This step carries out conversions like $[\mathbf{europe_n}]_{np} \rightsquigarrow \mathbf{europe_{np}}$, $[\mathbf{nobody_n}]_{np} \rightsquigarrow \mathbf{no_{n,np}person_n}$, and $[\mathbf{water_n}]_{np} \rightsquigarrow \mathbf{a_{n,np}water_n}$ (see Figure 7). Inserted $\mathbf{a_{n,np}}$ merely plays a role of an existential quantifier.

- Several CCG analyses are altered in order to reflect formal semantics, e.g., attributive modifiers are pushed *under* a relative clause: $\mathbf{big}\,(\mathbf{which\ run\ mouse}) \rightsquigarrow \mathbf{which\ run}\,(\mathbf{big\ mouse})$; and PPs are attached to nouns rather than NPs: $\mathbf{in}\,(\mathbf{a\ box})(\mathbf{every\ pug}) \rightsquigarrow \mathbf{every}\,(\mathbf{in}\,(\mathbf{a\ box})\,\mathbf{pug})$.

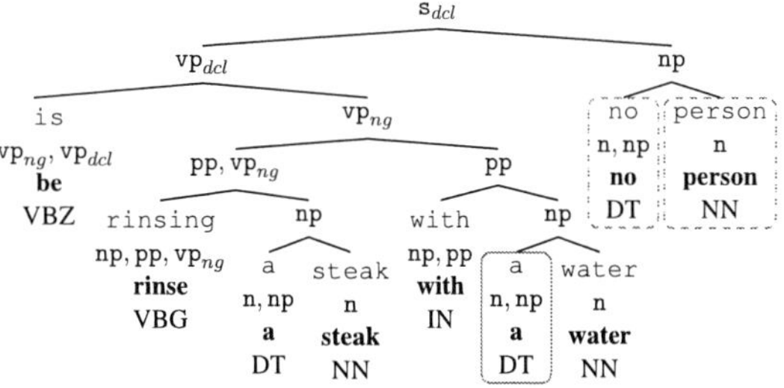

Figure 7: The corrected version of the CCG term of Figure 6, with inserted and decomposed terms.

LLFs are obtained from corrected CCG terms by type-raising QNPs from np to the type (vp, s) of generalized quantifiers. Hence, several LLFs are produced from a single CCG tree due to quantifier scope ambiguity, e.g., (3–5) are some of the LLFs obtained from the CCG term of Figure 7.[6]

$$N\big(\mathbf{be}\big(\lambda z.\, S\big(\lambda x.\, W\big(\lambda y.\, \mathbf{rinse}\, x\, (\mathbf{with}\, y)z\big)\big)\big)\big) \quad (3)$$

$$N\big(\mathbf{be}\big(\lambda z.\, W\big(\lambda y.\, S\big(\lambda x.\, \mathbf{rinse}\, x\, (\mathbf{with}\, y)z\big)\big)\big)\big) \quad (4)$$

$$W\big(\lambda y.\, S\big(\lambda x.\, N(\mathbf{be}\, (\mathbf{rinse}\, x\, (\mathbf{with}\, y))\big)\big)\big) \quad (5)$$

Since LLFs encode instructions for semantic composition, they can be used to compositionally derive semantics in other meaning representations (Figure 4), e.g., first-order logic (FOL) or Discourse Representation Theory (DRT). For this application, LLFgen can be used as an independent tool. Given a CCG derivation in the Prolog format (supported by both C&C and EasyCCG), LLFgen can return LLFs in XML, HTML or LaTeX formats. For a CCG tree, it is also possible to get either only the first LLF, e.g., (3), often reflecting the natural order of quantifiers, or a list of LLFs with various quantifier scope orders (possibly including semantically equivalent LLFs, like (3) and (4)).

---

[5] To handcraft the rules, we used a development set of 1.7K CCG derivations obtained by parsing the sentences from FraCaS (Cooper et al., 1996) and the trial portion of SICK (Marelli et al., 2014) with CCG-based parsers: C&C (Clark and Curran, 2007) and EasyCCG (Lewis and Steedman, 2014).

[6] The LLFs use the following abbreviations: $S = \mathbf{a_q\ steak_n}$, $W = \mathbf{a_q\ water_n}$, and $N = \mathbf{no_q\ person_n}$, where $\mathbf{q} = (\mathbf{n, vp, s})$.

4 Natural Logic Theorem Prover

The tableau theorem prover for natural logic (NLogPro) represents a core part of LangPro (Figure 1). It is responsible for checking a set of linguistic expressions on (in)consistency. NLogPro consists of four components: the *Proof Engine* builds tableau proofs by applying the rules from the *inventory of Rules*; the rule applications are validated by the properties of lexical terms (encoded in the *Signature*) and the lexical knowledge (available from the *Knowledge Base*). We used the same development data for LLFgen and NLogPro.

4.1 Signature

The signature (SG) lists lexical terms that have algebraic properties relevant for inference, e.g., monotonicity, intersectivity, and implicativity. The lexical items in the SG come with an argument structure where each argument position is associated with a set of algebraic properties. For example, **every** is characterized in the SG as `[dw,up]`, meaning that in its first argument **every** is downward monotone while being upward monotone in the second one. Currently, the SG lists about 20 lexical items, mostly generalized quantifiers (GQs), that were found in the development data.

4.2 The Inventory of Rules

The inventory of rules (IR) contains all inference rules used by the prover. Currently there are ca. 80 rules in the IR (some in Figure 3). Around a quarter of the rules are from Muskens (2010) and the rest are manually collected while exploring the development data. The rules cover a plethora of phenomena. Some of them are of a formal nature like Boolean connectives and monotonicity and others of linguistic nature: adjectives, prepositions, definite NPs, expletives, open compound nouns, light verbs, copula, passives and attitude verbs.

The IR involves around 25 *derivable* rules—the rules that represent shortcuts of several rule applications. One such rule is ($\text{NO}_\mathbb{T}^n$) in Figure 3, which is a specific version of ($\text{NO}_\mathbb{T}$). Use of derivable rules yields shorter tableau proofs but raises a problem of performing the same rule application several times. NLogPro avoids this by maintaining a subsumption relation between the rules and keeping track of rule applications per branch.

A user can introduce new rules in the IR as Prolog rules (Code 1): the head of the rule encodes antecedent nodes ===> consequent nodes, and the body is a list of Prolog goals specifying the conditions the rule has to meet.

```
r(Name, Feats, ConstIndx, KeyWrd, KB,
  br([nd(Mod1, LLF1, Arg1, Sign1),...
      nd(ModN, LLFN, ArgN, SignN)],
    Signature) ===>
 [br([nd(Mod3, LLF3, Arg3, Sign3),...],
     Signature3),
   br([nd(Mod4, LLF4, Arg4, Sign4),...],
     Signature4)]
:- Goal1, ..., GoalN. %conditions
```

Code 1: The Prolog format of tableau rules. `Feats` denotes efficiency features, `ConstIndx` and `KB` are the KB and indexing of constants respectively (fixed for every rule), and `KeyWrd` denotes fixed lexical terms occurring in the rule. Each branch maintains its own signature of entities introduced during the proof.

4.3 Knowledge Base

The knowledge base (BS) is based on the Prolog version of WordNet 3.0 (Fellbaum, 1998). At this moment only the hyponymy/hypernymy, similarity and antonymy relations are included in the KB. For simplicity, LangPro does not do any word sense disambiguation (WSD) but allows multiple word senses for a lexical term. For example, $A \sqsubseteq B$ iff $SynSet_A$ is a hyponym of $SynSet_B$, or there are similar $Sense_A$ and $Sense_B$, where $Sense_A \in SynSet_A$ and $Sense_B \in SynSet_B$. In the prover, a user can restrict the number of word senses per word by specifying a cutoff N, i.e. the N most frequent senses per word.

In addition to the WN relations, a user can introduce new lexical relations in the KB as Prolog facts, e.g., `is_(crowd, group)`.

4.4 The Proof Engine

The proof engine (PE) is the component that builds proof trees. While applying rules it takes into account computational efficiency of each rule where the efficiency depends on the following categories:

- *Branching*: a rule is either branching (e.g., $\forall_\mathbb{T}$) or non-branching (e.g., AUX).

- *Semantic equivalence*: this depends whether the antecedents of a rule is semantically equivalent to its consequents. For example, ($\wedge_F$) encodes the semantic equivalence while ($\text{NO}_\mathbb{T}$) does not.

- *Producing*: depending on whether a rule produces a fresh entity, it is a producer or a non-producer. ($\exists_\mathbb{T}$) is a producer while ($\forall_\mathbb{T}$) is not.

- *Consuming*: a rule is a consumer iff it employs an old entity from the branch during application. The consumer rules are $(\forall_\mathbb{T})$ and $(\text{NO}_\mathbb{T})$ but $(\exists_\mathbb{T})$.

The most efficient combination of these features is non-branching, semantic equivalence, non-producing and non-consuming. Depending on a priority order between these categories, called an efficiency criterion, one can define a partial efficiency order over the rules. In particular, (6) is one of the best efficiency criteria on SICK (Abzianidze, 2016a, Ch. 6). According to (6), $(\wedge_\mathbb{F})$ is more efficient than $(\text{NO}_\mathbb{T}^n)$ since the equivalence is the most prominent category in (6), and $(\wedge_\mathbb{F})$ is equivalence in contrast to $(\text{NO}_\mathbb{T}^n)$

$$[\texttt{equi}, \texttt{nonBr}, \texttt{nonProd}, \texttt{nonCons}] \qquad (6)$$

A user can change the default criterion (6) by passing a criterion via the Prolog predicate `effCr/1`.

The PE builds two structures: a tree (see Figure 2) and a list. The latter represents a list of the tree branches. The list structure is the main data structure that guides the computation process while the tree structure is optional (activated with the predicate `prooftree/0`) and is used for displaying proofs in a compact way. A few of the predicates that control the proof procedure are:

- `ral/1` sets a rule application limit to n, which means that after n rules are applied the proof is terminated. $n = 400$ by default.

- `thE/0` always permits existential import from definite NPs: it makes $(\exists_\mathbb{T})$ applicable to the entry $\textbf{the}_{n,vp,s}\ \textbf{dog}_n\ \textbf{bark}_{vp} : \mathbb{F}$.

- `allInt/0` allows to treat lexical modifiers of the form $c_{n,n}^{\text{VB.}|\text{JJ}|\text{NN}}$ as intersective by default unless stated differently in the SG. This permits to infer $\textbf{baby}_n : c : \mathbb{T}$ and $\textbf{kangaroo}_n : c : \mathbb{T}$ from $\textbf{baby}_{n,n}\textbf{kangaroo} : c : \mathbb{T}$, for better or worse.

- `the/0`, `a2the/0`, and `s2the/0` are used as flags and treat bare, indefinite, and plural NPs as definite NPs, respectively.

5 LangPro: Natural Language Prover

The tableau-based theorem prover for natural language is obtained by chaining a CCG parser, `LLFgen` and `NLogPro`. In order to detect a semantic relation between a set of premises $\{p_i\}_{i=1}^n$ and a hypothesis h, first the corresponding LLFs $\{P_i\}_{i=1}^n$ and H are obtained via a CCG parser and `LLFgen` (i.e. for simplicity, a single LLF per sentence). Then based on the lexical terms of the

LLFs, relevant sets of relations K and rules R are collected from the KB and the IR, respectively. To refute both entailment and contradiction relations `NLogPro` builds two proof trees using K and R. One starts with the counterexample (7) for entailment and another with the counterexample (8) for contradiction. The semantic relation which could not be refuted (i.e. its tableau for the counterexample was closed) is said to be proved. The relation is considered to be neutral iff both tableaux have the same closure status: open or closed.

$$\{P_1 : \mathbb{T},\ \ldots,\ P_n : \mathbb{T},\ H : \mathbb{F}\} \qquad (7)$$
$$\{P_1 : \mathbb{T},\ \ldots,\ P_n : \mathbb{T},\ H : \mathbb{T}\} \qquad (8)$$

Entailment relations often do not depend on semantics of phrases shared by premises and hypotheses. To bypass analyzing the common phrases, `LangPro` can use an optional CCG term aligner in `LLFgen` (Figure 1), which identifies the common CCG sub-terms and treats them as constants. The sub-terms that are downward monotone or indefinite NPs are excluded from alignments as they do not behave semantically as constants. After aligning CCG terms, aligned LLFs are obtained from them via the type-raising. Tableau proofs with aligned LLFs are shorter. Thus, first, a tableau with aligned LLFs is built, and if the tableau did not close, then non-aligned LLFs are used since alignment might prevent the tableau from closing. On SICK, the aligner boosts the accuracy by 1%. If stronger alignment is used (i.e. aligning indefinite NPs), the accuracy on SICK is increased by 2%. Both weak and strong alignment options can be chosen in `LangPro`.

The parser component of `LangPro` can be filled by C&C or EasyCCG. This results in two versions of `LangPro`, `ccLangPro` and `easyLangPro` respectively. Both versions achieve similar results on FraCaS and SICK, and a simple aggregation of their judgments (`coLangPro`) improves the accuracy on the unseen portion of SICK by 1%.

With respect to its rule-based nature, `LangPro` is fast. Given ready CCG derivations, on average 100 SICK problems are classified in 3.5 seconds.[7] Details about speed and impact of parameters on the performance are given in Abzianidze (2016a).

In addition to an entailment judgment, `LangPro` can output the actual tableau proof trees (similar

---

[7]This is measured on 8×2.4 GHz CPU machine, when proving problems in parallel (via the `paralle/0` predicate) with the strong aligner option and the rule application limit 50—the configuration that achieves high performance both in terms of speed and accuracy.

to Figure 2) in three formats: a drawing of a proof tree via the XPCE GUI, a LaTeX source code, an XML output, or an HTML file.

6 Related work

Theorem proving techniques (Bos and Markert, 2005) or ideas from Natural Logic (MacCartney, 2009) were already used in recognizing textual entailment (RTE). But the combination of these two is a novel approach to RTE. The underlying higher-order logic of LangPro guarantees sound reasoning over several premises, including some complex semantic phenomena. This is in contrast to the RTE systems that cannot reason over several premises or cannot account for Booleans and quantifiers, including the ones (MacCartney, 2009) inspired by Natural Logic, and in contrast to those ones that use FOL representations and cannot cover higher-order phenomena like generalized quantifiers or subsective adjectives.

LangPro achieves state-of-the-art semantic competence (with accuracy of 87%) on the FraCaS sections commonly used for evaluation (Abzianidze, 2016b,a). On SICK, the prover obtains 82.1% of accuracy (Abzianidze, 2015a, 2016a) while state-of-the-art systems score in the range of 81-87% and average performance of human on the dataset is around 84%. Detailed comparison of LangPro to the related RTE systems is discussed in (Abzianidze, 2015a, 2016b,a).

7 Conclusion

The presented natural language prover involves a unique combination of natural logic, higher-order logic and a tableau method. Its natural logic side simplifies generation of the logical forms and makes the prover to be relatively easily scaled up. Due to its higher-order virtue, the prover easily accounts for complex semantic phenomena untameable in FOL. Because of its high reliability (less than 3% of its entailment and contradiction judgments are incorrect), the judgments of the prover can be successfully borrowed by other RTE systems. Further scaling-up for longer sentences (e.g., newswire text) and automated knowledge acquisition present future challenges to the prover.

Acknowledgments

This work has been supported by the NWO-VICI grant "Lost in Translation – Found in Meaning" (288-89-003).

References

Lasha Abzianidze. 2015a. A tableau prover for natural logic and language. In *Proceedings of the 2015 Conference on Empirical Methods in Natural Language Processing*, pages 2492–2502. ACL.

Lasha Abzianidze. 2015b. Towards a wide-coverage tableau method for natural logic. In Tsuyoshi Murata, Koji Mineshima, and Daisuke Bekki, editors, *New Frontiers in Artificial Intelligence: Revised Selected Papers of JSAI-isAI 2014 Workshops, LENLS, JURISIN, and GABA*, pages 66–82. Springer.

Lasha Abzianidze. 2016a. *A natural proof system for natural language*. Ph.D. thesis, Tilburg University.

Lasha Abzianidze. 2016b. Natural solution to fracas entailment problems. In *Proceedings of the Fifth Joint Conference on Lexical and Computational Semantics*, pages 64–74. ACL.

Johan Bos and Katja Markert. 2005. Recognising textual entailment with logical inference. In *Proceedings of Human Language Technology Conference and Conference on Empirical Methods in Natural Language Processing*, pages 628–635.

Stephen Clark and James R. Curran. 2007. Wide-coverage efficient statistical parsing with CCG and log-linear models. *Computational Linguistics*, 33.

Robin Cooper, Dick Crouch, Jan Van Eijck, Chris Fox, Josef Van Genabith, Jan Jaspars, Hans Kamp, David Milward, Manfred Pinkal, Massimo Poesio, Steve Pulman, Ted Briscoe, Holger Maier, and Karsten Konrad. 1996. *FraCaS: A Framework for Computational Semantics*. Deliverable D16.

Christiane Fellbaum, editor. 1998. *WordNet: An Electronic Lexical Database*. MIT Press.

Mike Lewis and Mark Steedman. 2014. A* CCG parsing with a supertag-factored model. In *Proceedings of the 2014 Conference on Empirical Methods in Natural Language Processing*, pages 990–1000. ACL.

Bill MacCartney. 2009. *Natural language inference*. Phd thesis, Stanford University.

Marco Marelli, Stefano Menini, Marco Baroni, Luisa Bentivogli, Raffaella Bernardi, and Roberto Zamparelli. 2014. A sick cure for the evaluation of compositional distributional semantic models. In *Proceedings of LREC'14*. ELRA.

Reinhard Muskens. 2010. An analytic tableau system for natural logic. In Maria Aloni, Harald Bastiaanse, Tikitu de Jager, and Katrin Schulz, editors, *Logic, Language and Meaning*, volume 6042 of *LNCS*, pages 104–113. Springer.

Mark Steedman. 2000. *The Syntactic Process*. MIT Press, Cambridge, MA, USA.

Interactive Visualization and Manipulation of Attention-based Neural Machine Translation

Jaesong Lee and **Joong-Hwi Shin** and **Jun-Seok Kim**
NAVER Corp.
{jaesong.lee,joonghwi.shin,jun.seok}@navercorp.com

Abstract

While neural machine translation (NMT) provides high-quality translation, it is still hard to interpret and analyze its behavior. We present an interactive interface for visualizing and intervening behavior of NMT, specifically concentrating on the behavior of beam search mechanism and attention component. The tool (1) visualizes search tree and attention and (2) provides interface to adjust search tree and attention weight (manually or automatically) at real-time. We show the tool help users understand NMT in various ways.

1 Introduction

Recent advances in neural machine translation (NMT) (Sutskever et al., 2014) have changed the direction of machine translation community. Compared to traditional phrase-based statistical machine translation (SMT) (Koehn, 2010), NMT provides more accurate and fluent translation results. Companies also have started to adopt NMT for their machine translation service.

However, it is still challenging to analyze translation behavior of NMT. While SMT provides interpretable features (like phrase table), NMT directly learns complex features which are obscure to human. This is especially problematic in the case of wrong translation, since it is even hard to understand why the system generated such sentences.

To help the analysis, we propose a tool for visualizing and intervening NMT behavior, concentrated on beam search decoder and attention. The features can be grouped by two categories:

- Visualizing decoder result, including how decoder assigns probability to each token

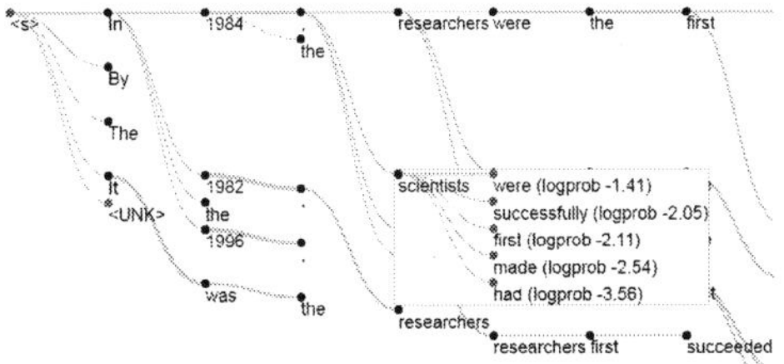

Figure 1: Beam search tree interface. Beam search result is shown as a tree (section 3.1). By hovering mouse over node, its corresponding output candidates can be seen. User may click the candidate to expand node which are discarded during search (section 3.3).

(word, sub-word, etc.), how beam search maintains and discards intermediate hypotheses, and how attention layer assigns attention weight. This enables detailed observation of decoder behavior.

- Intervening in decoder behavior, including manually expanding hypothesis discarded during search and adjusting attention weight. This helps understanding how the components affect translation quality.

We show the mechanism of visualization (Section 3.1 and 3.2) and manipulation (Section 3.3 and 3.4) and its usefulness with examples.

2 Related Work

There have been various methods proposed for visualizing and intervening neural models for NLP. (Li et al., 2015) provides a concise literature review.

Visualization and manipulation of NMT could be grouped into three parts: RNN (of encoder and decoder), attention (of decoder), and beam search (of decoder).

121

Proceedings of the 2017 EMNLP System Demonstrations, pages 121–126
Copenhagen, Denmark, September 7–11, 2017. ©2017 Association for Computational Linguistics

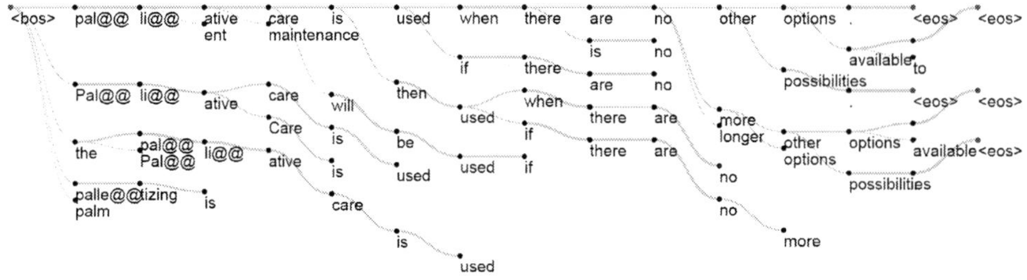

Figure 2: Beam search tree of de-en NMT.

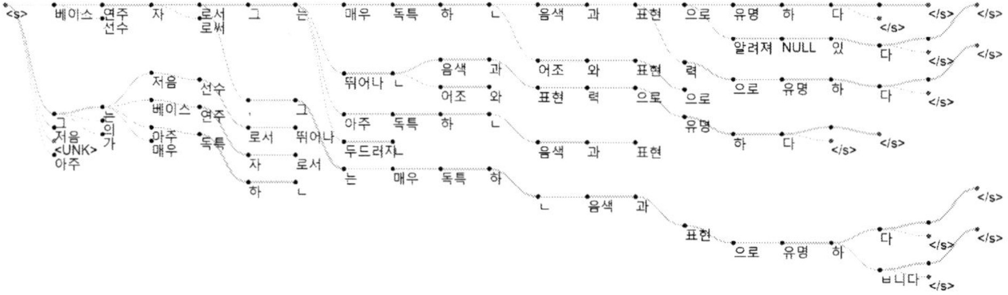

Figure 3: Beam search tree of en-ko NMT. Input sentence is: "As a bass player, he is known for his highly distinctive tone and phrasing."

RNN plays a central role in recognizing source sentences and generating target sentences. Although we here treat RNN as a black-box, there exists various methods to understand RNNs, e.g. by observing intermediate values (Strobelt et al., 2016; Karpathy et al., 2015; Li et al., 2015) or by removing some parts of them (Goh, 2016; Li et al., 2016).

Attention (Bahdanau et al., 2014; Luong et al., 2015) is an important component for improving NMT quality. Since the component behaves like alignment in traditional SMT, it has been proposed to utilize attention during training (Cheng et al., 2015; Tu et al., 2016b) or during decoding (Wu et al., 2016). In this work, we propose a way to manipulate attention and to understand the behavior.

Beam search is known to improve quality of NMT translation output. However, it is also known that larger beam size does not always helps but rather hurts the quality (Tu et al., 2016a). Therefore it is important to understand how beam search affects quality. (Wu et al., 2016; Freitag and Al-Onaizan, 2017) proposed several penalty functions and pruning methods for beam search. We directly visualize beam search result as a tree and manually explore hypotheses discarded by decoder.

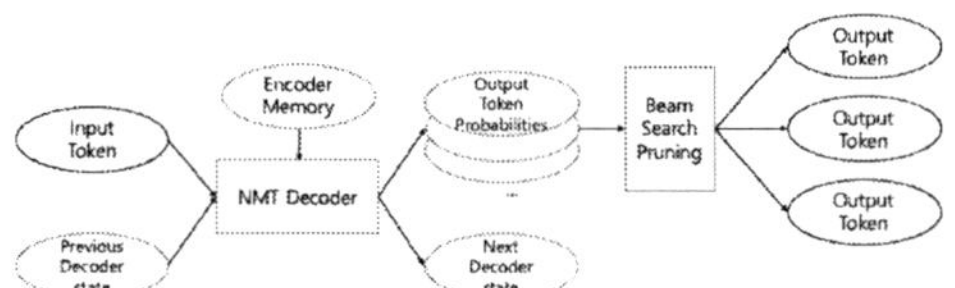

Figure 4: Diagram of NMT decoder step. Search tree visualization (Figure 2) shows input and output tokens as a tree.

3 Interactive Beam Search

We propose an interactive tool for visualizing and manipulating NMT decoder behavior. The system consists of two parts: back-end NMT server and front-end web interface. NMT server is responsible for NMT computation. Web interface is responsible for requesting computation to NMT server and showing results at real time.

For back-end implementation, we use two NMT models. For English-Korean (en-ko), we use a model used in Naver Papago (Lee et al., 2016) service[1] ported to TensorFlow. For German-English (de-en), we adopted Nematus[2] and pretrained models provided by (Sennrich et al., 2016). For front-end we implemented JavaScript-based web

[1] https://papago.naver.com/
[2] https://github.com/rsennrich/nematus

122

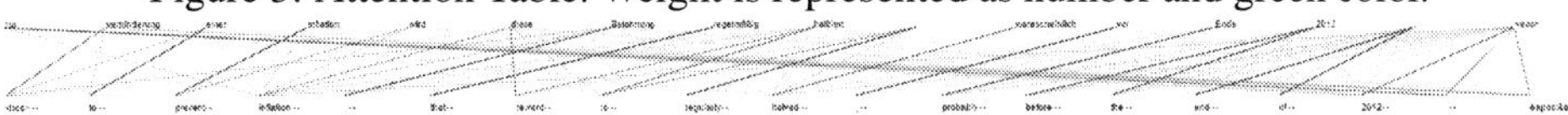

	zur	Verhinderung	einer	Inflation	wird	diese	Belohnung	regelmäßig	halbiert	,	wahrscheinlich	vor	Ende	2012	.	<eos>
<bos> → to	0.046	0.500	0.167	0.008	0.019	0.024	0.157	0.011	0.029	0.004	0.002	0.012	0.004	0.001	0.000	0.018
to → prevent	0.010	0.074	0.850	0.014	0.013	0.001	0.005	0.001	0.009	0.002	0.000	0.000	0.000	0.001	0.000	0.019
prevent → inflation	0.002	0.005	0.011	0.709	0.258	0.001	0.005	0.004	0.001	0.000	0.000	0.000	0.000	0.001	0.000	0.003
inflation → ,	0.072	0.006	0.029	0.065	0.103	0.317	0.159	0.005	0.074	0.023	0.003	0.006	0.003	0.003	0.001	0.131
, → that	0.015	0.008	0.003	0.006	0.064	0.029	0.737	0.047	0.049	0.010	0.002	0.006	0.002	0.001	0.000	0.021
that → reward	0.000	0.000	0.000	0.000	0.001	0.002	0.003	0.984	0.002	0.002	0.000	0.000	0.000	0.000	0.000	0.004
reward → is	0.002	0.007	0.004	0.001	0.001	0.468	0.024	0.031	0.357	0.076	0.003	0.005	0.002	0.000	0.000	0.019
is → regularly	0.003	0.003	0.003	0.000	0.000	0.084	0.007	0.002	0.536	0.332	0.004	0.011	0.001	0.000	0.000	0.014
regularly → halved	0.002	0.002	0.002	0.000	0.001	0.028	0.003	0.002	0.022	0.923	0.006	0.001	0.002	0.000	0.000	0.007
halved → ,	0.026	0.033	0.001	0.004	0.003	0.022	0.040	0.002	0.074	0.084	0.549	0.022	0.048	0.009	0.004	0.079
, → probably	0.002	0.001	0.000	0.000	0.000	0.004	0.005	0.001	0.008	0.002	0.026	0.892	0.020	0.002	0.001	0.034
probably → before	0.002	0.002	0.001	0.001	0.001	0.021	0.002	0.000	0.002	0.011	0.004	0.014	0.741	0.089	0.002	0.108
before → the	0.001	0.001	0.001	0.002	0.002	0.001	0.000	0.000	0.000	0.001	0.000	0.006	0.013	0.748	0.155	0.067
the → end	0.002	0.001	0.004	0.002	0.004	0.001	0.000	0.000	0.001	0.001	0.000	0.005	0.021	0.800	0.082	0.076
end → of	0.004	0.001	0.001	0.004	0.001	0.001	0.000	0.000	0.001	0.000	0.000	0.001	0.009	0.071	0.873	0.033
of → 2012	0.001	0.000	0.000	0.003	0.001	0.000	0.000	0.000	0.000	0.000	0.000	0.000	0.000	0.055	0.903	0.034
2012 → .	0.139	0.028	0.009	0.028	0.020	0.048	0.013	0.016	0.029	0.014	0.021	0.011	0.008	0.035	0.032	0.550
. → <eos>	0.513	0.081	0.002	0.011	0.011	0.010	0.016	0.003	0.004	0.000	0.004	0.013	0.002	0.003	0.001	0.326

Figure 5: Attention Table. Weight is represented as number and green color.

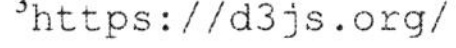

Figure 6: Attention Graph Dialog. Weight is represented as red color.

page with d3.js[3].

3.1 Search Tree Visualization

To understand how beam search decoder selects and discards intermediate hypothesis, we first plot all hypotheses as a tree (Figure 2, 3). For each input token (word or sub-word) and decoder (RNN) state vector, the decoder computes output probability of all possible output token, then beam search routine selects token based on its probability value (Figure 4). We plot each input and output token as tree node, and input-output relation as edge. If a node is mouse-hovered, it shows its next possible tokens with highest probability, including pruned ones (Figure 1). We also visualize output probability of node using edge thickness; thicker edge means higher probability.

3.2 Attention Visualization

We show the attention weight of (partially) generated sentence as table (Figure 5) and as graph (Figure 6). Table interface provides detailed information, and graph interface provides more concise view therefore better for long sentences.

3.3 Search Tree Manipulation

We implemented an interface to manually expand nodes which are discarded during beam search. In search tree visualization (Figure 7) or attention manipulation dialog (Figure 9), a user can click one of output candidate (green node) then the system computes its next outputs and extends the tree.

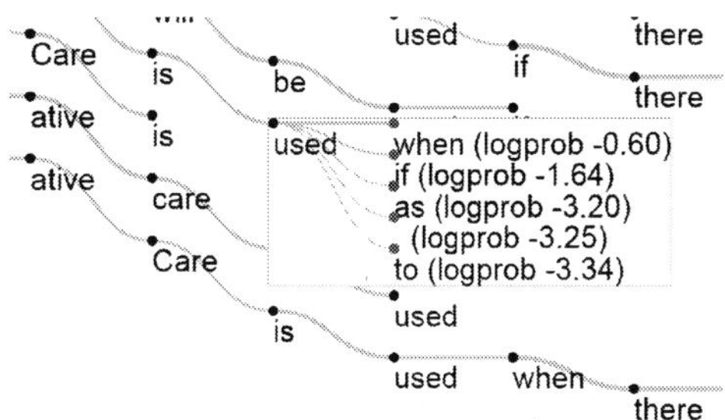

Figure 7: Manual expansion of nodes not explored at Figure 2. For the partial sentence "the Pal@@ li@@ ative Care is", new subtree "... used when there ..." are created.

This enables exploration of hypotheses not covered by decoder but worth to analyze.

3.4 Attention Manipulation

We are interested in understanding attention layer of (Bahdanau et al., 2014; Luong et al., 2015), especially the role and effect of attention weights. To achieve it, we modified NMT decoder to accept arbitrary attention weight instead of what the decoder computes (Figure 8).

3.4.1 Manual Adjustment of Attention Weight

For given memory cells (encoder outputs) $(m_1, \cdots, m_n)$ and decoder internal state h, the attention layer first computes relevance score of memory cell $s_i = f(m_i, h)$ and attention weight $w_i = \mathrm{softmax}(s_1, \cdots, s_n)_i$. Then memory cells

[3] https://d3js.org/

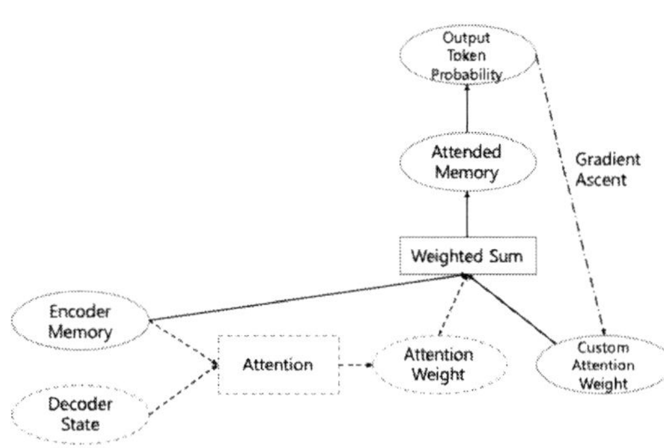

Figure 8: Diagram of attention manipulation mechanism. The dashed components are original component of NMT decoder. Here "attention weight" is replaced by "custom attention weight" which is given by user or computed to maximize probability of output token.

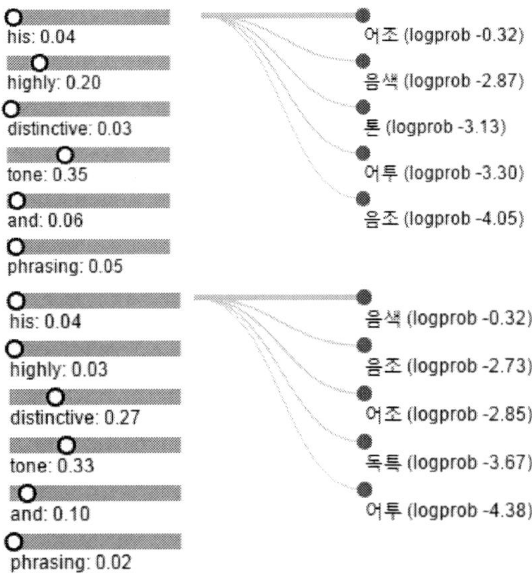

Figure 9: Result of attention manipulation for two output tokens "어조" and "음색".

are summarized into one fixed vector ($\tilde{m}$) via weighted sum: $\tilde{m} = \sum_i w_i m_i$. The summarized vector is fed to next layer to compute output token probabilities: $p(y_j) = g(\tilde{m}, h)_j$.

We modified the decoder to accept custom weight $w' = (w'_1, \cdots w'_n)$ instead of original ones w, when w' is provided by user. We also implemented front-end interface to adjust custom weight (Figure 9). If user drags circle on the bar, the weights are adjusted and the system computes new output probabilities using the weight. It helps to understand what is encoded in memory cell and how decoder utilizes the attended memory $\tilde{m}$. For example, user may increase or decrease weight of specific memory cell and observe its effect.

Figure 9 shows an illustrative example that how adjusting attention weight could change output probability distribution. When weight of "highly" and "tone" are high, NMT puts high probability to "어조" ("tone of voice"). When weight of "distinctive" is high, NMT recognizes "tone" in current context (musical instrument) and puts high probability to "음색" ("timbre").

3.4.2 Automatic Adjustment of Attention Weight

We also implemented a method to find attention weight maximizing output probability of a specific token. For attention weight w and token y, we see this problem as a constrained optimization: maximize $\log p(y|w, \cdots)$ s.t. $w_i \geq 0, \sum_i w_i = 1$. Since the toolkits we use (TensorFlow[4] and Theano[5]) provide unconstrained gradient descent optimizer, we cast the original problem to unconstrained optimization: instead of weight w, we optimize unnormalized score s before softmax, initialized as $s_i = \log w_i$. The method can be used to optimize weight for specific time step (Figure 9) or for whole sentence (Figure 10).

For English-Korean, this technique is particularly useful because the original attention weight is sometimes hard to interpret. Due to ordering differences between two languages, en-ko NMTs tend to generate diverse sentences and they have very different orderings among each other. In Figure 3, input sentence is "As a *bass* player, *he* is …". NMT puts high probability to output sentences starting with either "베이스" ("bass") or "그" ("he"), since both are valid. Therefore,

[4]https://www.tensorflow.org/
[5]http://deeplearning.net/software/theano/

124

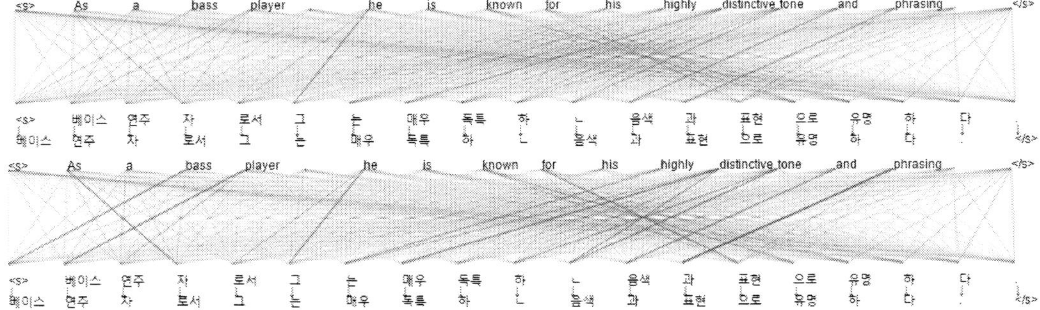

Figure 10: Two attention graphs of en-ko NMT. The first one shows attention weights from NMT. The second one shows attention weights adjusted to maximize target sentence. It reveals clearer and more interpretable relation than original attention.

corresponding source words have high attention weights (0.14 for "bass" and 0.07 for "he"). Since output token is chosen after attention, the attention weights do not necessarily look like alignment between source and output sentences, but rather look like a *mixture* of alignments of possible output sentences.

Once output token is chosen, we can find new attention weight which increases probability of output token, which would be more interpretable than the original weight. An example of such adjustment is shown at Figure 10.

4 Conclusion

We propose a web-based interface for visualizing, investigating and understanding neural machine translation (NMT). The tool provides several methods to understand beam search and attention mechanism in an interactive way, by visualizing search tree and attention, expanding search tree manually, and changing attention weight either manually or automatically. We show the visualization and manipulation helps understanding NMT behavior.

References

Dzmitry Bahdanau, Kyunghyun Cho, and Yoshua Bengio. 2014. Neural machine translation by jointly learning to align and translate. In *Proceedings of the International Conference on Learning Representations*.

Yong Cheng, Shiqi Shen, Zhongjun He, Wei He, Hua Wu, Maosong Sun, and Yang Liu. 2015. Agreement-based joint training for bidirectional attention-based neural machine translation. *CoRR*, abs/1512.04650.

Markus Freitag and Yaser Al-Onaizan. 2017. Beam search strategies for neural machine translation. *CoRR*, abs/1702.01806.

Gabriel Goh. 2016. Decoding the thought vector.

Andrej Karpathy, Justin Johnson, and Li Fei-Fei. 2015. Visualizing and understanding recurrent networks. *arXiv preprint arXiv:1506.02078*.

Philipp Koehn. 2010. *Statistical Machine Translation*, 1st edition. Cambridge University Press, New York, NY, USA.

Hyoung-Gyu Lee, Jun-Seok Kim, Joong-Hwi Shin, Jaesong Lee, Ying-Xiu Quan, and Young-Seob Jeong. 2016. papago: A machine translation service with word sense disambiguation and currency conversion. In *Proceedings of COLING 2016, the 26th International Conference on Computational Linguistics: System Demonstrations*, pages 185–188, Osaka, Japan. The COLING 2016 Organizing Committee.

Jiwei Li, Xinlei Chen, Eduard Hovy, and Dan Jurafsky. 2015. Visualizing and understanding neural models in nlp. *arXiv preprint arXiv:1506.01066*.

Jiwei Li, Will Monroe, and Dan Jurafsky. 2016. Understanding neural networks through representation erasure. *CoRR*, abs/1612.08220.

Minh-Thang Luong, Hieu Pham, and Christopher D. Manning. 2015. Effective approaches to attention-based neural machine translation. In *Proceedings of the 2015 Conference on Empirical Methods in Natural Language Processing*, pages 1412–1421, Lisbon, Portugal. Association for Computational Linguistics.

Rico Sennrich, Barry Haddow, and Alexandra Birch. 2016. Edinburgh neural machine translation systems for wmt 16. In *Proceedings of the First Conference on Machine Translation*, pages 371–376, Berlin, Germany. Association for Computational Linguistics.

Hendrik Strobelt, Sebastian Gehrmann, Bernd Huber, Hanspeter Pfister, and Alexander M. Rush. 2016. Visual analysis of hidden state dynamics in recurrent neural networks. *CoRR*, abs/1606.07461.

Ilya Sutskever, Oriol Vinyals, and Quoc V Le. 2014. Sequence to sequence learning with neural networks. In *Advances in neural information processing systems*, pages 3104–3112.

Zhaopeng Tu, Yang Liu, Lifeng Shang, Xiaohua Liu, and Hang Li. 2016a. Neural machine translation with reconstruction. *CoRR*, abs/1611.01874.

Zhaopeng Tu, Zhengdong Lu, Yang Liu, Xiaohua Liu, and Hang Li. 2016b. Coverage-based neural machine translation. *CoRR*, abs/1601.04811.

Yonghui Wu, Mike Schuster, Zhifeng Chen, Quoc V. Le, Mohammad Norouzi, Wolfgang Macherey, Maxim Krikun, Yuan Cao, Qin Gao, Klaus Macherey, Jeff Klingner, Apurva Shah, Melvin Johnson, Xiaobing Liu, Łukasz Kaiser, Stephan Gouws, Yoshikiyo Kato, Taku Kudo, Hideto Kazawa, Keith Stevens, George Kurian, Nishant Patil, Wei Wang, Cliff Young, Jason Smith, Jason Riesa, Alex Rudnick, Oriol Vinyals, Greg Corrado, Macduff Hughes, and Jeffrey Dean. 2016. Google's neural machine translation system: Bridging the gap between human and machine translation. *CoRR*, abs/1609.08144.

Association for Computational Linguistics
209 N. Eighth Street
Stroudsburg, Pennsylvania 18360

ISBN 978-1-5108-4780-4